Hands-On Dependency Injection in Go

Develop clean Go code that is easier to read, maintain, and test

Corey Scott

BIRMINGHAM - MUMBAI

Hands-On Dependency Injection in Go

Copyright © 2018 Packt Publishing

Commissioning Editor: Aaron Lazar
Acquisition Editor: Shriram Shekhar
Content Development Editor: Akshada Iyer
Technical Editor: Riddesh Dawne
Copy Editor: Safis Editing
Project Coordinator: Prajakta Naik
Proofreader: Safis Editing
Indexer: Tejal Daruwale Soni
Graphics: Jisha Chirayil
Production Coordinator: Jyoti Chauhan

First published: November 2018

Production reference: 1231118

Published by Packt Publishing Ltd.
Livery Place
35 Livery Street
Birmingham
B3 2PB, UK.

ISBN 978-1-78913-276-2

www.packtpub.com

To my wife, May; this book would be far less without your help and support, as would I.
- Corey Scott

`mapt.io`

Mapt is an online digital library that gives you full access to over 5,000 books and videos, as well as industry leading tools to help you plan your personal development and advance your career. For more information, please visit our website.

Why subscribe?

- Spend less time learning and more time coding with practical ebooks and videos from over 4,000 industry professionals

- Improve your learning with Skill Plans built especially for you

- Get a free eBook or video every month

- Mapt is fully searchable

- Copy and paste, print, and bookmark content

Packt.com

Did you know that Packt offers eBook versions of every book published, with PDF and ePub files available? You can upgrade to the eBook version at `www.packt.com` and as a print book customer, you are entitled to a discount on the eBook copy. Get in touch with us at `customercare@packtpub.com` for more details.

At `www.packt.com`, you can also read a collection of free technical articles, sign up for a range of free newsletters, and receive exclusive discounts and offers on Packt books and eBooks.

Contributors

About the author

Corey Scott is a senior software engineer currently living in Melbourne, Australia. He's been programming professionally since 2000, with the last 5 years spent building large-scale distributed services in Go.

An occasional technical speaker and blogger on a variety of software-related topics, he is passionate about designing and building quality software. He believes that software engineering is a craft that should be honed, debated, and continuously improved. He takes a pragmatic, non-zealot approach to coding and is always up for a good debate about software engineering, continuous delivery, testing, or clean coding.

> *I would firstly like to thank my wife, May, for encouraging me to take on this project, reviewing the content, and getting me through the project.*
>
> *I would also like to thank my reviewer, Ryan. Your reviews were spot on, and the many suggestions served to make the book notably better.*
>
> *I would like to thank Chang and Ang for reviewing the outline and for your fantastic suggestions.*
>
> *Finally, I would like to thank Shriram and Packt for the opportunity.*

About the reviewer

Ryan Law is a software engineer who enjoys spending time understanding how the world around him works. Being an early engineer in Grab, he has experience of working with many different technologies at scale, from building web portals, to designing distributed services in Go, to managing all of Grab's cloud infrastructure.

I would like to thank all my family and friends that have given me the time and opportunity to review this book. As always, it has been a pleasure working with Corey on getting his book published.

Packt is searching for authors like you

If you're interested in becoming an author for Packt, please visit authors.packtpub.com and apply today. We have worked with thousands of developers and tech professionals, just like you, to help them share their insight with the global tech community. You can make a general application, apply for a specific hot topic that we are recruiting an author for, or submit your own idea.

Table of Contents

Preface

Howdy! This book intends to be a hands-on introduction to dependency injection with Go. It may surprise you to learn that there are many different methods for applying dependency injection available in the Go language and, in this book, we will discuss six different and occasionally complementary options.

Dependency injection, like many software engineering concepts, is easily and often misunderstood, so this text seeks to address that. It delves into related concepts, such as the principles of SOLID, code smells, and test-induced damage, so as to offer a broader and more practical view.

The aim of *Hands-On Dependency Injection in Go* is not only to teach you how to apply dependency injection, but also when, where, and when not to. Each of the methods is clearly defined; we discuss its advantages and disadvantages, and when the method is best applied. Also, each method is applied step by step using significant examples.

As much as I love dependency injection, it's not always the right tool for the job. This book will also help you spot situations where applying dependency injection is perhaps not the best option.

As each dependency injection method is introduced, I would ask you to pause for a moment, step back, and consider the following. What problem is the technique trying to resolve? And what would your code look like after you apply this method? Don't worry if the answers to these questions don't come quickly; by the end of the book, they will.

Happy coding!

Who this book is for

This book is designed for developers who wish that their code was easy to read, test, and maintain. It is intended for developers coming from an object-oriented background who want to get more out of Go, as well as for developers who believe that quality code is about more than delivering one particular feature.

After all, writing code is easy. Similarly, getting a single test case to pass is simple. Creating code whose tests continue to pass after months or years of adding additional features is heading toward the impossible.

For us to be able to deliver code at that level consistently, we require a lot of nifty tricks. This book hopes to not only equip you with those tricks, but also to give you the wisdom to apply them effectively.

What this book covers

Chapter 1, *Never Stop Aiming for Better*, aims to define dependency injection, outline why dependency injection is important for Go development, and introduce several code smells that may be addressed with dependency injection.

Chapter 2, *SOLID Design Principles for Go*, introduces the SOLID software design principles and how they relate to both dependency injection and programming in Go.

Chapter 3, *Coding for User Experience*, addresses often overlooked concepts in programming, namely testing and the code's user experience. It also introduces many other concepts, including mocks, stubs, test-induced damage and the dependency graph, that we will use throughout the book.

Chapter 4, *Introduction to the ACME Registration Service*, introduces a small, fake service that forms the basis for many of our examples in later chapters. It highlights the issues with the service's current implementation and outlines the goals we are hoping to achieve by applying dependency injection.

Chapter 5, *Dependency Injection with Monkey Patching*, examines monkey patching as a way to swap out dependencies during our tests. This chapter applies monkey patching to our sample service to decouple our tests from the database, and to decouple the different layers from each other, all without resorting to significant refactoring.

Chapter 6, *Dependency Injection with Constructor Injection*, introduces perhaps the most traditional form of dependency injection – constructor injection. This chapter will examine its many advantages, its disadvantages, and show how to successfully apply constructor injection.

Chapter 7, *Dependency Injection with Method Injection*, introduces the second most common form of dependency injection – method injection. This chapter discusses the advantages and disadvantages of method injection and shows how to successfully apply the method for request-scoped dependencies.

Chapter 8, *Dependency Injection by Config*, introduces config injection. Config injection is an extension of constructor and method injection that intends to improve the usability of the code by reducing the number of parameters.

`Chapter 9`, *Just-in-Time Dependency Injection*, discusses another unusual form of dependency injection – just-in-time injection. Just-in-time (JIT) injection is a strategy that gives us many of the benefits of dependency injection, such as decoupling and testability, without adding parameters to our constructors or methods.

`Chapter 10`, *Off-the-Shelf Injection*, introduces the final dependency injection method – dependency injection using a framework. This chapter outlines the advantages and disadvantages related to adopting a dependency injection framework and also introduces and applies Google Go Cloud's wire framework to our sample service.

`Chapter 11`, *Curb Your Enthusiasm*, examines some of the ways in which dependency injection can go wrong. It offers many examples where applying dependency injection is either unnecessary or detrimental to the code.

`Chapter 12`, *Reviewing Our Progress*, contrasts the state of our sample service after applying dependency injection with the state it was in when it was introduced. It also discusses the steps we could have taken if we were starting a new service with dependency injection.

To get the most out of this book

While dependency injection and many of the other programming concepts discussed in this book are not simple or intuitive, this book introduces them with little assumed knowledge.

That said, the following is assumed:

- You have a basic level of experience with building and testing Go code.
- You are comfortable with the idea of objects/classes due to prior experience with Go or an object-oriented language, such as Java or Scala.

Additionally, it would be beneficial to have at least a passing understanding of building and consuming HTTP-based REST APIs. In `Chapter 4`, *Introduction to the ACME Registration Service*, we will introduce an example REST service that will form the basis for many of the examples in the book. To be able to run this sample service, you will need to be able to install and configure a MySQL database service on your development environment and be able to customize the supplied configuration to match your local environment. All of the commands provided in this book were developed and tested under OSX and should work without modification on any Linux- or Unix-based system. Developers with Windows-based development environments will need to adjust the commands before running them.

Download the example code files

You can download the example code files for this book from your account at `www.packt.com`. If you purchased this book elsewhere, you can visit `www.packt.com/support` and register to have the files emailed directly to you.

You can download the code files by following these steps:

1. Log in or register at `www.packt.com`.
2. Select the **SUPPORT** tab.
3. Click on **Code Downloads & Errata**.
4. Enter the name of the book in the **Search** box and follow the onscreen instructions.

Once the file is downloaded, please make sure that you unzip or extract the folder using the latest version of:

- WinRAR/7-Zip for Windows
- Zipeg/iZip/UnRarX for Mac
- 7-Zip/PeaZip for Linux

The code bundle for the book is also hosted on GitHub at `https://github.com/PacktPublishing/Hands-On-Dependency-Injection-in-Go`. In case there's an update to the code, it will be updated on the existing GitHub repository.

We also have other code bundles from our rich catalog of books and videos available at `https://github.com/PacktPublishing/`. Check them out!

Download the color images

We also provide a PDF file that has color images of the screenshots/diagrams used in this book. You can download it here: `http://www.packtpub.com/sites/default/files/downloads/Bookname_ColorImages.pdf`.

Conventions used

There are a number of text conventions used throughout this book.

`CodeInText`: Indicates code words in text, database table names, folder names, filenames, file extensions, pathnames, dummy URLs, user input, and Twitter handles. Here is an example: "Mount the downloaded `WebStorm-10*.dmg` disk image file as another disk in your system."

A block of code is set as follows:

```
html, body, #map {
  height: 100%;
  margin: 0;
  padding: 0
}
```

When we wish to draw your attention to a particular part of a code block, the relevant lines or items are set in bold:

```
[default]
exten => s,1,Dial(Zap/1|30)
exten => s,2,Voicemail(u100)
exten => s,102,Voicemail(b100)
exten => i,1,Voicemail(s0)
```

Any command-line input or output is written as follows:

```
$ mkdir css
$ cd css
```

Bold: Indicates a new term, an important word, or words that you see on screen. For example, words in menus or dialog boxes appear in the text like this. Here is an example: Select **System info** from the **Administration** panel."

Warnings or important notes appear like this.

Tips and tricks appear like this.

Get in touch

Feedback from our readers is always welcome.

General feedback: If you have questions about any aspect of this book, mention the book title in the subject of your message and email us at customercare@packtpub.com.

Errata: Although we have taken every care to ensure the accuracy of our content, mistakes do happen. If you have found a mistake in this book, we would be grateful if you would report this to us. Please visit www.packt.com/submit-errata, selecting your book, clicking on the Errata Submission Form link, and entering the details.

Piracy: If you come across any illegal copies of our works in any form on the internet, we would be grateful if you would provide us with the location address or website name. Please contact us at copyright@packt.com with a link to the material.

If you are interested in becoming an author: If there is a topic that you have expertise in, and you are interested in either writing or contributing to a book, please visit authors.packtpub.com.

Reviews

Please leave a review. Once you have read and used this book, why not leave a review on the site that you purchased it from? Potential readers can then see and use your unbiased opinion to make purchase decisions, we at Packt can understand what you think about our products, and our authors can see your feedback on their book. Thank you!

For more information about Packt, please visit packt.com.

1
Never Stop Aiming for Better

Do you want code that is easier to maintain? How about easier to test? Easier to extend? **Dependency Injection** (**DI**) might be just the tool you need.

In this chapter, we will define DI, perhaps in a somewhat atypical way, and explore the code smells that could indicate you need DI. We will also talk briefly about Go and how I would like you to approach the ideas presented in this book.

Are you ready to join me on a journey to better Go code?

We will cover the following topics:

- Why does DI matter?
- What is DI?
- When should I apply DI?
- How can I improve as a Go programmer?

Technical requirements

Hopefully, you will have Go installed. It is downloadable from `https://golang.org/` or your preferred package manager.

All code in this chapter is available at `https://github.com/PacktPublishing/Hands-On-Dependency-Injection-in-Go/tree/master/ch01`.

Why does DI matter?

As professionals, we should never stop learning. Learning is the one true way to ensure we stay in demand and continue delivering value to our customers. Doctors, lawyers, and scientists are all highly respected professionals and all focus on continuously learning. Why should programmers be different?

In this book, we will take a journey that will start with some code that *gets the job done* and, by selectively applying various DI methods available in Go, together, we will transform it into something a hell of a lot easier to maintain, test, and extend.

Not everything in this book is *traditional* or perhaps even *idiomatic*, but I would ask you to *try it before you deny it*. If you like it, fantastic. If not, at least you learned what you don't want to do.

So, how do I define DI?

DI is *coding in such a way that those resources (that is, functions or structs) that we depend on are abstractions*. Because these dependencies are abstract, changes to them do not necessitate changes to our code. The fancy word for this is **decoupling**.

The use of the word abstraction here may be a little misleading. I do not mean an abstract class like you find in Java; Go does not have that. Go does, however, have interfaces and function literals (also known as **closures**).

Consider the following example of an interface and the `SavePerson()` function that uses it:

```
// Saver persists the supplied bytes
type Saver interface {
  Save(data []byte) error
}

// SavePerson will validate and persist the supplied person
func SavePerson(person *Person, saver Saver) error {
  // validate the inputs
  err := person.validate()
  if err != nil {
    return err
  }

  // encode person to bytes
  bytes, err := person.encode()
  if err != nil {
```

```
      return err
   }

   // save the person and return the result
   return saver.Save(bytes)
}

// Person data object
type Person struct {
   Name  string
   Phone string
}

// validate the person object
func (p *Person) validate() error {
   if p.Name == "" {
      return errors.New("name missing")
   }

   if p.Phone == "" {
      return errors.New("phone missing")
   }

   return nil
}

// convert the person into bytes
func (p *Person) encode() ([]byte, error) {
   return json.Marshal(p)
}
```

In the preceding example, what does Saver do? It saves some bytes somewhere. How does it do this? We don't know and, while working on the SavePerson function, we don't care.

Let's look at another example that uses a function literal:

```
// LoadPerson will load the requested person by ID.
// Errors include: invalid ID, missing person and failure to load
// or decode.
func LoadPerson(ID int, decodePerson func(data []byte) *Person) (*Person,
error) {
   // validate the input
   if ID <= 0 {
      return nil, fmt.Errorf("invalid ID '%d' supplied", ID)
   }

   // load from storage
```

```
bytes, err := loadPerson(ID)
if err != nil {
  return nil, err
}

// decode bytes and return
return decodePerson(bytes), nil
}
```

What does `decodePerson` do? It converts the `bytes` into a person. How? We don't need to know to right now.

This is the first advantage of DI that I would highlight to you:

DI reduces the knowledge required when working on a piece of code, by expressing dependencies in an abstract or generic manner

Now, let's say that the preceding code came from a system that stored data in a **Network File Share** (**NFS**). How would we write unit tests for that? Having access to an NFS at all times would be a pain. Any such tests would also fail more often than they should due to entirely unrelated issues, such as network connectivity.

On the other hand, by relying on an abstraction, we could swap out the code that saves to the NFS with fake code. This way, we are only testing our code in isolation from the NFS, as shown in the following code:

```
func TestSavePerson_happyPath(t *testing.T) {
    // input
    in := &Person{
        Name:  "Sophia",
        Phone: "0123456789",
    }

    // mock the NFS
    mockNFS := &mockSaver{}
    mockNFS.On("Save", mock.Anything).Return(nil).Once()

    // Call Save
    resultErr := SavePerson(in, mockNFS)

    // validate result
    assert.NoError(t, resultErr)
    assert.True(t, mockNFS.AssertExpectations(t))
}
```

Don't worry if the preceding code looks unfamiliar; we will examine all of the parts in depth later in this book.

Which brings us to the second advantage of DI:

DI enables us to test our code in isolation of our dependencies

Considering the earlier example, how could we test our error-handling code? We could shut down the NFS through some external script every time we run the tests, but this would likely be slow and would definitely annoy anyone else that depended on it.

On the other hand, we could quickly make a fake `Saver` that always failed, as shown in the following code:

```
func TestSavePerson_nfsAlwaysFails(t *testing.T) {
    // input
    in := &Person{
        Name:  "Sophia",
        Phone: "0123456789",
    }

    // mock the NFS
    mockNFS := &mockSaver{}
    mockNFS.On("Save", mock.Anything).Return(errors.New("save
failed")).Once()

    // Call Save
    resultErr := SavePerson(in, mockNFS)

    // validate result
    assert.Error(t, resultErr)
    assert.True(t, mockNFS.AssertExpectations(t))
}
```

The above test is fast, predictable, and reliable. Everything we could want from tests!

This gives us the third advantage of DI:

DI enables us to quickly and reliably test situations that are otherwise difficult or impossible
Let's not forget about the traditional sales pitch for DI. Tomorrow, if we decided to save to a NoSQL database instead of our NFS, how would our `SavePerson` code have to change? Not one bit. We would only need to write a new `Saver` implementation, giving us the fourth advantage of DI:

DI reduces the impact of extensions or changes
At the end of the day, DI is a tool—a handy tool, but no magic bullet. It's a tool that can make code easier to understand, test, extend, and reuse—a tool that can also help reduce the likelihood of circular dependency issues that commonly plague new Go developers.

Code smells that indicate you might need DI

The saying *to a man with only a hammer, every problem looks like a nail* is old and yet is never truer than in programming. As professionals, we should be continually striving to acquire more tools to be better equipped for whatever our job throws at us. DI, while a highly useful tool, is useful only for particular nails. In our case, these nails are **code smells**. Code smells are indications in the code of a potentially deeper problem.

There are many different types of code smell; in this section, we will examine only those that can be alleviated by DI. In later chapters, we will reference these smells as we attempt to remove them from our code.

Code smells generally fall into four different categories:

- Code bloat
- Resistance to change
- Wasted effort
- Tight coupling

Code bloat

Code bloat smells are cases where unwieldy slabs of code have been added to structs or functions so that they have become hard to understand, maintain, and test. Frequently found in older code, they are often the result of a gradual degradation and lack of maintenance rather than intentional choices.

They can be found with a visual scan of the source code or by employing a cyclomatic complexity checker (a software metric that indicates the complexity of a piece of code) such as gocyclo (`https://github.com/fzipp/gocyclo`).

These smells include the following:

- **Long methods**: While the code is run on computers, it is written for humans. Any method of more than about 30 lines should be split into smaller chunks. While it makes no difference to the computer, it makes it easier for us humans to understand.
- **Long structs**: Similar to long methods, the longer a struct, the harder it is to understand and therefore maintain. Long structs typically also indicate the struct is doing too much. Splitting one struct into several smaller ones is also a great way to increase the reusability potential of the code.

- **Long parameter lists**: Long parameter lists also indicate that the method is likely doing more than it should. When adding new features, it is tempting to add a new parameter to an existing function to account for the new use case. This is a slippery slope. This new parameter is either optional/unnecessary for the existing use cases or is an indication of a significant increase in complexity in the method.
- **Long conditional blocks**: Switch statements are amazing. The problem is they are very easy to abuse and tend to multiply like proverbial rabbits. Perhaps the most significant problem, however, is their effect on the readability of the code. Long conditional blocks take up a lot of space and interrupt the readability of the function. Consider the following code:

```
func AppendValue(buffer []byte, in interface{}) []byte{
    var value []byte

    // convert input to []byte
    switch concrete := in.(type) {
    case []byte:
        value = concrete

    case string:
        value = []byte(concrete)

    case int64:
        value = []byte(strconv.FormatInt(concrete, 10))

    case bool:
        value = []byte(strconv.FormatBool(concrete))

    case float64:
        value = []byte(strconv.FormatFloat(concrete, 'e', 3, 64))
    }

    buffer = append(buffer, value...)
    return buffer
}
```

By taking `interface{}` as input, anywhere we wish to use it, we are almost forced to have a switch like this one. We would be better off changing from `interface{}` to an interface and then adding the necessary operations to the interface. This approach is better illustrated by the `json.Marshaller` and `driver.Valuer` interfaces in the standard library.

Applying DI to these smells will typically reduce the complexity of individual pieces of code by breaking them into smaller, separate pieces, which in turn makes them easier to understand, maintain, and test.

Resistance to change

These are cases where it is difficult and/or slow to add new features. Similarly, tests are often harder to write, especially tests for failure conditions. Similar to code bloat, these smells can be the result of a gradual degradation and lack of maintenance, but they can also be caused by a lack of up-front planning or poor API design.

They can be found by examining the pull request log or commit history and, in particular, determining if new features require many small changes in different parts of the code. If your team tracks feature velocity and you notice it is declining, this is also a likely cause.

These smells include the following:

- **Shotgun surgery**: This is when small changes made to one struct necessitate changes in other structs. These changes imply that the organisation or abstraction used was incorrect. Typically, all of these changes should be in one class. In the following example, you can see how adding an email field to the person data would result in changing all three structs (`Presenter`, `Validator`, and `Saver`):

```go
// Renderer will render a person to the supplied writer
type Renderer struct{}

func (r Renderer) render(name, phone string, output io.Writer) {
  // output the person
}

// Validator will validate the supplied person has all the
// required fields
type Validator struct{}

func (v Validator) validate(name, phone string) error {
  // validate the person
  return nil
}

// Saver will save the supplied person to the DB
type Saver struct{}

func (s *Saver) Save(db *sql.DB, name, phone string) {
  // save the person to db
}
```

- **Leaking implementation details**: One of the more popular idioms in the Go community is *accept interfaces, return structs*. It's a catchy turn of phrase, but its simplicity masks its cleverness. When a function accepts a struct, it ties the user to a particular implementation—a strict relationship that makes future changes or additional usage difficult. By extension, if that implementation detail were to change, the API changes and forces changes on its users.

Applying DI to these smells is typically a good investment in the future. While not fixing them is not fatal, the code will progressively degrade until you are dealing with the proverbial *big ball of mud*. You know the type—a package that no-one understands, no-one trusts, and only the brave or stupid are willing to make changes to. DI enables you to decouple from the implementation choices, thereby making it easier to refactor, test, and maintain small chunks of code in isolation.

Wasted effort

These smells are cases where the cost to maintain the code is higher than it needs to be. They are typically caused by laziness or lack of experience. It's always easier to copy/paste code than to carefully refactor it. The problem is, coding like this is like eating unhealthy snacks. It feels great in the moment, but the long-term consequences suck.

They can be found by taking a critical look at the source code and asking yourself *do I really need this code?* Or, *can I make this easier to understand?*

Using tools such as dupl (`https://github.com/mibk/dupl`) or PMD (`https://pmd.github.io/`) will also help you identify areas of the code to investigate.

These smells include the following:

- **Excessive duplicated code**: Firstly, please, please do not become a zealot about this one. While in most cases, duplicated code is a bad thing, sometimes copying code can result in a system that is easier to maintain and can evolve. We will deal with a common source of this smell in `Chapter 8`, *Dependency Injection by Config*.
- **Excessive comments**: Leaving a note for those that come after you, even it is only you 6 months from now, is a friendly and professional thing to do. But when that note becomes an essay, then it's time to refactor:

```
// Excessive comments
func outputOrderedPeopleA(in []*Person) {
  // This code orders people by name.
  // In cases where the name is the same, it will order by
  // phone number.
```

```
// The sort algorithm used is a bubble sort
// WARNING: this sort will change the items of the input array
for _, p := range in {
   // ... sort code removed ...
}

outputPeople(in)
}

// Comments replaced with descriptive names
func outputOrderedPeopleB(in []*Person) {
   sortPeople(in)
   outputPeople(in)
}
```

- **Overly complicated code**: The harder code is for other people to understand, the worse it is. Typically, this is the result of someone trying to be too fancy or not putting enough effort into structure or naming. Taking a more selfish view, if you are the only one who understands a piece of code, you are the only one that can work on it. Meaning, you are doomed to maintain it forever. What does the following code do:

```
for a := float64(0); a < 360; a++ {
   ra := math.Pi * 2 * a / 360
   x := r*math.Sin(ra) + v
   y := r*math.Cos(ra) + v
   i.Set(int(x), int(y), c)
}
```

- **DRY/WET code**: The **Don't Repeat Yourself (DRY)** principle is aimed at reducing duplicated efforts by grouping responsibilities together and providing clean abstractions. By contrast, in WET code, sometimes called **Waste Everyone's Time** code, you will find the same responsibility in many places. This smell often appears in formatting or conversion code. This sort of code should exist at the system boundaries, that is, converting user input or formatting output.

While many of these smells can be fixed without DI, DI provides an easier way to *lift and shift* the duplication into an abstraction that can then be used to reduce the duplication and improve the readability and maintainability of the code.

Tight coupling

For people, tight coupling might be a good thing. For Go code, it's really not. Coupling is a measure of how objects relate to or depend on each other. When the tight coupling is present, this interdependence forces the objects or packages to evolve together, adding complexity and maintenance costs.

Coupling-related smells are perhaps the most insidious and obstinate but by far the most rewarding when dealt with. They are often the result of a lack of object-oriented design or insufficient use of interfaces.

Sadly, I don't have a handy tool to help you find these smells but I am confident that, by the end of this book, you will have no trouble spotting and dealing with them.

Frequently, I find it useful to implement a feature in a tightly coupled form first and then work backward to decouple and thoroughly unit test my code before submitting it. For me, it is especially helpful in cases where the correct abstractions are not obvious.

These smells include the following:

- **Dependence on God objects**: These are large objects that *know too much* or *do too much*. While this is a general code smell and something that should be avoided like the plague, the problem from a DI perspective is that too much of the code is dependent on this one object. When they exist and we are not careful, it won't be long before Go will be refusing to compile due to a circular dependency. Interestingly, Go considers dependencies and imports not at an object level but at a package level. So we have to avoid God packages as well. We will address a very common God object problem in `Chapter 8`, *Dependency Injection by Config*.
- **Circular dependencies**: These are where package A depends on package B, and package B depends on package A. This is an easy mistake to make and sometimes a hard one to get rid of.

    In the following example, while the config is arguably a `God` object and therefore a code smell, I am hard pressed to find a better way to import the config from a single JSON file. Instead, I would argue that the problem to be solved is the use of the `config` package by `orders` package. A typical config God object follows:

    ```
    package config

    import ...

    // Config defines the JSON format of the config file
    type Config struct {
        // Address is the host and port to bind to.
    ```

```
    // Default 0.0.0.0:8080
    Address string

    // DefaultCurrency is the default currency of the system
    DefaultCurrency payment.Currency
}

// Load will load the JSON config from the file supplied
func Load(filename string) (*Config, error) {
    // TODO: load currency from file
    return nil, errors.New("not implemented yet")
}
```

In the attempted usage of the `config` package, you can see that the `Currency` type belongs to the `Package` package and so including it in `config`, as shown in the preceding example, causes a circular dependency:

```
package payment

import ...

// Currency is custom type for currency
type Currency string

// Processor processes payments
type Processor struct {
    Config *config.Config
}

// Pay makes a payment in the default currency
func (p *Processor) Pay(amount float64) error {
    // TODO: implement me
    return errors.New("not implemented yet")
}
```

- **Object orgy**: These occur when an object has too much knowledge of and/or access to the internals of another or, to put it another way, *insufficient encapsulation between objects*. Because the objects are *joined at the hip*, they will frequently have to evolve together, increasing the cost of understanding the code and maintaining it. Consider the following code:

```
type PageLoader struct {
}

func (o *PageLoader) LoadPage(url string) ([]byte, error) {
    b := newFetcher()
```

```go
    // check cache
    payload, err := b.cache.Get(url)
    if err == nil {
        // found in cache
        return payload, nil
    }

    // call upstream
    resp, err := b.httpClient.Get(url)
    if err != nil {
        return nil, err
    }
    defer resp.Body.Close()

    // extract data from HTTP response
    payload, err = ioutil.ReadAll(resp.Body)
    if err != nil {
        return nil, err
    }

    // save to cache asynchronously
    go func(key string, value []byte) {
        b.cache.Set(key, value)
    }(url, payload)

    // return
    return payload, nil
}

type Fetcher struct {
    httpClient http.Client
    cache      *Cache
}
```

In this example, `PageLoader` repeatedly calls the member variable of the `Fetcher`. So much so that, if the implementation of `Fetcher` changed, it's highly likely that `PageLoader` would be affected. In this case, these two objects should be merged together as `PageLoader` has no extra functionality.

- **Yo-yo problem**: The standard definition of this smell is *when the inheritance graph is so long and complicated that the programmer has to keep flipping through the code to understand it.* Given that Go doesn't have inheritance, you would think we would be safe from this problem. However, it is possible if you try hard enough, with excessive composition. To address this issue, it's better to keep relationships as shallow and abstract as possible. In this way, we can concentrate on a much smaller scope when making changes and compose many small objects into a larger system.

- **Feature envy**: When a function makes extensive use of another object, it is envious of it. Typically, an indication that the function should be moved away from the object it is envious of. DI may not be the solution to this, but this smell does indicate high coupling and, therefore, is an indicator to consider applying DI techniques:

```go
func doSearchWithEnvy(request searchRequest) ([]searchResults,
error) {
   // validate request
   if request.query == "" {
     return nil, errors.New("search term is missing")
   }
   if request.start.IsZero() || request.start.After(time.Now()) {
     return nil, errors.New("start time is missing or invalid")
   }
   if request.end.IsZero() || request.end.Before(request.start) {
     return nil, errors.New("end time is missing or invalid")
   }

   return performSearch(request)
}

func doSearchWithoutEnvy(request searchRequest) ([]searchResults,
error) {
   err := request.validate()
   if err != nil {
     return nil, err
   }

   return performSearch(request)
}
```

As your code becomes less coupled, you will find the individual parts (packages, interfaces, and structs) will become more focused. This is referred to as having **high cohesion**. Both low coupling and high cohesion are desirable as they make the code easier to understand and work with.

Healthy skepticism

As we journey through this book, you will look at some fantastic coding techniques and some not so great. I would ask you to spend some time pondering which is which. Continuous learning should be tempered with a healthy dose of skepticism. For each technique, I will lay out the pros and cons, but I would ask you to dig deeper. Ask yourself the following:

- What is this technique trying to achieve?
- What would my code look like after I apply this technique?
- Do I really need it?
- Are there any downsides to using this method?

Even when your inner skeptic dismisses the technique, you've at least learned to identify something you don't like and don't want to use, and learning is always a win.

A quick word about idiomatic Go

Personally, I try to avoid using the term **idiomatic Go** but a Go book is arguably not complete without addressing it in some form. I avoid it because I have seen it too often used as a stick to beat people. Essentially, *this is not idiomatic, therefore it's wrong* and, by extension, *I am idiomatic and therefore better than you*. I believe that programming is a craft and, while a craft should have some form of consistency in its application, it should, as with all crafts, be flexible. After all, innovation is often found by bending or breaking the rules. So what does idiomatic Go mean to me?

I'll define it as loosely as I can:

- **Format your code with** `gofmt`: Truly one less thing for us programmers to argue about. It's the official style, supported with official tools. Let's find something more substantive to argue about.
- **Read, apply, and regularly revisit the ideas in** *Effective Go* (`https://golang.org/doc/effective_go.html`) **and** *Code Review Comments* (`https://github.com/golang/go/wiki/CodeReviewComments`): There is a huge amount of wisdom in these pages, so much so that it's perhaps impossible to glean it all from just one reading.
- **Aggressively apply the** *Unix philosophy*: It state that we should *design code that does a single thing, but to does it well and works well together well with other code.*

While these three things are the minimum for me, there are a couple of other ideas that resonate:

- **Accepting interfaces and returning structs**: While accepting interfaces leads to nicely decoupled code, the returning structs might strike you as a contradiction. I know they did with me at first. While outputting an interface might feel like it's more loosely coupled, it's not. Output can only be one thing—whatever you code it to be. Returning an interface is fine if that's what you need, but forcing yourself to do so just ends up with you writing more code.
- **Reasonable defaults**: Since switching to Go, I've found many cases where I want to offer my user the ability to configure the module but such configuration is frequently not used. In other languages, this could lead to multiple constructors or seldom used parameters, but by applying this pattern we end up with a much cleaner API and less code to maintain.

Leave your baggage at the door

If you were to ask me *what is the most frequent mistake new Go programmers make?*, I would not hesitate to tell you that it's bringing other language patterns into Go. I know this was my biggest early mistake. My first Go service looked like a Java app written in Go. Not only was the result subpar but it was rather painful, particularly while I was trying to achieve things such as inheritance. I've had a similar experience programming Go in a functional style, as you might see in `Node.js`.

In short, please don't do it. Re-read *Effective Go* and Go blogs as often as you need to until you find yourself using small interfaces, firing off Go routines without reservation, loving channels, and wondering why you ever needed more than composition to achieve nice polymorphism.

Summary

In this chapter, we started a journey—a journey that will lead to code that is easier to maintain, extend, and test.

We started by defining DI and examining some of the benefits it can bring us. With the help of a few examples, we saw how this might look in Go.

After that, we started identifying code smells to look out for and that could be addressed or alleviated by applying DI.

Finally, we examined what I believe Go code looks like, and I challenged you to be skeptical and apply a critical eye to techniques presented in this book.

Questions

1. What is DI?
2. What are the four highlighted advantages of DI?
3. What sorts of issues does it address?
4. Why is it important to be skeptical?
5. What does idiomatic Go mean to you?

Further reading

Packt has many other great resources for learning about DI and Go:

- `https://www.packtpub.com/application-development/java-9-dependency-injection`
- `https://www.packtpub.com/application-development/dependency-injection-net-core-20`
- `https://www.packtpub.com/networking-and-servers/mastering-go`

SOLID Design Principles for Go

2

In 2002, *Robert "Uncle Bob" Martin* published the book *Agile Software Development, Principles, Patterns, and Practices* in which he defined the five principles of reusable programs, which he called SOLID principles. While it might seem strange to include these principles in a book about a programming language invented 10 years later, these principles are still relevant today.

In this chapter, we will briefly examine each of these principles, how they relate to **dependency injection** (**DI**) and what that means for Go. SOLID is an acronym for five popular object-oriented software design principles:

- Single responsibility principle
- Open/closed principle
- Liskov substitution principle
- Interface segregation principle
- Dependency inversion principle

Technical requirements

The only requirement for this chapter is a basic understanding of objects and interfaces and an open mind.

All code in this chapter is available at `https://github.com/PacktPublishing/Hands-On-Dependency-Injection-in-Go/tree/master/ch02`.

You will find links to additional information and other references mentioned in this chapter in the *Further reading* section at the end of this chapter.

Single responsibility principle (SRP)

"A class should have one, and only one, reason to change."
–Robert C. Martin

Go doesn't have classes, but if we squint a little and replace the word *class* with *objects* (structs, functions, interfaces or packages), then the concept still applies.

Why do we want our objects to do only one thing? Let's look at a couple of objects that do one thing:

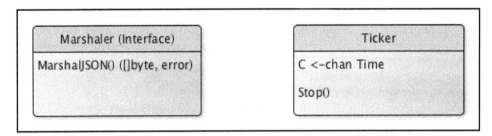

These objects are simple and easy to use, and have a wide range of uses.

Designing objects so that they all do only one thing sounds okay in the abstract. But you are probably thinking that doing so for an entire system would add a lot more code. Yes, it will. However, what it doesn't do is add complexity; in fact, it significantly reduces it. Each piece of code would be smaller and easier to understand, and therefore easier to test. This fact gives us the first advantage of SRP:

SRP reduces the complexity by decomposing code into smaller, more concise pieces

With a name like single responsibility principle, it would be safe to assume that it is all about responsibility, but so far, all we have talked about is change. Why is this? Let's look at an example:

```
// Calculator calculates the test coverage for a directory
// and it's sub-directories
type Calculator struct {
  // coverage data populated by `Calculate()` method
  data map[string]float64
}

// Calculate will calculate the coverage
func (c *Calculator) Calculate(path string) error {
  // run `go test -cover ./[path]/...` and store the results
```

```
    return nil
  }

  // Output will print the coverage data to the supplied writer
  func (c *Calculator) Output(writer io.Writer) {
    for path, result := range c.data {
      fmt.Fprintf(writer, "%s -> %.1f\n", path, result)
    }
  }
}
```

The code looks reasonable—one member variable and two methods. It does not, however, conform to SRP. Let's assume that the app was successful, and we decided that we also needed to output the results to CSV. We could add a method to do that, as shown in the following code:

```
// Calculator calculates the test coverage for a directory
// and it's sub-directories
type Calculator struct {
  // coverage data populated by `Calculate()` method
  data map[string]float64
}

// Calculate will calculate the coverage
func (c *Calculator) Calculate(path string) error {
  // run `go test -cover ./[path]/...` and store the results
  return nil
}

// Output will print the coverage data to the supplied writer
func (c Calculator) Output(writer io.Writer) {
  for path, result := range c.data {
    fmt.Fprintf(writer, "%s -> %.1f\n", path, result)
  }
}

// OutputCSV will print the coverage data to the supplied writer
func (c Calculator) OutputCSV(writer io.Writer) {
  for path, result := range c.data {
    fmt.Fprintf(writer, "%s,%.1f\n", path, result)
  }
}
```

We have changed the struct and added another Output() method. We have added more responsibilities to the struct and, in doing so, we have added complexity. In this simple example, our changes are confined to one method, so there's no risk that we broke the previous code. However, as the struct gets bigger and more complicated, our changes are unlikely to be so clean.

Conversely, if we were to break the responsibilities into `Calculate` and `Output`, then adding more outputs would mere define new structs. Additionally, should we decide that we don't like the default output format, we could change it separately from other parts.

Let's try a different implementation:

```go
// Calculator calculates the test coverage for a directory
// and it's sub-directories
type Calculator struct {
  // coverage data populated by `Calculate()` method
  data map[string]float64
}

// Calculate will calculate the coverage
func (c *Calculator) Calculate(path string) error {
  // run `go test -cover ./[path]/...` and store the results
  return nil
}

func (c *Calculator) getData() map[string]float64 {
  // copy and return the map
  return nil
}

type Printer interface {
  Output(data map[string]float64)
}

type DefaultPrinter struct {
  Writer io.Writer
}

// Output implements Printer
func (d *DefaultPrinter) Output(data map[string]float64) {
  for path, result := range data {
    fmt.Fprintf(d.Writer, "%s -> %.1f\n", path, result)
  }
}

type CSVPrinter struct {
  Writer io.Writer
}

// Output implements Printer
func (d *CSVPrinter) Output(data map[string]float64) {
```

```
for path, result := range data {
    fmt.Fprintf(d.Writer, "%s,%.1f\n", path, result)
  }
}
```

Do you notice anything significant about the printers? They have no connection at all to the calculation. They could be used for any data in the same format. This leads to the second advantage of SRP:

SRP increases the potential reusability of code.

In the first implementation of our coverage calculator, to test the `Output()` method we would be first call the `Calculate()` method. This approach increases the complexity of our tests by coupling the calculation with the output. Consider the following scenarios:

- How do we test for no results?
- How do we test edge conditions, such as 0% or 100% coverage?

After decoupling these responsibilities, we should encourage ourselves to consider the inputs and outputs of each part in a less interdependent manner, hence making the tests easier to write and maintain. This leads to the third advantage of SRP:

SRP makes tests simpler to write and maintain.

SRP is also an excellent way to improve general code readability. Take a look at this next example:

```
func loadUserHandler(resp http.ResponseWriter, req *http.Request) {
  err := req.ParseForm()
  if err != nil {
    resp.WriteHeader(http.StatusInternalServerError)
    return
  }
  userID, err := strconv.ParseInt(req.Form.Get("UserID"), 10, 64)
  if err != nil {
    resp.WriteHeader(http.StatusPreconditionFailed)
    return
  }

  row := DB.QueryRow("SELECT * FROM Users WHERE ID = ?", userID)

  person := &Person{}
  err = row.Scan(&person.ID, &person.Name, &person.Phone)
  if err != nil {
    resp.WriteHeader(http.StatusInternalServerError)
    return
```

```
    }

    encoder := json.NewEncoder(resp)
    encoder.Encode(person)
}
```

I'd bet that took more than five seconds to understand. How about this code?

```
func loadUserHandler(resp http.ResponseWriter, req *http.Request) {
    userID, err := extractIDFromRequest(req)
    if err != nil {
        resp.WriteHeader(http.StatusPreconditionFailed)
        return
    }

    person, err := loadPersonByID(userID)
    if err != nil {
        resp.WriteHeader(http.StatusInternalServerError)
        return
    }

    outputPerson(resp, person)
}
```

By applying SRP at the function level, we have reduced the function's bloat and increased its readability. The function's single responsibility is now to coordinate the calls to the other functions.

How does this relate to DI?

When applying DI to our code, we are unsurprisingly injecting our dependencies, typically in the form of a function parameter. If you see a function with many injected dependencies, this is a likely sign that the method is doing too much.

Additionally, applying SRP will inform our object design. As such, this helps us identify when and where to use DI.

What does this mean for Go?

In Chapter 1, *Never Stop Aiming for Better*, we mentioned Go's relationship with the Unix philosophy, which states that we should *design code that does a single thing, but to does it well and works well together well with other code*. After applying SRP, our objects will be perfectly in line with this principle.

Go interfaces, structs, and functions

At the interface and struct level, applying SRP results in many small interfaces. A function that complies with the SRP has few inputs and is quite short (that is, it has less than one screen of code). Both of these features inherently address the code bloat smells we mentioned in `Chapter 1`, *Never Stop Aiming for Better*.

By addressing the code bloat, we find that one of the less-advertised advantages of SRP is that it makes code easier to understand. Simply put, when a piece of code does one thing, its purpose is clearer.

When applying SRP to existing code, you will often break the code into smaller pieces. You may experience a natural aversion to this, due to the feeling that you might also then have to write more tests. In cases where you are splitting a struct or interface into multiple parts, this may be true. However, if the code you are refactoring has high unit-test coverage, then you probably already have many of the tests you need. They just need to be moved around a little bit.

On the other hand, when applying SRP to a function to reduce bloat, no new tests are required; the tests for the original function are perfectly acceptable. Let's look at an example of a test for our `loadUserHandler()`, which was shown in the preceding example:

```go
func TestLoadUserHandler(t *testing.T) {
    // build request
    req := &http.Request{
        Form: url.Values{},
    }
    req.Form.Add("UserID", "1234")

    // call function under test
    resp := httptest.NewRecorder()
    loadUserHandler(resp, req)

    // validate result
    assert.Equal(t, http.StatusOK, resp.Code)

    expectedBody := `{"ID":1,"Name":"Bob","Phone":"0123456789"}` + "\n"
    assert.Equal(t, expectedBody, resp.Body.String())
}
```

This test can be applied to either form of our function and will achieve the same thing. In this case, we were refactoring for readability, and we don't want anything to discourage us from that. Additionally, testing from the API (either a public method or a function called by others) is more stable, as the API contract is less likely to change than the internal implementation.

Go packages

Applying SRP at the package level is perhaps harder to do. Systems are often designed in layers. For example, it's common to see an HTTP REST service with layers arranged in the following manner:

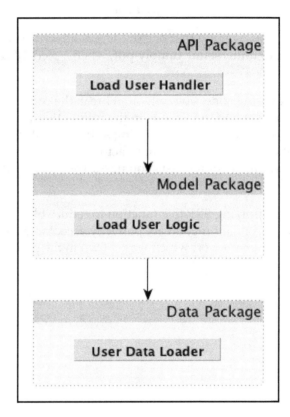

These abstractions are nice and clear; however, problems start to appear when our service has more than a few endpoints. We very quickly end up with monster packages full of entirely unrelated logic. Good packages, on the other hand, are small, concise, and clear of purpose.

It can be hard to find the right abstraction. Often, when I am in need of inspiration, I turn to the experts and examine the standard Go libraries. For example, let's take a look at the `encoding` package:

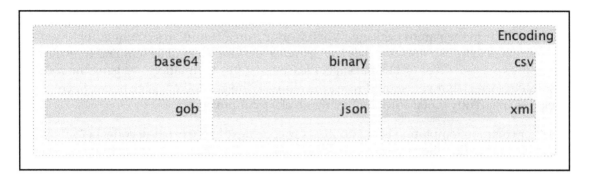

As you can see, each different type is neatly organized in its own package, but all of the packages are still grouped logically by the parent directory. Our REST service would break it down as shown in the following figure:

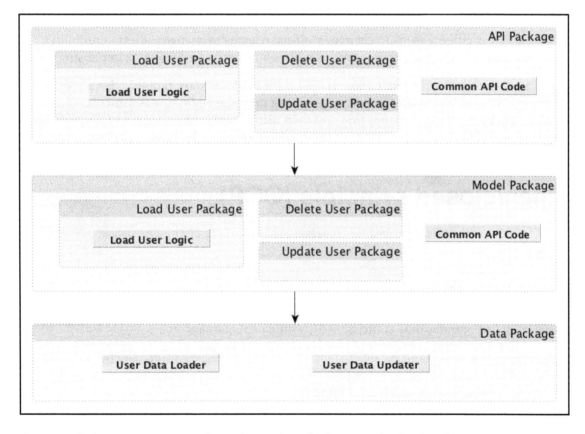

Our initial abstractions are on the right track, only from too high a level.

Another aspect of the `encoding` package that is not immediately apparent is that the shared code is in the parent package. When working on a feature, it's common for programmers to think *I need that code I wrote earlier,* and for them to be tempted to extract the code to a `commons` or `utils` package. Please resist this temptation—reusing the code is absolutely correct, but you should resist the allure of the general package name. Such packages inherently violate SRP by having no clear-cut purpose.

Another common temptation is to add the new code next to the existing code. Let's imagine that we were writing the `encoding` package mentioned previously and the first encoder we made was the JSON one. Next, we add the GobEncoder, and things are going great. Add a few more encoders, and suddenly we have a substantial package with lots of code and a large exported API. At some point, the documentation for our little `encoding` package becomes so long that it will be hard for users to follow. Similarly, we have so much code in the package that our extension and debugging work slows down because it's hard to find things.

SRP helps us identify reasons to change; multiple reasons to change indicate multiple responsibilities. Decoupling these responsibilities enables us to develop better abstractions.

If you have the time or the inclination to do it right from the start, fantastic. However, applying SRP and finding the correct abstractions from the beginning is difficult. You can counter this by breaking the rules first and then using subsequent changes to discover how the software wants to evolve, using the forces of evolution as the basis for refactoring.

Open/closed principle (OCP)

> *"Software entities (classes, modules, functions, etc.) should be open for extension, but closed for modification."*
>
>   *- Bertrand Meyer*

The terms *open* and *closed* are not something I often hear when discussing software engineering, so perhaps they could do with a little explanation.

Open means that we should be able to extend or adapt code by adding new behaviors and features. Closed means that we should avoid making changes to existing code, changes that could result in bugs or other kinds of regression.

These two characteristics might seem contradictory, but the missing piece of the puzzle is the scope. When talking about being open, we are talking about the design or structure of the software. From this perspective, being open means that it is easy to add new packages, new interfaces, or new implementations of an existing interface.

When we talk about being closed, we are talking about existing code and minimizing the changes we make to it, particularly the APIs that are used by others. This brings us to the first advantage of OCP:

OCP helps reduce the risk of additions and extensions

You can think of OCP as a risk-mitigation strategy. Modifying existing code always has some risk involved, and changes to the code used by others especially so. While we can and should be protecting ourselves from this risk with unit tests, these are restricted to scenarios that we intend and misuses that we can imagine; they will not cover everything our users can come up with.

The following code does not follow the OCP:

```
func BuildOutput(response http.ResponseWriter, format string, person
Person) {
  var err error

  switch format {
  case "csv":
    err = outputCSV(response, person)

  case "json":
    err = outputJSON(response, person)
  }

  if err != nil {
    // output a server error and quit
    response.WriteHeader(http.StatusInternalServerError)
    return
  }

  response.WriteHeader(http.StatusOK)
}
```

The first hint that something is amiss is the `switch` statement. It is not hard to imagine a situation where requirements change, and where we might need to add or even remove an output format.

Just how much would have to change if we needed to add another format? See the following:

- **We would need to add another case condition to the switch**: This method is already 18 lines long; how many more formats do we need to add before we cannot see it all on one screen? In how many other places does this `switch` statement exist? Will they need to be updated too?
- **We would need to write another formatting function**: This is one of three changes that are unavoidable
- **The caller of the method would have to be updated to use the new format**: This is the other unavoidable change
- **We would have to add another set of test scenarios to match the new formatting**: This is also unavoidable; however, the tests here will likely be longer than just testing the formatting in isolation

What started as a *small and simple change* is beginning to feel more arduous and risky than we intended.

Let's replace the format input parameter and the `switch` statement with an abstraction, as shown in the following code:

```
func BuildOutput(response http.ResponseWriter, formatter PersonFormatter,
person Person) {
  err := formatter.Format(response, person)
  if err != nil {
    // output a server error and quit
    response.WriteHeader(http.StatusInternalServerError)
    return
  }

  response.WriteHeader(http.StatusOK)
}
```

How many changes was it this time? Let's see:

- We need to define another implementation of the `PersonFormatter` interface
- The caller of the method has to be updated to use the new format
- We have to write test scenarios for the new `PersonFormatter`

That's much better: we are down to only the three unavoidable changes and *we changed nothing in the primary function at all*. This shows us the second advantage of OCP:

OCP can help reduce the number of changes needed to add or remove a feature.

Also, if there happens to be a bug in our new structure after adding the new formatter, it can only be in one place—the new code. This is the third advantage of OCP:

OCP narrows the locality of bugs to only the new code and its usage.

Let's look at another example, where we don't end up applying DI:

```go
func GetUserHandlerV1(resp http.ResponseWriter, req *http.Request) {
  // validate inputs
  err := req.ParseForm()
  if err != nil {
    resp.WriteHeader(http.StatusInternalServerError)
    return
  }
  userID, err := strconv.ParseInt(req.Form.Get("UserID"), 10, 64)
  if err != nil {
    resp.WriteHeader(http.StatusPreconditionFailed)
    return
  }

  user := loadUser(userID)
  outputUser(resp, user)
}

func DeleteUserHandlerV1(resp http.ResponseWriter, req *http.Request) {
  // validate inputs
  err := req.ParseForm()
  if err != nil {
    resp.WriteHeader(http.StatusInternalServerError)
    return
  }
  userID, err := strconv.ParseInt(req.Form.Get("UserID"), 10, 64)
  if err != nil {
    resp.WriteHeader(http.StatusPreconditionFailed)
    return
  }

  deleteUser(userID)
}
```

As you can see, both our HTTP handlers are pulling the data from the form and then converting it into a number. One day, we decide to tighten our input validation and ensure that the number is positive. The likely result? Some pretty nasty shotgun surgery. In this case, however, there is no way around. We made the mess; now we need to clean it up. The fix is hopefully pretty obvious—extracting the repeated logic to one place and then adding the new validation there, as shown in the following code:

```go
func GetUserHandlerV2(resp http.ResponseWriter, req *http.Request) {
  // validate inputs
  err := req.ParseForm()
  if err != nil {
    resp.WriteHeader(http.StatusInternalServerError)
    return
  }
  userID, err := extractUserID(req.Form)
  if err != nil {
    resp.WriteHeader(http.StatusPreconditionFailed)
    return
  }

  user := loadUser(userID)
  outputUser(resp, user)
}

func DeleteUserHandlerV2(resp http.ResponseWriter, req *http.Request) {
  // validate inputs
  err := req.ParseForm()
  if err != nil {
    resp.WriteHeader(http.StatusInternalServerError)
    return
  }
  userID, err := extractUserID(req.Form)
  if err != nil {
    resp.WriteHeader(http.StatusPreconditionFailed)
    return
  }

  deleteUser(userID)
}
```

Sadly, the original code has not reduced, but it's definitely easier to read. Beyond that, we have future-proofed ourselves against any further changes to the validation of the UserID field.

For both our examples, the key to meeting OCP was to find the correct abstraction.

How does this relate to DI?

In Chapter 1, *Never Stop Aiming for Better*, we defined DI as *coding in such a way that those resources that we depend on are abstractions*. By using OCP, we can discover cleaner and more durable abstractions.

What does this mean for Go?

Typically, when discussing OCP, the examples are littered with abstract classes, inheritance, virtual functions, and all kinds of things that Go doesn't have. Or does it?

What is an abstract class really? What is it actually trying to achieve?

It's trying to provide a place for code that is shared between several implementations. We can do that in Go—it's called **composition**. You can see it at work in the following code:

```go
type rowConverter struct {
}

// populate the supplied Person from *sql.Row or *sql.Rows object
func (d *rowConverter) populate(in *Person, scan func(dest ...interface{})
error) error {
  return scan(in.Name, in.Email)
}

type LoadPerson struct {
  // compose the row converter into this loader
  rowConverter
}

func (loader *LoadPerson) ByID(id int) (Person, error) {
  row := loader.loadFromDB(id)

  person := Person{}
  // call the composed "abstract class"
  err := loader.populate(&person, row.Scan)

  return person, err
}

type LoadAll struct {
  // compose the row converter into this loader
  rowConverter
}
```

```
func (loader *LoadPerson) All() ([]Person, error) {
  rows := loader.loadAllFromDB()
  defer rows.Close()

  output := []Person{}
  for rows.Next() {
    person := Person{}

    // call the composed "abstract class"
    err := loader.populate(&person, rows.Scan)
    if err != nil {
      return nil, err
    }
  }

  return output, nil
}
```

In the preceding example, we have extracted some of the shared logic into a `rowConverter` struct. Then, by embedding that struct in the other structs, we can use it without any changes. We have achieved the goals of the abstract class and OCP. Our code is open; we can embed wherever we like but closed. The embedded class has no knowledge of the fact that it was embedded, nor did it require any changes to be used.

Earlier, we defined *closed* as remaining unchanged, but restricted the scope to only the parts of the API that were exported or used by others. It is not reasonable to expect that internal implementation details, including private member variables, should never change. The best way to achieve this is to hide those implementation details. This is called **encapsulation**.

At the package level, encapsulation is simple: we make it private. A good rule of thumb here is to make everything private and only make things public when you really have to. Again, my justification is risk and work avoidance. The moment you export something is the moment that someone could rely on it. Once they rely on it, it should become closed; you have to maintain it, and any changes have a higher risk of breaking something. With proper encapsulation, changes within a package should be invisible to existing users.

At the object level, private doesn't mean what it does in other languages, so we have to learn to behave ourselves. Accessing private member variables leaves the objects tightly coupled, a decision that will come back to bite us.

One of my favorite features of Go's type system is the ability to attach methods to just about anything. Let's say you are writing an HTTP handler for a health check. It does nothing more than return the status 204 (No Content). The interface we need to satisfy is as follows:

```
type Handler interface {
    ServeHTTP(ResponseWriter, *Request)
}
```

A simple implementation might look as shown in the following code:

```
// a HTTP health check handler in long form
type healthCheck struct {
}

func (h *healthCheck) ServeHTTP(resp http.ResponseWriter, _ *http.Request)
{
    resp.WriteHeader(http.StatusNoContent)
}

func healthCheckUsage() {
    http.Handle("/health", &healthCheckLong{})
}
```

We could create a new struct to implement an interface, but that's going to be at least five lines. We can reduce it to three, as shown in the following code:

```
// a HTTP health check handler in short form
func healthCheck(resp http.ResponseWriter, _ *http.Request) {
    resp.WriteHeader(http.StatusNoContent)
}

func healthCheckUsage() {
    http.Handle("/health", http.HandlerFunc(healthCheck))
}
```

The secret sauce, in this case, is hidden in the standard library. We are casting our function into the `http.HandlerFunc` type, which has a `ServeHTTP` method attached to it. This nifty little trick makes it easy for us to satisfy the `http.Handler` interface. As we have already seen in this chapter, moving towards interfaces leads us to less coupled code that is easier to maintain and extend.

Liskov substitution principle (LSP)

"If for each object o1 of type S there is an object o2 of type T such that for all programs P defined in terms of T, the behavior of P is unchanged when o1 is substituted for o2 then S is a subtype of T."

-Barbara Liskov

After reading that three times, I am still not sure I have got it straight. Thankfully, Robert C. Martin made it easier on us and summarized it as follows:

"Subtypes must be substitutable for their base types."

-Robert C. Martin

That I can follow. However, isn't he talking about abstract classes again? Probably. As we saw in the section on OCP, while Go doesn't have abstract classes or inheritance, it does have a composition and interface implementation.

Let's step back for a minute and look at the motivation of this principle. LSP requires that *subtypes are substitutable for each other*. We can use Go interfaces, and this will always hold true.

But hang on, what about this code:

```go
func Go(vehicle actions) {
  if sled, ok := vehicle.(*Sled); ok {
    sled.pushStart()
  } else {
    vehicle.startEngine()
  }

  vehicle.drive()
}

type actions interface {
  drive()
  startEngine()
}

type Vehicle struct {
}

func (v Vehicle) drive() {
  // TODO: implement
}

func (v Vehicle) startEngine() {
  // TODO: implement
}

func (v Vehicle) stopEngine() {
  // TODO: implement
}

type Car struct {
```

```
  Vehicle
}

type Sled struct {
  Vehicle
}

func (s Sled) startEngine() {
  // override so that is does nothing
}

func (s Sled) stopEngine() {
  // override so that is does nothing
}

func (s Sled) pushStart() {
  // TODO: implement
}
```

It uses an interface, but it clearly violates LSP. We could fix this by adding more interfaces, as shown in the following code:

```
func Go(vehicle actions) {
   switch concrete := vehicle.(type) {
   case poweredActions:
      concrete.startEngine()

   case unpoweredActions:
      concrete.pushStart()
   }

   vehicle.drive()
}

type actions interface {
   drive()
}

type poweredActions interface {
   actions
   startEngine()
   stopEngine()
}

type unpoweredActions interface {
   actions
   pushStart()
}
```

```
type Vehicle struct {
}

func (v Vehicle) drive() {
    // TODO: implement
}

type PoweredVehicle struct {
    Vehicle
}

func (v PoweredVehicle) startEngine() {
    // common engine start code
}

type Car struct {
    PoweredVehicle
}

type Buggy struct {
    Vehicle
}

func (b Buggy) pushStart() {
    // do nothing
}
```

However, this isn't better. The fact that this code still smells indicates that we are probably using the wrong abstraction or the wrong composition. Let's try the refactor again:

```
func Go(vehicle actions) {
    vehicle.start()
    vehicle.drive()
}

type actions interface {
    start()
    drive()
}

type Car struct {
    poweredVehicle
}

func (c Car) start() {
    c.poweredVehicle.startEngine()
}
```

```
func (c Car) drive() {
  // TODO: implement
}

type poweredVehicle struct {
}

func (p poweredVehicle) startEngine() {
  // common engine start code
}

type Buggy struct {
}

func (b Buggy) start() {
  // push start
}

func (b Buggy) drive() {
  // TODO: implement
}
```

That's much better. The `Buggy` phrase is not forced to implement methods that make no sense, nor does it contain any logic it doesn't need, and the usage of both vehicle types is nice and clean. This demonstrates a key point about LSP:

LSP refers to behavior and not implementation.

An object can implement any interface that it likes, but that doesn't make it behaviorally consistent with other implementations of the same interface. Look at the following code:

```
type Collection interface {
    Add(item interface{})
    Get(index int) interface{}
}

type CollectionImpl struct {
    items []interface{}
}

func (c *CollectionImpl) Add(item interface{}) {
    c.items = append(c.items, item)
}

func (c *CollectionImpl) Get(index int) interface{} {
    return c.items[index]
}
```

```
type ReadOnlyCollection struct {
    CollectionImpl
}

func (ro *ReadOnlyCollection) Add(item interface{}) {
    // intentionally does nothing
}
```

In the preceding example, we met (as in delivered) the API contract by implementing all of the methods, but we turned the method we didn't need into a NO-OP. By having our `ReadOnlyCollection` implement the `Add()` method, it satisfies the interface but introduces the potential for confusion. What happens when you have a function that accepts a `Collection`? When you call `Add()`, what would you expect to happen?

The fix, in this case, might surprise you. Instead of making an `ImmutableCollection` out of a `MutableCollection`, we can flip the relation over, as shown in the following code:

```
type ImmutableCollection interface {
    Get(index int) interface{}
}

type MutableCollection interface {
    ImmutableCollection
    Add(item interface{})
}

type ReadOnlyCollectionV2 struct {
    items []interface{}
}

func (ro *ReadOnlyCollectionV2) Get(index int) interface{} {
    return ro.items[index]
}

type CollectionImplV2 struct {
    ReadOnlyCollectionV2
}

func (c *CollectionImplV2) Add(item interface{}) {
    c.items = append(c.items, item)
}
```

A bonus of this new structure is that we can now let the compiler ensure that we don't use `ImmutableCollection` where we need `MutableCollection`.

How does this relate to DI?

By following LSP, our code performs consistently regardless of the dependencies we are injecting. Violating LSP, on the other hand, leads us to violate OCP. These violations cause our code to have too much knowledge of the implementations, which in turn breaks the abstraction of the injected dependencies.

What does this mean for Go?

When using composition—particularly the unnamed variable form—to satisfy interfaces, LSP applies just as it would in object-oriented languages.

When implementing interfaces, we can use LSP's focus on *consistent* behavior as a way of detecting code smells related to incorrect abstractions.

Interface segregation principle (ISP)

> *"Clients should not be forced to depend on methods they do not use."*
> *–Robert C. Martin*

Personally, I prefer a much more direct definition—*interfaces should be reduced to the minimum possible size.*

Let's first discuss why fat interfaces might be a bad thing. Fat interfaces have more methods and are therefore likely to be harder to understand. They also require more work to use, whether this be through implementing, mocking, or stubbing them.

Fat interfaces indicate more responsibility and, as we saw with the SRP, the more responsibility an object has, the more likely it will want to change. If the interface changes, it causes a ripple effect through all its users, violating OCP and causing a massive amount of shotgun surgery. This is the first advantage of ISP:

ISP requires us to define thin interfaces

For many programmers, their natural tendency is to add to the existing interface rather than define a new one, thereby creating a fat interface. This leads to a situation where the, sometimes singular, implementation becomes tightly coupled with the users of the interface. This coupling then makes the interface, their implementations, and users all the more resistant to change. Consider the following example:

```go
type FatDbInterface interface {
    BatchGetItem(IDs ...int) ([]Item, error)
    BatchGetItemWithContext(ctx context.Context, IDs ...int) ([]Item, error)

    BatchPutItem(items ...Item) error
    BatchPutItemWithContext(ctx context.Context, items ...Item) error

    DeleteItem(ID int) error
    DeleteItemWithContext(ctx context.Context, item Item) error

    GetItem(ID int) (Item, error)
    GetItemWithContext(ctx context.Context, ID int) (Item, error)

    PutItem(item Item) error
    PutItemWithContext(ctx context.Context, item Item) error

    Query(query string, args ...interface{}) ([]Item, error)
    QueryWithContext(ctx context.Context, query string, args ...interface{})
([]Item, error)

    UpdateItem(item Item) error
    UpdateItemWithContext(ctx context.Context, item Item) error
}

type Cache struct {
    db FatDbInterface
}

func (c *Cache) Get(key string) interface{} {
    // code removed

    // load from DB
    _, _ = c.db.GetItem(42)

    // code removed
    return nil
}

func (c *Cache) Set(key string, value interface{}) {
    // code removed
```

```
    // save to DB
    _ = c.db.PutItem(Item{})

    // code removed
}
```

It's not hard to imagine all of these methods belonging to one struct. Method pairs such as GetItem() and GetItemWithContext() are quite likely to share much, if not almost all, of the same code. On the other hand, a user of GetItem() is not likely to also use GetItemWithContext(). For this particular use case, a more appropriate interface would be the following:

```
type myDB interface {
    GetItem(ID int) (Item, error)
    PutItem(item Item) error
}

type CacheV2 struct {
    db myDB
}

func (c *CacheV2) Get(key string) interface{} {
    // code removed

    // load from DB
    _, _ = c.db.GetItem(42)

    // code removed
    return nil
}

func (c *CacheV2) Set(key string, value interface{}) {
    // code removed

    // save from DB
    _ = c.db.PutItem(Item{})

    // code removed
}
```

Leveraging this new, thin interface makes the function signature far more explicit and flexible. This leads us to the second advantage of ISP:

ISP leads to explicit inputs.

A thin interface is also more straightforward to more fully implement, keeping us away from any potential problems with LSP.

In cases where we are using an interface as an input and the interface needs to be fat, this is a powerful indication that the method is violating SRP. Consider the following code:

```
func Encrypt(ctx context.Context, data []byte) ([]byte, error) {
    // As this operation make take too long, we need to be able to kill it
    stop := ctx.Done()
    result := make(chan []byte, 1)

    go func() {
        defer close(result)

        // pull the encryption key from context
        keyRaw := ctx.Value("encryption-key")
        if keyRaw == nil {
            panic("encryption key not found in context")
        }
        key := keyRaw.([]byte)

        // perform encryption
        ciperText := performEncryption(key, data)

        // signal complete by sending the result
        result <- ciperText
    }()

    select {
    case ciperText := <-result:
        // happy path
        return ciperText, nil

    case <-stop:
        // cancelled
        return nil, errors.New("operation cancelled")
    }
}
```

Do you see the issue? We are using the `context` interface, which is fantastic and highly recommended, but we are violating ISP. Being pragmatic programmers, we can argue that this interface is widely used and understood, and the value of defining our own interface to reduce it to the two methods that we need is unnecessary. In most cases, I would agree, but in this particular case, we should reconsider. We are using the `context` interface for two entirely separate purposes. The first is a control channel to allow us to stop short or timeout the task, and the second is to provide a value. In effect, our usage of `context` here is violating SRP and, as such, risks potential confusion and results in a greater resistance to change.

What happens if we decide to use the stop channel pattern not on a request level, but at the application level? What happens if the key value is not in the context, but from some other source? By applying the ISP, we can separate the concerns into two interfaces, as shown in the following code:

```
type Value interface {
    Value(key interface{}) interface{}
}

type Monitor interface {
    Done() <-chan struct{}
}

func EncryptV2(keyValue Value, monitor Monitor, data []byte) ([]byte,
error) {
    // As this operation make take too long, we need to be able to kill it
    stop := monitor.Done()
    result := make(chan []byte, 1)

    go func() {
        defer close(result)

        // pull the encryption key from Value
        keyRaw := keyValue.Value("encryption-key")
        if keyRaw == nil {
            panic("encryption key not found in context")
        }
        key := keyRaw.([]byte)

        // perform encryption
        ciperText := performEncryption(key, data)

        // signal complete by sending the result
        result <- ciperText
    }()

    select {
    case ciperText := <-result:
        // happy path
        return ciperText, nil

    case <-stop:
        // cancelled
        return nil, errors.New("operation cancelled")
    }
}
```

Our function now complies with the ISP, and both inputs are free to evolve separately. But what happens to the users of this function? Must they stop using `context`? Absolutely not. The method can be called as shown in the following code:

```
// create a context
ctx, cancel := context.WithCancel(context.Background())
defer cancel()

// store the key
ctx = context.WithValue(ctx, "encryption-key", "-secret-")

// call the function
_, _ = EncryptV2(ctx, ctx, []byte("my data"))
```

The repeated use of `context` as a parameter likely feels a little weird but, as you can see, it's for a good cause. This leads us to our final advantage of the ISP:

ISP helps to decouple the inputs from their concrete implementation, enabling them to evolve separately.

How does this relate to DI?

As we have seen, the ISP helps us to break down interfaces to logically separate parts, with each part providing a particular feature—a concept sometimes referred to as a role interface. By leveraging these role interfaces in our DI, our code becomes decoupled from the concrete implementation of the inputs.

Not only does this decoupling allow parts of the code to evolve separately, but it also tends to make it easier to identify test vectors. In the previous example, it's easier to scan through the inputs one at a time and consider their possible values and states. This process might result in a list of vectors like the following:

Test vectors for the *value* input include:

- **Happy path**: Returns a valid value
- **Error path**: Returns an empty value

Test vectors for the *monitor* input include:

- **Happy path**: Does not return a done signal
- **Error path**: Immediately returns a done signal

What does this mean for Go?

In Chapter 1, *Never Stop Aiming for Better*, we mentioned the popular Go idiom coined by *Jack Lindamood*—*accept interfaces, return structs*. Combine this idea with the ISP and things start to take off. The resultant functions are very concise about their requirements and, at the same time, they are quite explicit regarding their outputs. In other languages, we might have to define the outputs in the form of an abstraction or create adapter classes to decouple our function from our users entirely. However, given Go's support for implicit interfaces, there is no need for this.

Implicit interfaces are a language feature whereby the implementor (that is, the struct) does not need to define the interfaces that it implements, but rather only needs to define the appropriate methods to satisfy the interface, as shown in the following code:

```go
type Talker interface {
    SayHello() string
}

type Dog struct{}

// The method implicitly implements the Talker interface
func (d Dog) SayHello() string {
    return "Woof!"
}

func Speak() {
    var talker Talker
    talker = Dog{}

    fmt.Print(talker.SayHello())
}
```

This might seem like a neat trick to cut down on typing, and it is. However, that is not the only reason to use it. When using explicit interfaces, the implementing object becomes somewhat coupled with its dependents as there is a rather explicit link between them. However, perhaps the most significant reason is simplicity. Let's look at one of the most popular interfaces in Go that you've probably never heard of:

```go
// Stringer is implemented by any value that has a String method, which
// defines the "native" format for that value. The String method is used
// to print values passed as an operand to any format that accepts a
// string or to an unformatted printer such as Print.
type Stringer interface {
    String() string
}
```

This interface might not look impressive, but the fact that the `fmt` package supports this interface allows you to do the following:

```
func main() {
  kitty := Cat{}

  fmt.Printf("Kitty %s", kitty)
}

type Cat struct{}

// Implicitly implement the fmt.Stringer interface
func (c Cat) String() string {
  return "Meow!"
}
```

If we had explicit interfaces, imagine how many times we would have to declare that we implement `Stringer`. Perhaps where implicit interfaces give us the most significant advantage in Go is when they are combined with the ISP and DI. The combination of the three allows us to define input interfaces that are thin, specific to the particular use case, and decoupled from everything else, as we saw with the `Stringer` interface.

Furthermore, defining interfaces in the package in which they are used narrows the scope of knowledge required to work on a piece of code, which in turn makes it much easier to understand and test.

Dependency inversion principle (DIP)

"High level modules should not depend on low level modules. Both should depend on abstractions. Abstractions should not depend upon details. Details should depend on abstractions"

–Robert C. Martin

Have you ever found yourself standing in a shoe store wondering if you should get the brown or the black pair, only to get home and regret your choice? Sadly, once you've bought them, they're yours. Programming against concrete implementations is the same thing: once you choose, you are stuck with it, refunds and refactoring notwithstanding. But why choose when you don't have to? Look at the relationship shown in the following diagram:

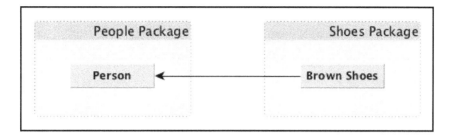

Not very flexible, is it? Let's convert the relationship into an abstraction:

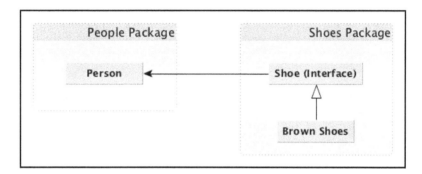

That's much better. Everything relies only on nice clean abstractions, satisfying both LSP and ISP. The packages are concise and clear, happily satisfying the SRP. The code even *seems* to satisfy *Robert C. Martin's* description of the DIP, but sadly, it doesn't. It's that pesky word in the middle, inversion.

In our example, the Shoes package owns the Shoe interface, which is entirely logical. However, problems arise when the requirements change. Changes to the Shoes package are likely to cause the Shoe interface to want to change. This will, in turn, require the Person object to change. Any new features that we add to the Shoe interface may be not be needed or relevant to the Person object. Therefore, the Person object is still coupled to the Shoe package.

In order to entirely break this coupling, we need to change the relationship from **Person** uses Shoe to **Person** requires **Footwear**, like this:

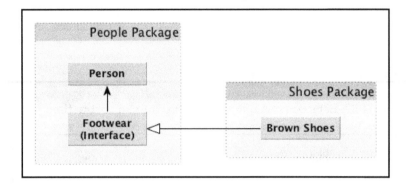

There are two key points here. Firstly, the DIP forces us to focus on the ownership of the abstractions. In our example, that means moving the interface into the package where it was used and changing the relationship from *uses* to *requires*; it's a subtle difference, but an important one.

Secondly, the DIP encourages us to decouple usage requirements from implementations. In our example, our `Brown Shoes` object implements `Footwear`, but it's not hard to imagine a lot more implementations and some might not even be shoes.

How does this relate to DI?

Dependency inversion is very easy to mistake for dependency injection, and many, including me for a long time, assume that they are equivalent. But as we have seen, dependency inversion focuses on the ownership of the dependencies' abstract definition, and DI is focused on using those abstractions.

By applying DIP with DI, we end up with very well-decoupled packages that are incredibly easy to understand, easy to extend, and simple to test.

What does this mean for Go?

We have talked before about Go's support for implicit interfaces and how we can leverage that to define our dependencies as interfaces in the same package, rather than importing an interface from another package. This approach is DIP.

Perhaps your inner skeptic is going crazy, yelling, *but this would mean I would have to define interfaces everywhere!* Yes, that might be true. It could even result in a small amount of duplication. You will find, however, that the interfaces you would have defined without dependency inversion would have been fatter and more unwieldy, a fact that would have cost you more to work with in the future.

After applying DIP, you are unlikely to have any circular dependency issues. In fact, you will almost certainly find that the number of imports in your code drops significantly and your dependency graph becomes rather flat. In fact, many packages will only be imported by the `main` package.

Summary

In this brief introduction of SOLID design principles, we learned how they apply not only to DI, but also to Go. During our examination of the various DI methods in the second section of this book, we will frequently reference these principles.

In the next chapter, we will continue to examine the aspects of coding that should be at the forefront of your mind when studying and experimenting with new techniques. I will also introduce you to a few handy tools that will make your coding life a little easier.

Questions

1. How does the single responsibility principle improve Go code?
2. How does the open/closed principle improve Go code?
3. How does the liskov substitution principle improve Go code?
4. How does the interface segregation principle improve Go code?
5. How does the dependency inversion principle improve Go code?
6. How is dependency inversion different from dependency injection?

Further reading

Packt has many other great resources for learning about SOLID principles:

- `https://www.packtpub.com/mapt/book/application_development/9781787121300/1`
- `https://www.packtpub.com/mapt/book/application_development/9781785884375/10/ch10lvl1sec50/the-solid-principles`
- `https://www.packtpub.com/mapt/book/application_development/9781785280832/8`

Coding for User Experience

3

In this chapter, we will examine several often overlooked, but valuable, aspects of programming, chiefly testing, user experience, and dependency graphs. While these topics might not feel like they have anything to do with; **Dependency Injection** (**DI**), they have been included to give you a solid but pragmatic foundation from which you can evaluate the techniques in the second part of this book.

The following topics will be covered in this chapter:

- Optimizing for humans
- A security blanket named *unit tests*
- Test-induced damage
- Visualizing your package dependencies with Godepgraph

Technical requirements

For this chapter, you need a basic understanding of Go.

All code in this chapter is available at `https://github.com/PacktPublishing/Hands-On-Dependency-Injection-in-Go/tree/master/ch03`.

Optimizing for humans

In recent years, we have seen the rise of the term UX, which stands for user experience. At its core, UX is about usability—understanding the user and crafting interactions and interfaces to be more intuitive or more natural for them to use.

UX typically refers to customers, which makes sense—that is, after all, where the money is. However, we programmers are missing out on something rather significant. Let me ask you, who are the users of the code you write? Not the customers that use the software itself. The users of the code are your colleagues and the future version of you. Would you like to make their life easier? Put in a different way, would you rather spend your future trying to figure out the purpose of a piece of code or extending the system? That is where the money is. As programmers, we get paid to deliver features rather than beautiful code, and code with good UX enables the faster delivery of features, and with less risk.

What does user experience mean for Go code?

What does UX mean for Go code? The short version is, *we should write code whose general intent is understood after a quick first read by any competent programmer.*

Did that sound a bit like hand waving? Yeah, it might be hand waving. It's a standard problem with solving problems in any creative endeavor; you know it when you see it, and you feel it when it doesn't exist. Perhaps the main reason it is so hard to define is that the definition of *competence* varies significantly based on the members of the team and the environment. Similarly, the reason it is often hard to achieve is due to the fact that code inherently makes more sense to the author than anyone else.

But first, let's look at some simple principles to start off in the right direction.

Start with simple – get complicated only when you must

As programmers, we should always strive to keep things simple, and resort to complexity when there is no other way. Let's see this principle in action. Try to determine what this next example does in three seconds or less:

```go
func NotSoSimple(ID int64, name string, age int, registered bool) string {
    out := &bytes.Buffer{}
    out.WriteString(strconv.FormatInt(ID, 10))
    out.WriteString("-")
    out.WriteString(strings.Replace(name, " ", "_", -1))
    out.WriteString("-")
    out.WriteString(strconv.Itoa(age))
    out.WriteString("-")
    out.WriteString(strconv.FormatBool(registered))
    return out.String()
}
```

How about this one:

```
func Simpler(ID int64, name string, age int, registered bool) string {
    nameWithNoSpaces := strings.Replace(name, " ", "_", -1)
    return fmt.Sprintf("%d-%s-%d-%t", ID, nameWithNoSpaces, age, registered)
}
```

Applying the approach embodied in the first code to an entire system will almost certainly make it run faster, but not only did it likely take longer to code, but it's also harder to read and therefore maintain and extend.

There will be times when you need to extract extreme performance from your code, but it's far better to wait until it cannot be avoided before burdening yourself with the extra complexity.

Apply just enough abstraction

Excessive abstraction leads to an excessive mental burden and excessive typing. While some may argue that any code fragment that could be swapped out or extended later deserves an abstraction, I would argue for a more pragmatic approach. Implement enough to deliver the business value we are tasked with and then refactor as needed. Look at the following code:

```
type myGetter interface {
    Get(url string) (*http.Response, error)
}

func TooAbstract(getter myGetter, url string) ([]byte, error) {
    resp, err := getter.Get(url)
    if err != nil {
        return nil, err
    }
    defer resp.Body.Close()

    return ioutil.ReadAll(resp.Body)
}
```

Compare the previous code to the following usage of the commonly understood concept:

```
func CommonConcept(url string) ([]byte, error) {
    resp, err := http.Get(url)
    if err != nil {
        return nil, err
    }
    defer resp.Body.Close()
```

```
    return ioutil.ReadAll(resp.Body)
}
```

Follow industry, team, and language conventions

Concepts, variables, and function names all *just make sense* when they follow conventions. Ask yourself, if you are working on a system about cars, what would you expect a variable called `flower` to be?

Coding style is arguably something that Go got right. For many years, I was part of the *bracket placement* and the *tab versus spaces* wars, but when switching to Go, all of that changed. There is a fixed, documented, and easily reproducible style—run `gofmt`, problem solved. There are still some places where you can hurt yourself. Coming from a language with unchecked exceptions, you might be tempted to use Go's `panic()` phrase; while possible, it is one of several conventions explicitly discouraged in the official Code Review Comments wiki (`https://github.com/golang/go/wiki/CodeReviewComments`).

Team conventions are a little bit harder to define, and perhaps sometimes to follow. Should a variable of the `channel` type be called `result`, `resultCh`, or `resultChan`? I have seen, and probably written, all three.

How about error logging? Some teams like to log errors at the point at which they are triggered, and others prefer to do so at the top of the call stack. I have a preference, as I am sure you do, but I have yet to see an overwhelmingly compelling argument for either.

Export only what you must

When you are careful and stingy about your exported API, many good things happen. Chiefly, it becomes easier for others to understand; when a method has fewer parameters, it is naturally easier to understand. Look at the following code:

```
NewPet("Fido", true)
```

What does `true` mean? It's hard to tell without opening the function or the documentation. However, what if we do the following:

```
NewDog("Fido")
```

In this case, the purpose is clear, mistakes are unlikely and, as a bonus, encapsulation is improved.

Similarly, interfaces and structs with fewer methods and packages with objects are all easier to understand, and are more likely to have a more definite purpose. Let's look at another example:

```
type WideFormatter interface {
  ToCSV(pets []Pet) ([]byte, error)
  ToGOB(pets []Pet) ([]byte, error)
  ToJSON(pets []Pet) ([]byte, error)
}
```

Compare the preceding code to the following:

```
type ThinFormatter interface {
  Format(pets []Pet) ([]byte, error)
}

type CSVFormatter struct {}

func (f CSVFormatter) Format(pets []Pet) ([]byte, error) {
  // convert slice of pets to CSV
}
```

Yes, in both of these cases, the result was more code. More straightforward code, but more code nonetheless. Providing a better UX for users will frequently incur a little bit more cost, but the productivity gains for the users are multiplicative. Considering the fact that, in many cases, one of the users of the code that you write is future you, you could say that a bit of extra work now saves you lots of work in the future.

Continuing along the line of looking out for *future me*, the second advantage this approach offers is it makes it easier to change your mind. Once a function or type is exported, it can be used; once used, it has to be maintained and takes much more effort to change. This approach makes such changes easier.

Aggressively apply the single responsibility principle

As we saw in `Chapter 2`, *SOLID Design Principles for Go*, applying the **single responsibility principle** (**SRP**) encourages objects to be more concise and more coherent and therefore easier to understand.

Discovering a good user experience

A good user experience does not need to be divined. It does not need to be handed down from some experienced guru either. In fact, the problem with experience is that what is easy, simple, and obvious to you today is vastly different from what it was last month, last year, or when you were starting out.

A good UX can be discovered through logic, persistence, and practice. To find out what a good UX looks like for your user, you can apply my UX discovery survey.

Ask yourself the following four questions:

- Who is the user?
- What are your users capable of?
- Why do users want to use your code?
- How do your users expect to use it?

Who is the user?

Much of the time, the answer will be *future me* and my colleagues. Your *future me* will be a better, smarter, and more handsome version of who you are now. Your colleagues, on the other hand, are harder to predict. If it helps, we can avoid considering the smart, fantastic ones; hopefully, whatever we do, they will understand. An intern, on the other hand, will be harder to predict. Chances are that if we can make our code make sense to them, then it will be just fine for everyone else.

If you ever have the chance to write software libraries for company-wide or general use, then this answer becomes a whole lot harder. In general, you want to aim low and only depart from a standard and straightforward format when there is no other choice.

What are your users capable of?

Now that we are clear on who the users are, we can develop a better understanding of their worldview. There is likely a massive disparity between the skills, experience, and domain knowledge between you and your users, and even between you and future you. This where most technical tools and software libraries fail. Think back to when you just started with Go. What did your code look like? Were there any language features in Go that you weren't using yet? Personally, I come from a Java background and, because of this, I entered the field with some preconceived ideas:

- I thought that threads were expensive (and that goroutines were threads)
- I thought that everything had to be in a struct
- Being used to explicit interfaces meant that I was not as enthusiastic about using the **interface segregation principle (ISP)** or the **dependency inversion principle (DSP)** as I am now
- I didn't understand the power of channels
- Passing lambdas around blew my mind

Over time, I have seen these sorts of things pop up over and over, particularly in code-review comments. There is quite an effective way of answering the question: *What are the users capable of?* Write an example and ask your colleagues the following questions:

- What does this do?
- How would you have done it?
- What do you expect this function to do?

If you don't have any users that you can quiz, another option is to ask yourself, *What else exists that is similar?* I am not suggesting that you follow other people's mistakes. The basic theory here is that if something else exists, and your users are comfortable with it then, if yours is similar, they will not have to learn to use it. This was perhaps best illustrated to me when using lambdas. Colleagues from a functional background were happy with it, but those from an object-oriented background found it either somewhat confounding or just not intuitive.

Why do users want to use your code?

The answer to the question of why your users would want to use your code could be long and varied. If it is, you might want to go back and re-read the *SRP* section. Beyond being able to split the code into smaller, more concise chunks, we need to make a list. We will apply the 80/20 rule to this list. Typically, 80% of usage comes from 20% of the use cases. Let me put this into perspective with an example.

Consider an **automated teller machine (ATM)**. A list of its use cases might look like the following:

- Withdraw money
- Deposit money
- Check balance
- Change PIN code

- Transfer money
- Deposit check

I reckon that on at least 80% of the occasions that a person uses an ATM, their purpose is to withdraw money. So what can we do with this information? We can optimize the interface to make the most common use cases as convenient as possible. In the case of the ATM, it could be as simple as putting the withdraw function on the first screen at the top so that users don't have to search for it. Now that we understand what our users are trying to achieve, we can build on this and consider how they expect to use it.

How do they expect to use it?

While the ATM example was clear, it was a system, and so you may be wondering how that could possibly apply to low-level concepts, such as functions. Let's look at an example:

```
// PetFetcher searches the data store for pets whose name matches
// the search string.
// Limit is optional (default is 100). Offset is optional (default 0).
// sortBy is optional (default name). sortAscending is optional
func PetFetcher(search string, limit int, offset int, sortBy string,
sortAscending bool) []Pet {
   return []Pet{}
}
```

That probably looks OK, right? The problem is that most of the usage looks like the following:

```
results := PetFetcher("Fido", 0, 0, "", true)
```

As you can see, most of the time we don't need all of those return values, and many of the inputs are ignored.

The first step to addressing this sort of situation is to look at the under-used parts of the code and ask yourself, do we really need them? If they exist only for testing, then it means they are *test-induced damage,* which we will look at later in this chapter.

If they exist for some infrequently used but compelling use case, then we can address it another way. The first option would be to split the function into multiple parts; this would allow users to adopt only the complexity they need. The second option is to merge the configuration into an object, allowing users to ignore the parts they don't use.

In both approaches, we are providing *reasonable defaults*, reducing the mental burden of the function by allowing users to only worry about what they need.

When to compromise

Having a great user experience is a desirable goal, but is not a necessity. There are always going to be situations where the UX needs to be compromised. The first and perhaps most common situation is team evolution.

As the team evolves and becomes more experienced with Go, it will inevitably find that some early software patterns no longer seem as effective. These might include things such as the use of global, panic, and loading configurations from environment variables, or even when to use functions rather than objects. As the team evolves, so does their definition of both good software and what is standard or intuitive.

The second, and in many cases, an overused excuse for poor UX, is performance. As we saw in an early example in this chapter, it's often possible to write faster code, but the faster code is often harder to understand. The best option here is to optimize it for humans first and then, only when the system has proven to not be quick enough, optimize it for speed. Even then, these optimizations should be selectively applied to those parts of the system that are shown, by measurement, to be worth the effort to refactor and the long-term cost of less-than-ideal UX.

The last situation is visibility; sometimes, you just can't see what a good UX might be. In these cases, the more effective option is to implement and then iteratively refactor based on usage and any inconveniences that arise.

Final thoughts on coding for user experience

Programmer time, your time, is expensive; you should conserve it in preference of CPU time. The user experience for developers is challenging because of our inherent need to solve problems and deliver useful software. However, it is possible to conserve programmer time. Try to remember the following:

- Making something more configurable doesn't make it more usable—it makes it more confusing to use
- Designing for all use cases makes the code inconvenient for everyone
- User competence and expectations play a prominent role in how your code is perceived, and in its adoption

Perhaps most pertinent—it is always better and easier to change the UX to match the user than the other way around.

A security blanket named unit tests

Many folks will tell you, *you must write unit tests for your code; they make sure you have no bugs*. They really don't do that at all. Nor do I write unit tests because someone tells me I must. I write unit tests for what they do for me. Unit tests are empowering. They actually reduce the amount of work I have to do. Perhaps these are not justifications you have heard before. Let's explore them in a little more detail.

Unit tests give you the freedom and confidence to refactor: I love to refactor, perhaps a little too much, but that's a different topic. Refactoring allows me to experiment with varying styles of code, implementations, and UX. By having unit tests in place, I can be adventurous and confident that I don't unintentionally break anything along the way. They can also give you the courage to try new technologies, libraries, or coding techniques.

Existing unit tests make adding new features easier: As we have mentioned before, adding new features does incur some risk—risk that we might break something. Having the tests in place provides a safety net that allows us to be less mindful of what already exists and focus more on adding the new feature. It might seem counterintuitive, but unit tests actually make you move faster. As the system expands, having a safety blanket of unit tests allows you to proceed with confidence and not to have to worry about the things you might break.

Unit tests prevent repeated regression: There is no way around it—regression sucks. It makes you look bad and it causes you extra work, but it's going to happen. The best we can hope for is to not repeatedly fix the same bug. While tests do prevent some regression, they cannot stop it all. By writing a test that fails because of the bug and then fixing the bug, we achieve two things. First, we know when the bug is fixed because the test passes. Second, the bug does not happen again.

Unit tests document your intent: While I am not trying to suggest that tests can replace documentation, they are explicit, executable expressions of what you intended when you wrote the code. This is an exceptionally desirable quality when working in a team. It allows you to work on any part of the system without worrying about breaking code written by others or even perhaps fully understanding it.

Unit tests document your requirements from a dependency: In the second section of this book, we will work through some examples of applying DI to an existing code base. A significant part of this process will include grouping and extracting functionality into abstractions. These abstractions naturally become *units of work*. Each unit is then tested individually and in isolation. These tests are consequently more focused, and are easier to write and maintain.

Additionally, the tests on code that uses DI will often focus on how that function uses and reacts to the dependency. These tests effectively define the requirements contract for the dependency and help to prevent regression. Let's look at an example:

```go
type Loader interface {
  Load(ID int) (*Pet, error)
}

func TestLoadAndPrint_happyPath(t *testing.T) {
  result := &bytes.Buffer{}
  LoadAndPrint(&happyPathLoader{}, 1, result)
  assert.Contains(t, result.String(), "Pet named")
}

func TestLoadAndPrint_notFound(t *testing.T) {
  result := &bytes.Buffer{}
  LoadAndPrint(&missingLoader{}, 1, result)
  assert.Contains(t, result.String(), "no such pet")
}

func TestLoadAndPrint_error(t *testing.T) {
  result := &bytes.Buffer{}
  LoadAndPrint(&errorLoader{}, 1, result)
  assert.Contains(t, result.String(), "failed to load")
}

func LoadAndPrint(loader Loader, ID int, dest io.Writer) {
  loadedPet, err := loader.Load(ID)
  if err != nil {
    fmt.Fprintf(dest, "failed to load pet with ID %d. err: %s", ID, err)
    return
  }

  if loadedPet == nil {
    fmt.Fprintf(dest, "no such pet found")
    return
  }

  fmt.Fprintf(dest, "Pet named %s loaded", loadedPet.Name)
}
```

As you can see, this code expects the dependency to behave in a certain way. While the tests do not enforce this behavior from the dependency, they do serve to define this code's requirements.

Unit tests can help restore confidence and increase understanding: Do you have code in your system that you don't dare to change because if you do, something will break? How about code where you are really not sure what it does? Unit tests are fantastic for both of these situations. Writing tests against this code is an unobtrusive way to both learn what it does and validate that it does what you think it does. These tests have the added bonus that they can also be used as regression prevention for any future changes and to teach others what this code does.

So why do I write unit tests?

For me, the most compelling reason to write unit tests is that it makes me feels good. It feels great to go home at the end of the day or week and know that everything is working as intended and that the tests are making sure of it.

This is not to say that there are no bugs, but there are definitely fewer. Once fixed, bugs don't come back, saving me from embarrassment and saving me time. And, perhaps most importantly, fixing bugs means fewer support calls at nights and weekends because something is broken.

What should I test?

I wish I had a clear, quantifiable metric to give you as to what you should and should not test, but it's just not that clear. The first rule is definitely as follows:

 Don't test code that is too simple break.

This includes language features, such as those shown in the following code:

```go
func NewPet(name string) *Pet {
    return &Pet{
        Name: name,
    }
}

func TestLanguageFeatures(t *testing.T) {
    petFish := NewPet("Goldie")
    assert.IsType(t, &Pet{}, petFish)
}
```

This also includes simple functions, as shown in the following code:

```
func concat(a, b string) string {
    return a + b
}

func TestTooSimple(t *testing.T) {
    a := "Hello "
    b := "World"
    expected := "Hello World"

    assert.Equal(t, expected, concat(a, b))
}
```

After that, be pragmatic. We get paid to write code that works; tests are only a tool to ensure that it does and continues to do so. It is entirely possible to test too much. Excessive tests will not only lead to a lot of extra work, but will also cause tests to become brittle and frequently break during refactoring or extension.

For this reason, I recommend testing from a slightly higher and more *black-box* level. Take a look at the struct in this example:

```
type PetSaver struct{}

// save the supplied pet and return the ID
func (p PetSaver) Save(pet Pet) (int, error) {
    err := p.validate(pet)
    if err != nil {
        return 0, err
    }

    result, err := p.save(pet)
    if err != nil {
        return 0, err
    }

    return p.extractID(result)
}

// ensure the pet record is complete
func (p PetSaver) validate(pet Pet) (error) {
    return nil
}

// save to the datastore
func (p PetSaver) save(pet Pet) (sql.Result, error) {
    return nil, nil
}
```

```
// extract the ID from the result
func (p PetSaver) extractID(result sql.Result) (int, error) {
    return 0, nil
}
```

If we were to write tests for each method of this struct, then we will be discouraged from refactoring these methods or even extracting them from `Save()` in the first place, as we would have to refactor the corresponding tests as well. However, if we test the `Save()` method only, which is the only method that is used by others, then we can refactor the rest with far less hassle.

The types of tests are also important. Typically, we should test the following:

- **Happy path**: This is when everything goes as expected. These tests also tend to document how to use the code.
- **Input errors**: Incorrect and unexpected inputs can often cause the code to behave in strange ways. These tests ensure that our code handles these issues in a predictable way.
- **Dependency issues**: The other common cause of failure is when a dependency fails to perform as we need it to, either through coder error (such as regression) or environmental issues (such as a missing file or a failed call to a database).

Hopefully, by now you are sold on unit tests and are excited by what they can do for you. Another often neglected aspect of tests is their quality. By this, I'm not talking about use case coverage or code coverage percentage, but the raw code quality. It's sadly commonplace to write tests in a manner that we wouldn't allow ourselves to write for production code.

Duplication, poor readability, and lack of structure are all frequent mistakes. Thankfully, these issues can be easily addressed. The first step is just being mindful of the problem and applying the same level of effort and skill as we do with production code. The second requires breaking out some test-specific techniques; there are many but, in this chapter, I will introduce only three. These are as follows:

- Table-driven tests
- Stubs
- Mocks

Table-driven tests

Often, while writing tests, you will find that multiple tests for the same method result in a lot of duplication. Take this example:

```
func TestRound_down(t *testing.T) {
    in := float64(1.1)
    expected := 1

    result := Round(in)
    assert.Equal(t, expected, result)
}

func TestRound_up(t *testing.T) {
    in := float64(3.7)
    expected := 4

    result := Round(in)
    assert.Equal(t, expected, result)
}

func TestRound_noChange(t *testing.T) {
    in := float64(6.0)
    expected := 6

    result := Round(in)
    assert.Equal(t, expected, result)
}
```

There is nothing surprising, nor wrong with the intent here. Table-driven tests acknowledge the need for duplication and extract the variations into a *table*. It is this table that then drives a single copy of the code that would otherwise have been duplicated. Let's convert our tests in to table-driven tests:

```
func TestRound(t *testing.T) {
    scenarios := []struct {
        desc     string
        in       float64
        expected int
    }{
        {
            desc:     "round down",
            in:       1.1,
            expected: 1,
        },
        {
            desc:     "round up",
```

```
            in:        3.7,
            expected:  4,
        },
        {
            desc:      "unchanged",
            in:        6.0,
            expected:  6,
        },
    }

    for _, scenario := range scenarios {
        in := float64(scenario.in)

        result := Round(in)
        assert.Equal(t, scenario.expected, result)
    }
}
```

Our tests are now guaranteed to be consistent across all of the scenarios for this method, which in turn makes them more effective. If we had to change the function signature or call pattern, we have only one place in which to do so, resulting in less maintenance cost. Finally, reducing the inputs and outputs to a table makes it cheap to add new test scenarios, and helps to identify test scenarios by encouraging us to focus on the inputs.

Stubs

Sometimes referred to as *test doubles*, stubs are fake implementations of a dependency (that is, an interface) that provides a predictable, usually fixed result. Stubs are also used to help exercise code paths, such as errors, that otherwise might be very difficult or impossible to trigger.

Let's look at an example interface:

```
type PersonLoader interface {
    Load(ID int) (*Person, error)
}
```

Let's imagine that the production implementation of the fetcher interface actually calls an upstream REST service. Using our previous *types of tests* list, we want to test for the following scenarios:

- **Happy path**: The fetcher returns data
- **Input error**: The fetcher fails to find the `Person` we requested
- **System error**: The upstream service is down

There are more possible tests that we could implement, but this is enough for our purposes.

Let's think about how we would have to test without using a stub:

- **Happy path**: The upstream service has to be up and working correctly, and we would have to make sure we had a valid ID to request at all times.
- **Input error**: The upstream service has to be up and working correctly, but in this case, we would have to have an ID that was guaranteed to be invalid; otherwise, this test would be flaky.
- **System error**: The service would have to be down? If we assume that the upstream service belongs to another team or has users other than us, I don't think they would appreciate us shutting down the service every time we needed to test. We could configure an incorrect URL for the service, but then we would be running different configurations for our different test scenarios.

There are a lot of nonprogramming issues with the preceding scenarios. Let's see if a little code can solve the problem:

```
// Stubbed implementation of PersonLoader
type PersonLoaderStub struct {
    Person *Person
    Error error
}

func (p *PersonLoaderStub) Load(ID int) (*Person, error) {
    return p.Person, p.Error
}
```

With the preceding stub implementation, we can now create one stub instance per scenario with a table-driven test, as shown in the following code:

```
func TestLoadPersonName(t *testing.T) {
    // this value does not matter as the stub ignores it
    fakeID := 1

    scenarios := []struct {
        desc          string
        loaderStub    *PersonLoaderStub
        expectedName  string
        expectErr     bool
    }{
        {
            desc: "happy path",
            loaderStub: &PersonLoaderStub{
                Person: &Person{Name: "Sophia"},
            },
```

```
            expectedName: "Sophia",
            expectErr:    false,
        },
        {
            desc: "input error",
            loaderStub: &PersonLoaderStub{
                Error: ErrNotFound,
            },
            expectedName: "",
            expectErr:    true,
        },
        {
            desc: "system error path",
            loaderStub: &PersonLoaderStub{
                Error: errors.New("something failed"),
            },
            expectedName: "",
            expectErr:    true,
        },
    }

    for _, scenario := range scenarios {
        result, resultErr := LoadPersonName(scenario.loaderStub, fakeID)

        assert.Equal(t, scenario.expectedName, result, scenario.desc)
        assert.Equal(t, scenario.expectErr, resultErr != nil, scenario.desc)
    }
}
```

As you can see, our tests now cannot fail because of the dependency; they no longer require anything external to the project itself, and they probably even run faster. If you find writing stubs burdensome, I would recommend two things. Firstly, check the previous Chapter 2, *SOLID Design Principles for Go,* on the ISP and see if you can break the interface into something smaller. Secondly, check out one of the many fantastic tools in the Go community; you are sure to find one that suits your needs.

Mocks

Mocks are very much like stubs, but they have one fundamental difference. Mocks have expectations. When we used stubs, our tests did nothing to validate our usage of the dependency; with mocks, they will. Which you use depends very much on the type of test and the dependency itself. For example, you might want to use a stub for a logging dependency, unless you are writing a test that ensures the code logs in a specific situation. However, you will often need a mock for a database dependency. Let's change our previous tests from stubs to mocks to ensure that we make those calls:

```go
func TestLoadPersonName(t *testing.T) {
    // this value does not matter as the stub ignores it
    fakeID := 1

    scenarios := []struct {
        desc          string
        configureMock func(stub *PersonLoaderMock)
        expectedName  string
        expectErr     bool
    }{
        {
            desc: "happy path",
            configureMock: func(loaderMock *PersonLoaderMock) {
                loaderMock.On("Load", mock.Anything).
                    Return(&Person{Name: "Sophia"}, nil).
                    Once()
            },
            expectedName: "Sophia",
            expectErr:    false,
        },
        {
            desc: "input error",
            configureMock: func(loaderMock *PersonLoaderMock) {
                loaderMock.On("Load", mock.Anything).
                    Return(nil, ErrNotFound).
                    Once()
            },
            expectedName: "",
            expectErr:    true,
        },
        {
            desc: "system error path",
            configureMock: func(loaderMock *PersonLoaderMock) {
                loaderMock.On("Load", mock.Anything).
                    Return(nil, errors.New("something failed")).
                    Once()
            },
            expectedName: "",
            expectErr:    true,
        },
    }

    for _, scenario := range scenarios {
        mockLoader := &PersonLoaderMock{}
        scenario.configureMock(mockLoader)

        result, resultErr := LoadPersonName(mockLoader, fakeID)
```

```
        assert.Equal(t, scenario.expectedName, result, scenario.desc)
        assert.Equal(t, scenario.expectErr, resultErr != nil, scenario.desc)
        assert.True(t, mockLoader.AssertExpectations(t), scenario.desc)
    }
  }
```

In the preceding example, we are validating that the appropriate calls are made and that the inputs are as we expect. Given that mock-based tests are more explicit, they are often more brittle and verbose than their stub-based equivalents. The best advice I can give you about this is to choose the option that best fits the test you are trying to write and, if the amount of setup seems excessive, consider what this implies about the code you are testing. You could have issues with feature envy or an inefficient abstraction. Refactoring for the DIP or SRP might help.

Just as there are with stubs, there are many great tools in the community for generating mocks. I have personally used mockery (https://github.com/vektra/mockery) by Vektra.

You can install mockery with the following command:

```
$ go get github.com/vektra/mockery/.../
```

Once installed, we can generate a mock for our test interface using mockery from the command line, or by using the go generate tool provided with the Go SDK by merely adding a comment to our source code, as shown in the following code:

```
//go:generate mockery -name PersonLoader -testonly -inpkg -case=underscore
type PersonLoader interface {
    Load(ID int) (*Person, error)
}
```

Once this is done, we then run the following:

```
$ go generate ./...
```

The resulting mocks can then be used as we did in the previous example. We will be using mockery and the mocks it generates a great deal in the second section of this book. If you wish to download mockery, you will find a link to their GitHub project at the end of this chapter.

Test-induced damage

In a 2014 blog post, *David Heinemeier Hansson* expressed that changes to a system for the sole purpose of making tests easier or faster resulted in test-induced damage. While I agree with David's intent, I am not sure we agree on the details. He coined this term in response to what he felt was excessive application DI and **test-driven development** (**TDD**).

Personally, I take a pragmatic approach to both. They are tools. Please try them out. If they work for you, fantastic. If not, that's fine too. I have never been able to get TDD to be as productive for me as other methods. Generally, I will write my function, at least the happy path, and then apply my tests. Then I refactor and clean.

Warning signs of test-induced damage

While there are many ways in which testing could cause damage to your software design, the following are some of the more common kinds of damage.

Parameters, config options, or outputs that only exist because of tests

While an individual instance of this might not feel like it has a huge impact, the cost does eventually add up. Remember that each parameter, option, and output is something that a user has to understand. Similarly, each parameter, option, and output has to be tested, documented, and otherwise maintained.

Parameters that cause or are caused by leaky abstractions

It's common to see a database connection string or URL passed into the business-logic layer for the sole purpose of passing it down to the data layer (the database or HTTP client). Typically, the motivation is to pass the config through the layers so that we can swap out the live config for something friendlier for testing. This sounds good, but it breaks the encapsulation of the data layer. Perhaps more concerning is that if we were to change the data-layer implementation to something else, we would likely have extensive shotgun surgery on our hands. The actual problem here is not the testing, but how we have chosen to *swap out* the data layer. Using the DIP, we could define our requirements as an interface in the business-logic layer and then mock or stub it. This would completely decouple the business-logic layer from the data layer and remove the need to pass the test configuration.

Publishing mocks in production code

Mocks and stubs are tools for testing; as such, they should only ever exist in test code. In Go, this means an _test.go file. I have seen many well-meaning folks publish interfaces and their mocks in production code. The first problem with this is that it introduces a possibility, however remote, of this code ending up in production. Depending on where in the system this mistake was located, the results could be disastrous.

The second problem is a little more subtle. When publishing the interface and mock, the intent is to reduce duplication, which is fantastic. However, this also increases dependence and resistance to change. Once this code is published and adopted by others, modifying it will require changing all usage of it.

Excessive test coverage

Another problem that could arise is excessive test coverage. Yes, you read that right. Writing too many tests is possible. Programmers, being the technically minded folks that we are, love metrics. Unit-test coverage is one such metric. While it is possible to achieve 100% test coverage, realizing this goal is a huge time sink, and the resulting code can be rather terrible. Consider the following code:

```go
func WriteAndClose(destination io.WriteCloser, contents string) error {
    defer destination.Close()
    _, err := destination.Write([]byte(contents))
    if err != nil {
        return err
    }
    return nil
}
```

To achieve 100% coverage, we would have to write a test where the destination.Close() call fails. We can totally do this, but what would it achieve? What would we be testing? It would give us another test to write and maintain. If this line of code doesn't work, would you even notice? How about this example:

```go
func PrintAsJSON(destination io.Writer, plant Plant) error {
    bytes, err := json.Marshal(plant)
    if err != nil {
        return err
    }

    destination.Write(bytes)
    return nil
}
```

```
type Plant struct {
    Name string
}
```

Again, we can totally test for that. But would we really be testing? In this case, we'd be testing that the JSON package in the Go standard library works as it's supposed to. External SDKs and packages should have their own tests so that we can just trust that they do what they claim. If this is not the case, we can always write tests for them and send them back to the project. That way, the entire community benefits.

Visualizing your package dependencies with Godepgraph

In a book about DI, you can expect us to spend a lot of time talking about dependencies. Dependencies at the lowest level, functions, structs, and interfaces are easy to visualize; we can just read the code or, if we want a pretty picture, we can make a class diagram like the following:

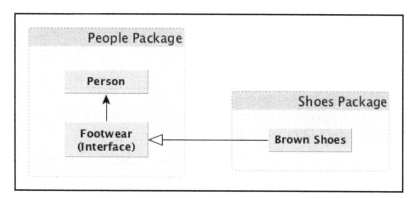

If we zoom out to the package level and try to map the dependencies between packages, then life gets a lot more difficult. This is where we rely again on the open source community's wealth of open-source tools. This time, we will need two tools called **godepgraph** and **Graphviz** (http://www.graphviz.org/). Godepgraph is a program for generating a dependency graph of Go packages, and Graphviz is a source graph-visualization software.

Installing the tools

A simple `go get` will install `godepgraph`, as shown in the following code:

```
$ go get github.com/kisielk/godepgraph
```

How you install Graphviz depends on your operating system. You can use Windows binaries, Linux packages, and both MacPorts and HomeBrew for OSX.

Generating a dependency graph

Once everything is installed, the following command:

```
$ godepgraph github.com/kisielk/godepgraph | dot -Tpng -o godepgraph.png
```

Will produce the following pretty picture for you:

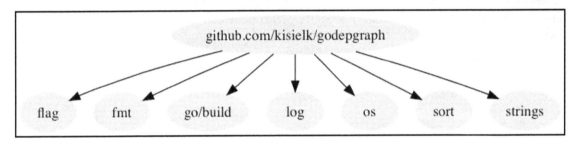

As you can see, the dependency graph for `godepgraph` is nice and flat, and only relies on packages from the standard library (the green circles).

Let's try something a little more complicated: let's generate the dependency graph for the code we are going to use in the second part of this book:

```
$ godepgraph github.com/PacktPublishing/Hands-On-Dependency-Injection-in-Go/ch04/acme/ | dot -Tpng -o acme-graph-v1.png
```

This gives us an incredibly complicated graph that will never fit on the page. Please take a look at `ch03/04_visualizing_dependencies/acme-graph-v1.png` if you want to see just how complicated it is. Don't worry too much about trying to make out the details; it's not in a super useful form right now.

The first thing we can do to fix this is remove the standard library imports (which have the −s flag), as shown in the following code. We can assume that using the standard library is acceptable, and is not something we need to turn into an abstraction or use DI on:

```
$ godepgraph -s github.com/PacktPublishing/Hands-On-Dependency-Injection-
in-Go/ch04/acme/ | dot -Tpng -o acme-graph-v2.png
```

We could use this graph, but it's still too complicated for me. Assuming we don't recklessly adopt external dependencies, we can treat them like the standard library and hide them from the graph (with the −o flag), as shown in the following code:

```
$ godepgraph -s -o github.com/PacktPublishing/Hands-On-Dependency-
Injection-in-Go/ch04/acme/ github.com/PacktPublishing/Hands-On-Dependency-
Injection-in-Go/ch04/acme/ | dot -Tpng -o acme-graph-v3.png
```

This gives us the following:

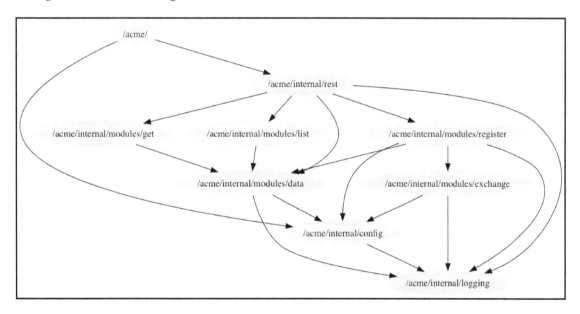

With all of the external packages removed, we can see how our packages relate and depend on each other.

If you are using OSX or Linux, I have included a Bash script called depgraph.sh that I use to generate these graphs in the source code for this chapter.

Interpreting the dependency graph

Like a lot of things in the programming world, what a dependency graph says is very much open to interpretation. I use the graph to discover potential problems that I can then go searching for in the code.

So, what would a *perfect* graph look like? If there were one, it would be very flat, with pretty much everything hanging from the main package. In such a system, all of the packages would be completely decoupled from each other and would have no dependencies beyond their external dependencies and the standard library.

This is really not feasible. As you will see with the various DI methods in the second part of this book, the goal is frequently to decouple the layers so that dependencies flow only in one direction—from the top down.

From an abstract perspective, this looks something like the following:

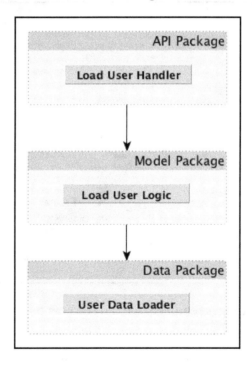

With this in mind, what potential issues do we see with our graph?

The first thing to consider when looking at any package is how many arrows are pointing into or out of it. This is a fundamental measure of coupling. Every arrow pointing into a package indicates a user of this package. Therefore, every arrow pointing inward means that the package may have to change if we make changes to the current package. The same can be said in reverse—the more packages the current package depends on, the more likely it will be to have to change as a result of them.

Considering the DIP, while adopting an interface from another package is the quick and easy thing to do, defining our own interface allows us to depend on ourselves, and reducing the likelihood of change.

The next thing that jumps out is the config package. Just about every package depends on it. As we have seen, with this amount of responsibility, making changes to that package is potentially tricky. Not far behind in terms of trickiness is the logging package. Perhaps what is most concerning is that the config package depends on the logging package. This means that we are one bad import away from circular dependency problems. These are both issues that we will need to leverage DI to deal with in later chapters.

Otherwise, the graph is pretty good; it flows out like a pyramid from the main package, and almost all of the dependencies are in one direction. The next time you are looking for ways to improve your code base or are experiencing a circular dependency problem, why don't you fire up `godepgraph` and see what it says about your system. The dependency graph will not tell you exactly where there is a problem or where there isn't a problem, but it will give you hints as to where to start looking.

Summary

Congratulations! We made it to the end of the first section! Hopefully, at this point, you've discovered a few new things, or perhaps have been reminded of some software design concepts that you had forgotten.

Programming, like any professional endeavor, deserves constant discussion, learning, and a healthy dose of skepticism.

In the second section, you will find several very different techniques for DI, some that you might like, some that you might not. Armed with everything we have examined so far, you will have no trouble in determining how and when each technique could work for you.

Questions

1. Why is the usability of code important?
2. Who benefits the most from code with great UX?
3. How do you construct a good UX?
4. What can unit testing do for you?
5. What kind of test scenarios should you consider?
6. How do table-driven tests help?
7. How can testing damage your software design?

4
Introduction to the ACME Registration Service

In this chapter, we will introduce a small but fake service called the *ACME registration service*. The code for this service will serve as the basis for most of the examples in the rest of the book. We will examine the business environment in which this service lives, discuss the goals for the service and the code, and finally, we will look at some examples of the problems that we can fix by applying **dependency injection** (**DI**).

By the end of this chapter, you should have enough knowledge to join the team as we work our way through the improvements we will make in the following chapters.

The following topics will be covered in this chapter:

- Goals for our system
- Introduction to our system
- Known issues

Technical requirements

As we are learning about the system that we are going to use for the rest of the book, I would strongly recommend downloading the source code and running it in your favorite IDE.

All of the code in this chapter is available at `https://github.com/PacktPublishing/Hands-On-Dependency-Injection-in-Go/tree/master/ch04`.

Instructions on how to obtain the code and configure the sample service are available in the README file, found at `https://github.com/PacktPublishing/Hands-On-Dependency-Injection-in-Go/`.

You can find the code for the service in the `ch04/acme` file.

Goals for our system

Have you ever tried to grow your own vegetables from seed? It's a long, slow, but gratifying experience. Building great code is no different. In gardening, it's perhaps more common to skip the first step and buy plants as seedlings from the nursery, and programming is much the same. Most of the time, when we join a project, the code already exists; sometimes it's happy and healthy, but often it's sick and dying.

In this situation, we are adopting a system. It works, but has a few thorns—Ok, maybe more than a few. With some tender loving care, we will turn this system into something healthy and thriving.

So, how do we define a healthy system? The system we have works; it does what the business needs it to do. That's enough, right?

Absolutely not! We might explicitly be paid to deliver a certain amount of features, but we are implicitly paid to provide code that can be maintained and extended. Beyond considering why we are paid, let's take a more selfish view: do you want your work tomorrow to be easier or harder than it is today?

A healthy code base has the following key features:

- High readability
- High testability
- Low coupling

We have talked about or alluded to all of these asks in part 1, but their importance means that we will go over them one more time.

High readability

Simply put, high readability means being able to read the code and understand it. Code that is not readable will slow you down and could lead to mistakes, where you assume it does one thing but in fact it does something else.

Let's look at an example, shown in the following code:

```
type House struct {
    a string
    b int
    t int
    p float64
}
```

In this example, the code has a problem with its naming. Short variable names seem like a win; less typing means less work, right? In the short term, yes, but in the long run, they are hard to understand. You are forced to read the code to determine what the variable means and then re-read the code within that context, whereas a good name would have saved us from the first step. This does not indicate that super-long names are right either; they also add to the mental burden and waste screen real estate. A good variable is typically one word, with a commonly understood meaning or purpose.

There are two situations in which the aforementioned principles should not be followed. The first is methods. Perhaps it's because of my time using C++ and Java and the lack of a `this` operator in Go, but I find short method receivers to be useful, probably because of the fact that they are consistent throughout the struct, and only the short variable differentiates them from all the others.

The second situation is when we are working with test names. Tests are essentially mini stories; in this case, long names are often entirely appropriate. Comments would work too, but less effectively, as the test runner outputs the test's name when it fails and not the comments.

Let's update the preceding example with these ideas in mind and see if it's any better, as shown in the following code:

```
type House struct {
    address string
    bedrooms int
    toilets int
    price float64
}
```

For more on readability, flip back to the *Optimizing for humans* section in `Chapter 3`, *Coding for User Experience*.

High testability

Writing automated tests can feel like *extra work*, something that takes time away from our real purpose of writing features. In fact, the primary goal of automated tests is to ensure that code performs as expected, and continues to do so despite any changes or additions we might make to the code base as a whole. Automated tests do, however, have a cost: you have to write and maintain them. Therefore, if our code is easy to test, we will be less inclined to skimp on the tests and rush on to that exciting next feature.

Let's look at an example, as shown in the following code:

```
func longMethod(resp http.ResponseWriter, req *http.Request) {
    err := req.ParseForm()
    if err != nil {
        resp.WriteHeader(http.StatusPreconditionFailed)
        return
    }
    userID, err := strconv.ParseInt(req.Form.Get("UserID"), 10, 64)
    if err != nil {
        resp.WriteHeader(http.StatusPreconditionFailed)
        return
    }

    row := DB.QueryRow("SELECT * FROM Users WHERE userID = ?", userID)

    person := &Person{}
    err = row.Scan(person.ID, person.Name, person.Phone)
    if err != nil {
        resp.WriteHeader(http.StatusInternalServerError)
        return
    }

    encoder := json.NewEncoder(resp)
    err = encoder.Encode(person)
    if err != nil {
        resp.WriteHeader(http.StatusInternalServerError)
        return
    }
}
```

So what's wrong with the example? The simplest answer is that it knows too much, or if I was being more selfish, it makes me know too much.

It contains boundary-layer (HTTP and database) logic, and it also contains business logic. It is rather long, meaning that I have to keep more context in my head. It's basically one massive violation of the **single responsibility principle** (**SRP**). There are many reasons it could change. The input format could change. The database format could change. The business rules could change. Any such change would mean that every test for this code would likely also need to change. Let's look at what a test for the preceding code might look like, as shown in the following code:

```go
func TestLongMethod_happyPath(t *testing.T) {
    // build request
    request := &http.Request{}
    request.PostForm = url.Values{}
    request.PostForm.Add("UserID", "123")

    // mock the database
    var mockDB sqlmock.Sqlmock
    var err error

    DB, mockDB, err = sqlmock.New()
    require.NoError(t, err)
      mockDB.ExpectQuery("SELECT .* FROM people WHERE ID = ?").
     WithArgs(123).
     WillReturnRows(
        sqlmock.NewRows(
           []string{"ID", "Name", "Phone"}).
           AddRow(123, "May", "0123456789"))

    // build response
    response := httptest.NewRecorder()

    // call method
    longMethod(response, request)

    // validate response
    require.Equal(t, http.StatusOK, response.Code)

    // validate the JSON
    responseBytes, err := ioutil.ReadAll(response.Body)
    require.NoError(t, err)

    expectedJSON := `{"ID":123,"Name":"May","Phone":"0123456789"}` + "\n"
    assert.Equal(t, expectedJSON, string(responseBytes))
}
```

As you can see, the test is verbose and unwieldy. Perhaps worst of all, any other tests for this method will involve copying this test and making minor changes. This sounds effective, but there are two issues. The small differences will likely be hard to spot among all this boilerplate code, and any change to the feature we are testing will need to be made to all these tests as well.

While there are many ways to fix the testability of our example, perhaps the simplest option is to separate the different concerns and then do the bulk of our testing one method at a time, as shown in the following code:

```go
func shortMethods(resp http.ResponseWriter, req *http.Request) {
    userID, err := extractUserID(req)
    if err != nil {
        resp.WriteHeader(http.StatusInternalServerError)
        return
    }

    person, err := loadPerson(userID)
    if err != nil {
        resp.WriteHeader(http.StatusInternalServerError)
        return
    }

    outputPerson(resp, person)
}

func extractUserID(req *http.Request) (int64, error) {
    err := req.ParseForm()
    if err != nil {
        return 0, err
    }

    return strconv.ParseInt(req.Form.Get("UserID"), 10, 64)
}

func loadPerson(userID int64) (*Person, error) {
    row := DB.QueryRow("SELECT * FROM people WHERE ID = ?", userID)

    person := &Person{}
    err := row.Scan(&person.ID, &person.Name, &person.Phone)
    if err != nil {
        return nil, err
    }
    return person, nil
}

func outputPerson(resp http.ResponseWriter, person *Person) {
```

```
encoder := json.NewEncoder(resp)
err := encoder.Encode(person)
if err != nil {
   resp.WriteHeader(http.StatusInternalServerError)
   return
}
}
```

For more on what unit testing can do for you, flip back to the *A security blanket named unit tests* section in `Chapter 3`, *Coding for User Experience*.

Low coupling

Coupling is a measure of how an object or package relates to others. An object is considered to have high coupling if changes to it will likely result in changes to other objects, or vice versa. Conversely, when an object has low coupling, it is independent of other objects or packages. In Go, low coupling is best achieved through implicit interfaces and stable and minimal exported APIs.

Low coupling is desirable as it leads to code where changes are localized. In the following example, by using an implicit interface to define our requirements we are able to insulate ourselves from changes to our dependency:

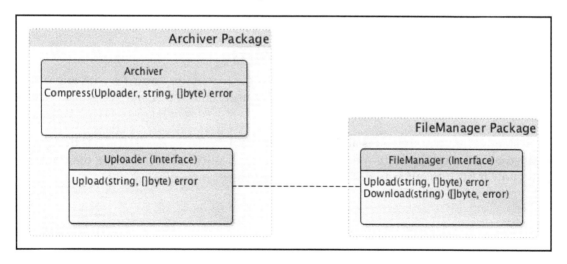

As you can see from the preceding example, we no longer depend on the **FileManager Package**, and this helps us in other ways. This lack of dependence also means that we have less context to remember when reading the code and fewer dependencies when writing our tests.

For more on how to achieve low coupling, flip back to the SOLID principles covered in `Chapter 2`, *SOLID Design Principles for Go*.

Final thoughts on goals

By now, you might be seeing a pattern. All of these goals will lead to code that is easy to read, understand, test, and extend—that is to say, code that is maintainable. While these may seem like selfish or perfectionist goals, I would argue that it is imperative for the business in the long term. In the short term, delivering value to the users, typically in the form of features, is essential. But when this is done poorly, the rate at which features can be added, the number of programmers required to add features, and the number of bugs that are introduced because of changes will all increase and cost the business more than the cost of developing good code.

So now that we have defined the goals that we have for our service, let's take a look at its current state.

Introduction to our system

Welcome to the project! So what do you need to know to join the team? As with any project, the first thing you want to know is what it does, its users, and the business environment in which it is deployed.

The system we are working on is an HTTP-based event registration service. It is designed to be called by our web application or native mobile applications. The following diagram shows how it fits into our network:

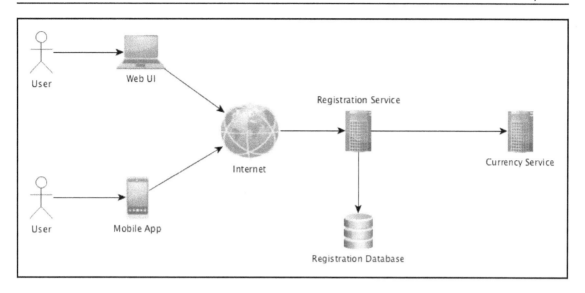

Currently, there are three endpoints, listed as follows:

- **Register**: This will create a new registration record
- **Get**: This will return the full details of an existing registration record
- **List**: This will return a list of all the registrations

All request and response payloads are in JSON. The data is stored in a MySQL database.

We also have an upstream currency conversion service—which we call during registration—to convert the registration price of 100 euros to the requested currency of the user.

If you wish to run the service or the tests locally, please refer to the ch04/README.md file for instructions.

Software architecture

Conceptually, our code has three layers, as shown in the following diagram:

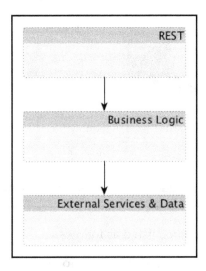

These layers are as follows:

- **REST**: This package accepts the HTTP requests and converts them into function calls in the business logic. It then converts the business logic response back into HTTP.
- **Business Logic**: This is where the magic happens. This layer uses the external service and data layer to perform the business functions.
- **External Services and Data**: This layer consists of code that accesses the database and the upstream services that provides the currency exchange rates.

I used the word *conceptually* at the beginning of this section because our import graph shows a slightly different story:

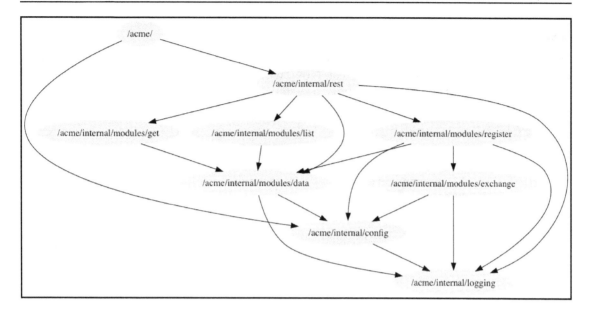

As you can see, we have a quasi-fourth layer with the config and logging packages, and what's worse, everything seems to depend on them. This is likely going to cause us problems somewhere down the road.

There is one less obvious problem that is shown here. See the link between the rest and data packages? This indicates that our HTTP layer depends on the data layer. This is risky because they have different life cycles and different reasons to change. We will look at this and some other nasty surprises in the next section.

Known issues

Every system has its skeletons, parts of the code we are not proud of. Sometimes, they are parts of the code that we would have done better if we'd just had more time. This project is no different. Let's examine the issues that we currently know about.

Testability

Despite being a small and working service, we have quite a few issues, perhaps the most egregious of which is its difficulty to test. Now, we don't want to start introducing test-induced damage, but we do want to have a system that we are confident in. To achieve this, we are going to need to reduce the complexity and verbosity of the tests. Take a look at the following test:

```go
func TestGetHandler_ServeHTTP(t *testing.T) {
    // ensure the test always fails by giving it a timeout
    ctx, cancel := context.WithTimeout(context.Background(), 5*time.Second)
    defer cancel()

    // Create and start a server
    // With out current implementation, we cannot test this handler
    // without a full server as we need the mux.
    address, err := startServer(ctx)
    require.NoError(t, err)

    // build inputs
    response, err := http.Get("http://" + address + "/person/1/")

    // validate outputs
    require.NoError(t, err)
    require.Equal(t, http.StatusOK, response.StatusCode)

    expectedPayload :=
[]byte(`{"id":1,"name":"John","phone":"0123456780","currency":"USD","price"
:100}` + "\n")
    payload, _ := ioutil.ReadAll(response.Body)
    defer response.Body.Close()

    assert.Equal(t, expectedPayload, payload)
}
```

This test is for our most straightforward endpoint, `Get`. Ask yourself, how could this test break? What changes, technical or business-related, would cause this test to need to be updated? What parts of the system must be working correctly for this test to pass?

Some potential answers to these questions include following:

- If the URL path changed, this test would break
- If the output format changed, this test would break
- If the `config` file wasn't configured correctly, this test would break
- If the database wasn't working, this test would break

- If the record ID 1 were missing from the database, this test would break
- If the business logic layer had a bug, this test would break
- If the database layer had a bug, this test would break

This list is rather nasty for a simple endpoint. The fact that this test can break in so many ways means it's a brittle test. Brittle tests are exhausting to maintain and often exhausting to write as well.

Duplication of effort

Let's examine the test for the `Get` endpoint in the business layer, as shown in the following code:

```
func TestGetter_Do(t *testing.T) {
    // inputs
    ID := 1
    name := "John"

    // call method
    getter := &Getter{}
    person, err := getter.Do(ID)

    // validate expectations
    require.NoError(t, err)
    assert.Equal(t, ID, person.ID)
    assert.Equal(t, name, person.FullName)
}
```

This test is almost the same as the one in the previous section. Perhaps this is logical, given that it's the same endpoint. But let's take a selfish view—what does this test give us, other than better unit test coverage, that the previous one did not?

Nothing. Because the previous test was effectively an integration test, it tested the entire stack. This test is also an integration test, but one layer down. Because it tests code that was tested by the previous example, we have performed double the work, have double the amount of tests to maintain, and have gained nothing.

Lack of isolation in tests

The lack of isolation shown in our preceding code is a symptom of high coupling between the layers. In the following section, we will be applying DI and the **dependency inversion principle** (**DIP**) to fix this.

High coupling between the data and REST packages

Our REST package is using the Person struct defined in the data package. On the surface, this makes some sense. Less code means less work to write and maintain that code; however, this means that the output format and the data format are tied to each other. Consider what happens if we start storing private information relating to the customer, such as a password or IP address. This information might be necessary for some functions, but it is very unlikely that it should need to be published via the Get or List endpoints.

There is another consideration that we should bear in mind. As the volume of data that is stored or the amount of usage grows, it might be necessary to change the format of the data. Any such change to this struct would break the API contract and, therefore, our users.

Perhaps the most significant risk here is simply human error; if you are working on the data package, you may not remember that the REST package uses that struct, or how. Let's say that we added the ability for users to log in to our system. The most straightforward implementation of this would be to add a password field to the database. What happens if our Get endpoint was building its output as shown in the following code?

```
// output the supplied person as JSON
func (h *GetHandler) writeJSON(writer io.Writer, person *data.Person) error
{
    return json.NewEncoder(writer).Encode(person)
}
```

Our Get endpoint payload would now include the password. Whoops!

This issue is an SRP violation, and the fix for this is to ensure that these two use cases are decoupled and allowed to evolve separately.

High coupling with the config package

As we saw in our dependency graph, just about everything depends on the config package. The primary cause of this is code that directly references a public global variable to configure itself. The first issue with this is how it affects the tests. All tests now pretty much make sure that the config global has been properly initialized before being run. Because all of the tests are using the same global variable, we are forced to choose between not changing the config, which hampers our ability to test, or running the tests in serial, which wastes our time.

Let's look at an example, as shown in the following code:

```
// bind stop channel to context
ctx := context.Background()

// start REST server
server := rest.New(config.App.Address)
server.Listen(ctx.Done())
```

In this code, we are starting our REST server and passing it the address (host and port) to bind to. If we decided that we wanted to start multiple servers to test different things in isolation, then we would have to change the value stored in `config.App.Address`. However, by doing so in one test, we could accidentally influence a different test.

The second issue doesn't appear as often, but this coupling also means that this code cannot be easily used by other projects, packages, or use cases beyond its original intent.

The final issue is perhaps the most annoying: you cannot use custom data types, defined outside of the `Config` package, in your config as a result of a circular dependency issue.

Consider the following code:

```
// Currency is a custom type; used for convenience and code readability
type Currency string

// UnmarshalJSON implements json.Unmarshaler
func (c *Currency) UnmarshalJSON(in []byte) error {
    var s string
    err := json.Unmarshal(in, &s)
    if err != nil {
        return err
    }

    currency, valid := validCurrencies[s]
    if !valid {
        return fmt.Errorf("'%s' is not a valid currency", s)
    }
    *c = currency

    return nil
}
```

Say that your config included the following:

```
type Config struct {
    DefaultCurrency currency.Currency `json:"default_currency"`
}
```

In this case, any attempt to use the config package in the same package as our `Currency` type would be prevented.

Downstream currency service

The exchange package makes HTTP calls to an external service for exchange rates. Currently, when the tests are run, it will make calls to that service. This means that our tests have the following features:

- They require an internet connection
- They are dependent on the downstream service being accessible and working properly
- They require proper credentials and quotas from the downstream service

All of these factors are either out of our control or otherwise wholly unrelated to our service. If we take the perspective that the reliability of our tests is a measure of the quality of our work, then our quality is now dependent on things we cannot control. This is far from ideal.

We could create a fake currency service and change our config to point to that, and when testing the exchange package, I would likely do just that. But having to do this in other places is annoying and prone to error.

Summary

In this chapter, we introduced a small service that is in pretty rough shape. We are going to improve this service with a series of refactorings as we explore the many DI techniques. In the following chapters, we will tackle the problems we have outlined in this chapter by applying the different DI techniques available in Go.

For each different technique, keep in mind the code smells, the SOLID principles, the code UX, and all the other ideas we discussed in part 1. Also, remember to bring along your inner skeptic.

Always ask yourself, what does this technique achieve? How does this technique make the code better/worse? How could you apply this technique to improve other code that belongs to you?

Questions

1. Which of the goals that are defined for our service is most important to you personally?
2. Which of the issues outlined seem to be the most urgent or important?

5
Dependency Injection with Monkey Patching

Do you have code that relies on a global variable? Do you have code that is dependent on the filesystem? Have you ever tried to test your database error handling code?

In this chapter, we will examine monkey patching as a way to *swap out* dependencies during our tests and test in a manner that is otherwise impossible. It doesn't matter if these dependencies are objects or functions. We will apply monkey patching to our sample service so that we can decouple our tests from the database; decouple the different layers from each other and all without resorting to significant refactoring.

In continuing with our pragmatic, skeptical approach, we will also discuss the advantages and disadvantages of monkey patching.

The following topics will be covered in this chapter:

- Monkey magic—an introduction to monkey patching
- Advantages of monkey patching
- Applying monkey patching
- Disadvantages of monkey patching

Technical requirements

It would be beneficial to be familiar with the code for our service that we introduced in Chapter 4, *Introduction to ACME registration service*. You might also find it useful to read and run the full versions of the code for this chapter, which are available at https://github.com/PacktPublishing/Hands-On-Dependency-Injection-in-Go/tree/master/ch05.

Instructions to obtain the code and configure the sample service are available in the README here `https://github.com/PacktPublishing/Hands-On-Dependency-Injection-in-Go/`.

You can find the code for our service, with the changes from this chapter already applied, in `ch05/acme`.

Monkey magic!

Monkey patching is changing a program at runtime, typically by replacing a function or variable.

While this is not a traditional form of **dependency injection** (**DI**), it can be used in Go to facilitate testing. In fact, monkey patching can be used to test in ways that are otherwise impossible.

Let's consider a real-world analogy first. Let's say you want to test the effects of a car crash on the human body. You probably wouldn't be volunteering to be the human that was in the car during testing. Nor are you allowed to make changes to the vehicle to facilitate your testing. But you could swap out (monkey patch) the human for a crash test dummy during your test.

The same process holds true for monkey patching in code; the changes only exist during the test and in many cases can be applied with little impact on the production code.

A quick note for those of you familiar with dynamic languages such as Ruby, Python, and JavaScript: it is possible to monkey patch individual class methods, and in some cases, patch the standard library. Go only offers us the ability to patch variables, which can be objects or functions, as we will see in this chapter.

Advantages of monkey patching

Monkey patching as a form of DI is very different from the other methods presented in this book in both implementation and effect. As such, there are some situations in which monkey patching is either the only option or the only succinct one. Monkey patching's other advantages are detailed in this section.

DI via monkey patching is cheap to implement—In this book, we have talked a lot about decoupling, which is the idea that separate pieces of our code should be kept separate, even though they use/depend on each other. We introduce abstractions and inject them into each other. Let's step back for a moment and consider why we want the code decoupled in the first place. It's not only about making it easier to test. It's also about allowing the code to evolve separately and provide us with small groups, mental boxes if you will, with which we can think about different parts of the code individually. It is this decoupling or separation with which monkey patching can be applied.

Consider this function:

```go
func SaveConfig(filename string, cfg *Config) error {
    // convert to JSON
    data, err := json.Marshal(cfg)
    if err != nil {
        return err
    }

    // save file
    err = ioutil.WriteFile(filename, data, 0666)
    if err != nil {
        log.Printf("failed to save file '%s' with err: %s", filename, err)
        return err
    }

    return nil
}
```

How do we decouple this function from the operating system? Let me put it a different way: how do we test how this function behaves when the file is missing?

We could replace the filename with `*os.File` or `io.Writer`, but that just pushes the problem somewhere else. We could refactor this function into a struct, change the call to `ioutil.WriteFile` into an abstraction, and then mock it. But that sounds like a lot of work.

With monkey patching, there is a far cheaper option:

```go
func SaveConfig(filename string, cfg *Config) error {
    // convert to JSON
    data, err := json.Marshal(cfg)
    if err != nil {
        return err
    }

    // save file
```

```
    err = writeFile(filename, data, 0666)
    if err != nil {
        log.Printf("failed to save file '%s' with err: %s", filename, err)
        return err
    }

    return nil
}

// Custom type that allows us to Monkey Patch
var writeFile = ioutil.WriteFile
```

With one line, we have given ourselves the ability to replace `writeFile()` with a mock that will allow us to test both happy path and error scenarios with ease.

Allows us to mock other packages, without fully understanding its internals—In the previous example, you may have noticed that we are mocking a standard library function. Do you know how to make `ioutil.WriteFile()` fail? Sure, we could go rooting around in the standard library; while that's a great way to improve your Go skills, it's not what we get paid for. How `ioutil.WriteFile()` could fail is not even significant in this case. What is actually important is how our code reacts to errors.

Monkey patching, like other forms of mocking, offers us the ability to not care about the internals of the dependency and yet be able to get it to behave as we need it to.

I propose that testing *from the outside* is the way to go anyway. Decoupling how we think about the dependency ensures that any tests have less knowledge of the internals and are not therefore susceptible to changes in implementation or environment. Should any changes occur to the internal implementation details of `io.WriteFile()`, they cannot break our tests. Our tests are only dependent on our code, so their reliability is entirely on us.

DI via monkey patching has minimal impact on existing code—In the previous example, we defined the external dependency as follows:

```
var writeFile = ioutil.WriteFile
```

Let's change this slightly:

```
type fileWriter func(filename string, data []byte, perm os.FileMode) error

var writeFile fileWriter = ioutil.WriteFile
```

Does this remind you of anything? In this version, we are explicitly defining our requirements, just like we did in the *Dependency inversion principle* section in `Chapter 2`, *SOLID Design Principles for Go*. While this change is entirely superfluous, it does raise some interesting questions.

Let's double back and examine what kinds of changes we would have to make to test our method without monkey patching. The first option would be injecting `io.WriteFile` into the function, as shown in the following code:

```go
func SaveConfig(writer fileWriter, filename string, cfg *Config) error {
    // convert to JSON
    data, err := json.Marshal(cfg)
    if err != nil {
        return err
    }

    // save file
    err = writer(filename, data, 0666)
    if err != nil {
        log.Printf("failed to save file '%s' with err: %s", filename, err)
        return err
    }

    return nil
}

// This custom type is not strictly needed but it does make the function
// signature a little cleaner
type fileWriter func(filename string, data []byte, perm os.FileMode) error
```

What is wrong with that? Personally, I have three problems with it. Firstly, this is a small, simple function with only one dependency; the function would get really ugly really quickly if we had more dependencies. To put it another way, the code UX is terrible.

Secondly, it breaks the encapsulation (information hiding) of the implementation of the function. This might feel like I am taking up a zealot-like argument, but I don't think of it this way. Imagine what happens if we refactor the implementation of our `SaveConfig()` such that we need to change `io.WriteFile` to something else. In that situation, we would have to change every use of our function, potentially a lot of changes and therefore a lot of risk.

Lastly, this change is arguably test-induced damage, as we discussed in the *Test-induced damage* section of `Chapter 3`, *Coding for User Experience*, as it is a change that only serves to improve testing and does not enhance the non-test code.

Another option that might come to mind is to refactor our function into an object and then use a more traditional form of DI, as shown in the following code:

```
type ConfigSaver struct {
    FileWriter func(filename string, data []byte, perm os.FileMode) error
}

func (c ConfigSaver) Save(filename string, cfg *Config) error {
    // convert to JSON
    data, err := json.Marshal(cfg)
    if err != nil {
        return err
    }

    // save file
    err = c.FileWriter(filename, data, 0666)
    if err != nil {
        log.Printf("failed to save file '%s' with err: %s", filename, err)
        return err
    }

    return nil
}
```

Sadly, this refactor suffers from similar issues as the previous one, not least of which is that it has the potential to be a considerable amount of changes. As you can see, monkey patching required significantly fewer changes than traditional methods.

DI via monkey patching allows testing of globals and singletons—You probably think I am crazy, Go doesn't have singletons. Perhaps not in the strictest sense, but have you ever read the code for the math/rand standard library package (https://godoc.org/math/rand)? In it, you will find the following:

```
// A Rand is a source of random numbers.
type Rand struct {
    src Source

    // code removed
}

// Int returns a non-negative pseudo-random int.
func (r *Rand) Int() int {
    // code changed for brevity
    value := r.src.Int63()
    return int(value)
}
```

```
/*
 * Top-level convenience functions
 */

var globalRand = New(&lockedSource{})

// Int returns a non-negative pseudo-random int from the default Source.
func Int() int { return globalRand.Int() }

// A Source represents a source of uniformly-distributed
// pseudo-random int64 values in the range [0, 1<<63).
type Source interface {
    Int63() int64

    // code removed
}
```

How would you test the Rand struct? You could swap the Source with a mock that returned a predictable, non-random result, easy.

Now, how would you test the convenience function Int()? It's not so easy. This method, by definition, returns a random value. With monkey patching, however, we can, as shown in the following code:

```
func TestInt(t *testing.T) {
    // monkey patch
    defer func(original *Rand) {
        // restore patch after use
        globalRand = original
    }(globalRand)

    // swap out for a predictable outcome
    globalRand = New(&stubSource{})
    // end monkey patch

    // call the function
    result := Int()
    assert.Equal(t, 234, result)
}

// this is a stubbed implementation of Source that returns a
// predictable value
type stubSource struct {
}

func (s *stubSource) Int63() int64 {
    return 234
}
```

With monkey patching, we are able to test the usage of the singleton without any changes to the client code. To achieve this with other methods, we would have to introduce a layer of indirection, which in turn would necessitate changes to the client code.

Applying monkey patching

Let's apply monkey patching to our ACME registration service that we introduced in Chapter 4, *Introduction to ACME Registration Service*. One of the many things we would like to improve with our service is the test reliability and coverage. In this case, we will be working on the data package. Currently, we only have one test, and it looks like this:

```
func TestData_happyPath(t *testing.T) {
    in := &Person{
        FullName: "Jake Blues",
        Phone:    "01234567890",
        Currency: "AUD",
        Price:    123.45,
    }

    // save
    resultID, err := Save(in)
    require.Nil(t, err)
    assert.True(t, resultID > 0)

    // load
    returned, err := Load(resultID)
    require.NoError(t, err)

    in.ID = resultID
    assert.Equal(t, in, returned)
    // load all
    all, err := LoadAll()
    require.NoError(t, err)
    assert.True(t, len(all) > 0)
}
```

In this test, we are performing a save and then loading the newly saved registration back using both the Load() and LoadAll() methods.

This code has at least three major issues.

Firstly, we are only testing the *happy path*; we have not tested our error handling at all.

Secondly, the test relies on the database. Some people will argue this is fine, and I do not want to add to that debate. In this particular case, the use of a live database causes our test of `LoadAll()` to be not very specific, which makes our tests less thorough than they could be.

Lastly, we are testing all the functions together, rather than in isolation. Consider what happens when the following part of the test fails:

```
returned, err := Load(resultID)
require.NoError(t, err)
```

Where is the problem? Is `Load()` broken or is `Save()` broken? This is the basis for the argument regarding testing in isolation.

All of the functions in the `data` package depend on a global instance of `*sql.DB`, which represents a pool of database connections. We therefore will be monkey patching that global variable and introducing a mocked version.

Introducing SQLMock

The SQLMock package (`https://github.com/DATA-DOG/go-sqlmock`) describes itself as follows:

> *"A mock library implementing sql/driver. Which has one and only purpose - to simulate any sql driver behavior in tests, without needing a real database connection"*

I find SQLMock useful, but often more work than directly using the database. Being a pragmatic programmer, I am happy to use either. Typically, the choice of which to use is made based on how I want the tests to work. If I want to be very precise, have no potential for issues related to existing contents of the table, and have no possibility for data races caused by the concurrent usage of the table, then I will spend the extra effort to use SQLMock.

 A data race occurs when two or more goroutines access a variable at the same time, and at least one of the goroutines is writing to the variable.

Let's look at using SQLMock to test. Consider the following function:

```go
func SavePerson(db *sql.DB, in *Person) (int, error) {
    // perform DB insert
    query := "INSERT INTO person (fullname, phone, currency, price) VALUES
(?, ?, ?, ?)"
    result, err := db.Exec(query, in.FullName, in.Phone, in.Currency,
in.Price)
    if err != nil {
        return 0, err
    }

    // retrieve and return the ID of the person created
    id, err := result.LastInsertId()
    if err != nil {
        return 0, err
    }
    return int(id), nil
}
```

This function takes *Person and *sql.DB as input, saves the person into the database provided, and then returns the ID of the newly created record. This function is using a traditional form of DI to pass the database connection pool into the function. This allows us an easy way to swap out the real database connection with a fake one. Now, let's build the test. First, we create a mock database using SQLMock:

```go
testDb, dbMock, err := sqlmock.New()
require.NoError(t, err)
```

Then, we define the query we are expecting as a regular expression and use that to configure the mock database. In this case, we are expecting a single db.Exec call that returns 2, the ID of the newly created record, and 1, the affected row:

```go
queryRegex := `\QINSERT INTO person (fullname, phone, currency, price)
VALUES (?, ?, ?, ?)\E`

dbMock.ExpectExec(queryRegex).WillReturnResult(sqlmock.NewResult(2, 1))
```

Now we call the function:

```go
resultID, err := SavePerson(testDb, person)
```

And then, we validate the results and the mock's expectations:

```go
require.NoError(t, err)
assert.Equal(t, 2, resultID)
assert.NoError(t, dbMock.ExpectationsWereMet())
```

Now that we have an idea of how we can leverage SQLMock to test our database interactions, let's apply it to our ACME registration code.

Monkey patching with SQLMock

Firstly, a quick refresher: currently, the `data` package does not use DI, and therefore we cannot pass in the `*sql.DB` like we did in the previous example. The function currently looks as shown in the following code:

```
// Save will save the supplied person and return the ID of the newly
// created person or an error.
// Errors returned are caused by the underlying database or our connection
// to it.
func Save(in *Person) (int, error) {
   db, err := getDB()
   if err != nil {
      logging.L.Error("failed to get DB connection. err: %s", err)
      return defaultPersonID, err
   }

   // perform DB insert
   query := "INSERT INTO person (fullname, phone, currency, price) VALUES
(?, ?, ?, ?)"
   result, err := db.Exec(query, in.FullName, in.Phone, in.Currency,
in.Price)
   if err != nil {
      logging.L.Error("failed to save person into DB. err: %s", err)
      return defaultPersonID, err
   }

   // retrieve and return the ID of the person created
   id, err := result.LastInsertId()
   if err != nil {
      logging.L.Error("failed to retrieve id of last saved person. err:
%s", err)
      return defaultPersonID, err
   }
   return int(id), nil
}
```

We could refactor to this, and perhaps in the future we might, but at the moment we have almost no tests on this code and refactoring without tests is a terrible idea. You might be thinking something similar to *but if we write tests with monkey patching and then refactor to a different style of DI later, then we would have to refactor these tests*, and you are right; this example is a little contrived. That said, there is nothing wrong with writing tests to provide you with a safety net or a high level of confidence now, and then deleting them later. It might feel like double work, but it's bound to be both less humiliating than introducing regression into a running system that people are relying on, and potentially less work that debugging that regression.

The first thing that jumps out is the SQL. We are going to need almost exactly the same string in our tests. So, to make it easier to maintain the code in the long term, we are going to convert that to a constant and move it to the top of the file. As the test is going to be quite similar to our previous example, let's first examine just the monkey patching. From the previous example, we have the following:

```
// define a mock db
testDb, dbMock, err := sqlmock.New()
defer testDb.Close()

require.NoError(t, err)
```

In these lines, we are creating a test instance of `*sql.DB` and a mock to control it. Before we can monkey patch our test instance of `*sql.DB`, we first need to create a backup of the original one so that we can restore it after the test is complete. To do this, we are going to use the `defer` keyword.

For those not familiar with it, `defer` is a function that is run just before the current function exits, that is, between executing the `return` statement and returning control to the caller of the current function. Another significant feature of `defer` is the fact that the arguments are evaluated immediately. The combination of these two features allows us to take a copy of the original `sql.DB` when `defer` is evaluated and not worry about how or when the current function exits, saving us from potentially a lot of copying and pasting of *clean up* code. This code looks as follows:

```
defer func(original sql.DB) {
    // restore original DB (after test)
    db = &original
}(*db)

// replace db for this test
db = testDb
```

With this done, the test looks as follows:

```go
func TestSave_happyPath(t *testing.T) {
    // define a mock db
    testDb, dbMock, err := sqlmock.New()
    defer testDb.Close()
    require.NoError(t, err)

    // configure the mock db
    queryRegex := convertSQLToRegex(sqlInsert)
    dbMock.ExpectExec(queryRegex).WillReturnResult(sqlmock.NewResult(2, 1))

    // monkey patching starts here
    defer func(original sql.DB) {
        // restore original DB (after test)
        db = &original
    }(*db)

    // replace db for this test
    db = testDb
    // end of monkey patch

    // inputs
    in := &Person{
        FullName: "Jake Blues",
        Phone:    "01234567890",
        Currency: "AUD",
        Price:    123.45,
    }

    // call function
    resultID, err := Save(in)

    // validate result
    require.NoError(t, err)
    assert.Equal(t, 2, resultID)
    assert.NoError(t, dbMock.ExpectationsWereMet())
}
```

Fantastic, we have our happy path test done. Unfortunately, we've only tested 7 out of 13 lines of our function; perhaps more importantly, we don't know whether our error handling code even works correctly.

Testing error handling

There are three possible errors we need to handle:

- The SQL insert could fail
- Failure to get the database
- We could fail to retrieve the ID of the inserted record

So, how do we test for SQL insert failure? With SQLMock it's easy: we make a copy of the previous test and instead of returning `sql.Result`, we return an error, as shown in the following code:

```
// configure the mock db
queryRegex := convertSQLToRegex(sqlInsert)
dbMock.ExpectExec(queryRegex).WillReturnError(errors.New("failed to
insert"))
```

We can then change our expectations from a result to an error, as shown in the following code:

```
require.Error(t, err)
assert.Equal(t, defaultPersonID, resultID)
assert.NoError(t, dbMock.ExpectationsWereMet())
```

Moving on to testing *failure to get the database*, this time SQLMock can't help us, but monkey patching can. Currently, our `getDB()` function looks as shown in the following code:

```
func getDB() (*sql.DB, error) {
    if db == nil {
        if config.App == nil {
            return nil, errors.New("config is not initialized")
        }

        var err error
        db, err = sql.Open("mysql", config.App.DSN)
        if err != nil {
            // if the DB cannot be accessed we are dead
            panic(err.Error())
        }
    }

    return db, nil
}
```

Let's change the function to a variable, as shown in the following code:

```
var getDB = func() (*sql.DB, error) {
    // code removed for brevity
}
```

We have not otherwise changed the implementation of the function. We can now monkey patch that variable and the resulting test looks as follows:

```
func TestSave_getDBError(t *testing.T) {
    // monkey patching starts here
    defer func(original func() (*sql.DB, error)) {
        // restore original DB (after test)
        getDB = original
    }(getDB)

    // replace getDB() function for this test
    getDB = func() (*sql.DB, error) {
        return nil, errors.New("getDB() failed")
    }
    // end of monkey patch

    // inputs
    in := &Person{
        FullName: "Jake Blues",
        Phone:    "01234567890",
        Currency: "AUD",
        Price:    123.45,
    }

    // call function
    resultID, err := Save(in)
    require.Error(t, err)
    assert.Equal(t, defaultPersonID, resultID)
}
```

You may have noticed a high amount of duplication between the happy path and error path tests. This is somewhat common in Go tests and is perhaps driven by the fact that we are intentionally calling a function repeatedly with different inputs or environments, essentially documenting and enforcing a contract of behavior for the object we are testing.

Given these fundamental responsibilities, we should be looking to ensure that our tests are both easy to read and maintain. To achieve these goals we can apply one of my favorite features in Go, table-driven tests (https://github.com/golang/go/wiki/TableDrivenTests).

Reducing test bloat with table-driven tests

With table-driven tests, we define a slice of scenarios (often the function inputs, mock configuration, and our expectations) at the start of the test and then a scenario runner, which is typically part of the test that would otherwise have been duplicated. Let's see what this looks like as an example. The happy path test for the `Load()` function looks like this:

```go
func TestLoad_happyPath(t *testing.T) {
    expectedResult := &Person{
        ID:       2,
        FullName: "Paul",
        Phone:    "0123456789",
        Currency: "CAD",
        Price:    23.45,
    }

    // define a mock db
    testDb, dbMock, err := sqlmock.New()
    require.NoError(t, err)

    // configure the mock db
    queryRegex := convertSQLToRegex(sqlLoadByID)
    dbMock.ExpectQuery(queryRegex).WillReturnRows(
        sqlmock.NewRows(strings.Split(sqlAllColumns, ", ")).
            AddRow(2, "Paul", "0123456789", "CAD", 23.45))

    // monkey patching the database
    defer func(original sql.DB) {
        // restore original DB (after test)
        db = &original
    }(*db)

    db = testDb
    // end of monkey patch

    // call function
    result, err := Load(2)

    // validate results
    assert.Equal(t, expectedResult, result)
    assert.NoError(t, err)
    assert.NoError(t, dbMock.ExpectationsWereMet())
}
```

This function has about 11 functional lines (after removing the formatting), of which approximately 9 would be almost identical in our test for SQL load failure. Converting this to a table-driven test gives us this:

```
func TestLoad_tableDrivenTest(t *testing.T) {
    scenarios := []struct {
        desc           string
        configureMockDB func(sqlmock.Sqlmock)
        expectedResult  *Person
        expectError     bool
    }{
        {
            desc: "happy path",
            configureMockDB: func(dbMock sqlmock.Sqlmock) {
                queryRegex := convertSQLToRegex(sqlLoadAll)
                dbMock.ExpectQuery(queryRegex).WillReturnRows(
                    sqlmock.NewRows(strings.Split(sqlAllColumns, ", ")).
                        AddRow(2, "Paul", "0123456789", "CAD", 23.45))
            },
            expectedResult: &Person{
                ID:       2,
                FullName: "Paul",
                Phone:    "0123456789",
                Currency: "CAD",
                Price:    23.45,
            },
            expectError: false,
        },
        {
            desc: "load error",
            configureMockDB: func(dbMock sqlmock.Sqlmock) {
                queryRegex := convertSQLToRegex(sqlLoadAll)
                dbMock.ExpectQuery(queryRegex).WillReturnError(
                    errors.New("something failed"))
            },
            expectedResult: nil,
            expectError:    true,
        },
    }

    for _, scenario := range scenarios {
        // define a mock db
        testDb, dbMock, err := sqlmock.New()
        require.NoError(t, err)

        // configure the mock db
        scenario.configureMockDB(dbMock)
```

```
        // monkey db for this test
        original := *db
        db = testDb

        // call function
        result, err := Load(2)

        // validate results
        assert.Equal(t, scenario.expectedResult, result, scenario.desc)
        assert.Equal(t, scenario.expectError, err != nil, scenario.desc)
        assert.NoError(t, dbMock.ExpectationsWereMet())

        // restore original DB (after test)
        db = &original
        testDb.Close()
    }
}
```

Sorry, there's a lot going on there, so let's break this into its separate parts:

```
scenarios := []struct {
    desc            string
    configureMockDB func(sqlmock.Sqlmock)
    expectedResult  *Person
    expectError     bool
}{
```

These lines define a slice and an anonymous struct that will be our list of scenarios. In this case, our scenario contains the following:

- **A description**: This is useful for adding to test error messages.
- **Mock configuration**: As we are testing how our code reacts to different responses from the database, this is where most of the magic happens.
- **An expected result**: Fairly standard, given the inputs and environment (that is, mock configuration). This is what we want to get back.
- **A Boolean to indicate whether we expect an error**: We could use an error value here; it would be more precise. However, I prefer to use a custom error, which means the output is not constant. I have also found that error messages can change over time and therefore the narrowness of the check makes the tests brittle. Essentially, I am trading test specificity for durability.

Then we have our scenarios, one per test case:

```
{
    desc: "happy path",
    configureMockDB: func(dbMock sqlmock.Sqlmock) {
        queryRegex := convertSQLToRegex(sqlLoadAll)
        dbMock.ExpectQuery(queryRegex).WillReturnRows(
            sqlmock.NewRows(strings.Split(sqlAllColumns, ", ")).
                AddRow(2, "Paul", "0123456789", "CAD", 23.45))
    },
    expectedResult: &Person{
        ID:        2,
        FullName: "Paul",
        Phone:     "0123456789",
        Currency: "CAD",
        Price:     23.45,
    },
    expectError: false,
},
{
    desc: "load error",
    configureMockDB: func(dbMock sqlmock.Sqlmock) {
        queryRegex := convertSQLToRegex(sqlLoadAll)
        dbMock.ExpectQuery(queryRegex).WillReturnError(
            errors.New("something failed"))
    },
    expectedResult: nil,
    expectError: true,
},
```

Now there's the test runner, which is basically a loop over all the scenarios:

```
for _, scenario := range scenarios {
    // define a mock db
    testDb, dbMock, err := sqlmock.New()
    require.NoError(t, err)

    // configure the mock db
    scenario.configureMockDB(dbMock)

    // monkey db for this test
    original := *db
    db = testDb

    // call function
    result, err := Load(2)

    // validate results
```

```
        assert.Equal(t, scenario.expectedResult, result, scenario.desc)
        assert.Equal(t, scenario.expectError, err != nil, scenario.desc)
        assert.NoError(t, dbMock.ExpectationsWereMet())

        // restore original DB (after test)
        db = &original
        testDb.Close()
    }
```

The contents of this loop are quite similar to the contents of our original test. It's often easier to write the happy path test first and then convert it to a table-driven test by adding the additional scenarios.

Perhaps the only difference between our test runner and the original function is that we are monkey patching. We cannot use `defer` inside a `for` loop as `defer` only runs when the function exits; we therefore have to restore the database at the end of the loop instead.

The use of table-driven tests here not only reduced the duplication in our test code, but it also has two other significant advantages. Firstly, it has distilled the tests down to inputs equals outputs, making them very easy to understand and very easy to add more scenarios.

Secondly, the code that is likely to change, namely the function call itself, only exists in one place. If that function altered to accept another input or return another value, we would have to fix it in one place, compared to once per test scenario.

Monkey patching between packages

So far, we have looked at monkey patching a private global variable or function for the purposes of testing inside our `data` package. But what happens if we want to test other packages? Wouldn't it be nice to decouple the business logic layer from the database too? That would certainly stop our business logic layer tests from breaking for unrelated events, such as optimizing our SQL queries.

Again, we are faced with a dilemma; we could start large-scale refactoring, but as we've mentioned before, it's a lot of work and a lot of risk, especially without tests to keep us out of trouble. Let's look at the most straightforward business logic package we have, the `get` package:

```
// Getter will attempt to load a person.
// It can return an error caused by the data layer or
// when the requested person is not found
type Getter struct {
}
```

```
// Do will perform the get
func (g *Getter) Do(ID int) (*data.Person, error) {
    // load person from the data layer
    person, err := data.Load(ID)
    if err != nil {
        if err == data.ErrNotFound {
            // By converting the error we are encapsulating the
            // implementation details from our users.
            return nil, errPersonNotFound
        }
        return nil, err
    }

    return person, err
}
```

As you can see, this function does very little beyond loading the person from the database. You could argue therefore that it does not need to exist; don't worry, we will be giving it more responsibility later on.

So how do we test this without the database? The first thing that comes to mind might be to monkey patch the database pool or the `getDatabase()` function as we did before.

This would work, but it would be sloppy and pollute the public API for the `data` package with things that we don't want production code using, the very definition of test-induced damage. It would also do nothing to decouple this package from the internal implementation of the `data` package. In fact, it would make it worse. Any change to the implementation of the `data` package would likely break our test for this package.

Another aspect to consider is that we can make any alteration we want because the service is small and we own all the code. This is often not the case; the package could be owned by another team, it could be part of an external dependency, or even part of the standard library. It's better, therefore, to get into the habit of keeping our changes local to the package we are working on.

With that in mind, we can adopt a trick we looked at briefly in the previous section, *Advantages of monkey patching*. Let's intercept the call from the `get` package to the `data` package, as shown in the following code:

```
// Getter will attempt to load a person.
// It can return an error caused by the data layer or
// when the requested person is not found
type Getter struct {
}

// Do will perform the get
```

```go
func (g *Getter) Do(ID int) (*data.Person, error) {
    // load person from the data layer
    person, err := loader(ID)
    if err != nil {
        if err == data.ErrNotFound {
            // By converting the error we are hiding the
            // implementation details from our users.
            return nil, errPersonNotFound
        }
        return nil, err
    }

    return person, err
}

// this function as a variable allows us to Monkey Patch during testing
var loader = data.Load
```

Now, we can intercept the calls with monkey patching, as shown in the following code:

```go
func TestGetter_Do_happyPath(t *testing.T) {
    // inputs
    ID := 1234

    // monkey patch calls to the data package
    defer func(original func(ID int) (*data.Person, error)) {
        // restore original
        loader = original
    }(loader)

    // replace method
    loader = func(ID int) (*data.Person, error) {
        result := &data.Person{
            ID:       1234,
            FullName: "Doug",
        }
        var resultErr error

        return result, resultErr
    }
    // end of monkey patch

    // call method
    getter := &Getter{}
    person, err := getter.Do(ID)

    // validate expectations
    require.NoError(t, err)
```

```
    assert.Equal(t, ID, person.ID)
    assert.Equal(t, "Doug", person.FullName)
}
```

Now, our test is not dependent on the database or any internal implementation details of the `data` package. While we have not entirely decoupled the packages, we have significantly reduced the number of things that must happen correctly for the tests in the `get` package to pass. This is arguably one of the points of DI by monkey patching, reducing the ways tests could break by reducing the dependence on outside factors and increasing the focus of the tests.

When the magic fades

Earlier in the book, I challenged you to examine each method of DI presented in the book with a critical eye. With that in mind, we should consider the potential costs of monkey patching.

Data races—We saw in our examples that monkey patching is the process of replacing a global variable with a copy that performs in the way we need it to for a particular test. And that is perhaps the biggest problem. Swapping something global, and therefore shared, for something specific causes a data race on that variable.

To understand this data race a little more, we need to understand how Go runs tests. By default, tests within a package are executed sequentially. We can reduce our test execution time by marking our tests with `t.Parallel()`. With our current tests of the `data` package, marking the test as parallel would cause the data race to appear, resulting in unpredictable tests.

Another significant feature of Go testing is that Go executes multiple packages in parallel. Like `t.Parallel()`, this can be fantastic for our test execution time. With our current code, we are safe from this because we only monkey patched within the same package as the tests. If we had monkey patched across package boundaries, then the data race would appear.

If your tests are flaky and you suspect a data race, you can try Go's built-in race detection (`https://golang.org/doc/articles/race_detector.html`) with:

```
$ go test -race ./...
```

If that doesn't find the problem, you can try running all the tests sequentially with:

```
$ go test -p 1 ./...
```

If the tests start passing consistently, then you will need to start digging for data races.

Verbose tests—As you have seen in our tests, the code to monkey patch and restore can become rather lengthy. With a little bit of refactoring, it is possible to lessen the boilerplate. For example, look at this:

```
func TestSaveConfig(t *testing.T) {
    // inputs
    filename := "my-config.json"
    cfg := &Config{
        Host: "localhost",
        Port: 1234,
    }

    // monkey patch the file writer
    defer func(original func(filename string, data []byte, perm os.FileMode)
error) {
        // restore the original
        writeFile = original
    }(writeFile)

    writeFile = func(filename string, data []byte, perm os.FileMode) error {
        // output error
        return nil
    }

    // call the function
    err := SaveConfig(filename, cfg)

    // validate the result
    assert.NoError(t, err)
}
```

We could change it to this:

```
func TestSaveConfig_refactored(t *testing.T) {
    // inputs
    filename := "my-config.json"
    cfg := &Config{
        Host: "localhost",
        Port: 1234,
    }

    // monkey patch the file writer
    defer restoreWriteFile(writeFile)

    writeFile = mockWriteFile(nil)
```

```
    // call the function
    err := SaveConfig(filename, cfg)

    // validate the result
    assert.NoError(t, err)
}

func mockWriteFile(result error) func(filename string, data []byte, perm
os.FileMode) error {
    return func(filename string, data []byte, perm os.FileMode) error {
        return result
    }
}

// remove the restore function to reduce from 3 lines to 1
func restoreWriteFile(original func(filename string, data []byte, perm
os.FileMode) error) {
    // restore the original
    writeFile = original
}
```

After this refactoring, we have far less duplication in the tests, resulting in less to maintain, but more importantly, the tests are no longer overshadowed by all of the monkey-patching-related code.

Obfuscated dependency relationship—This is not a problem with monkey patching itself but with the style of dependency management in general. In traditional DI, the dependency is passed in as a parameter, making the relationship explicit and visible.

From a user perspective, this lack of parameters can be considered an improvement to the UX of the code; after all, fewer inputs typically makes a function easier to use. However, when it comes to testing, things get messy quickly.

In our previous example, the SaveConfig() function depends on ioutil.WriteFile() and so mocking that dependency to test SaveConfig() seems reasonable. However, what happens when we need to test a function that calls SaveConfig()?

How does the user of SaveConfig() know that they need to mock ioutil.WriteFile()?

Because the relationship is muddled, the knowledge required increases and, incidentally, so does the test length; it isn't long before we have half a screen of monkey patching of functions at the beginning of every test.

Summary

In this chapter, we have learned how to leverage monkey patching to *swap out* dependencies in our tests. With monkey patching, we have tested globals, decoupled packages, and removed our dependence on external resources such as databases and the filesystem. We've worked through some practical examples while improving our sample service's code, and we frankly discussed both the advantages and disadvantages of using monkey patching.

In the next chapter, we will look at the second and perhaps the most traditional DI technique, dependency injection with constructor injection. With it, we will improve our service's code even further.

Questions

1. How does monkey patching work?
2. What are the ideal use cases for monkey patching?
3. How can you use monkey patching to decouple two packages without changing the dependency package?

Further reading

Packt has many other great resources for learning about monkey patching:

- **Mastering JQuery**: https://www.packtpub.com/mapt/book/web_development/9781785882166/12/ch12lvl1sec100/monkey-patching
- **Learn to code with Ruby**: https://www.packtpub.com/mapt/video/application_development/9781788834063/40761/41000/monkey-patching-ii

6
Dependency Injection with Constructor Injection

After examining one of the most unique forms of **dependency injection** (**DI**), monkey patching, in this chapter, we take it to the other extreme and look at perhaps the most *normal* or traditional, constructor injection.

While constructor injection is so ubiquitous that you may even have used it without realizing it, it has many subtleties, particularly concerning advantages and disadvantages, that bear examination.

Similar to the previous chapter, we will apply this technique to our sample service, where we will reap significant improvements.

The following topics will be covered in this chapter:

- Constructor injection
- Advantages of constructor injection
- Applying constructor injection
- Disadvantages of constructor injection

Technical requirements

It would be beneficial to be familiar with the code for our service that we introduced in Chapter 4, *Introduction to the ACME Registration Service* .

You might also find it useful to read and run the full versions of the code for this chapter, which are available at https://github.com/PacktPublishing/Hands-On-Dependency-Injection-in-Go/tree/master/ch06.

Instructions to obtain the code and configure the sample service are available in the README here `https://github.com/PacktPublishing/Hands-On-Dependency-Injection-in-Go/`.

You can find the code for our service, with the changes from this chapter already applied, in `ch06/acme`.

Constructor injection

When an object requires a dependency to work, the easiest way to ensure that dependency is always available is to require all users to supply it as a parameter to the object's constructor. This is known as **constructor injection**.

Let's work through an example where we will extract a dependency, generalize it, and achieve constructor injection. Say we are we are building a website for an online community. For this site, we wish to send an email to new users when they sign up. The code for this could be like this:

```
// WelcomeSender sends a Welcome email to new users
type WelcomeSender struct {
    mailer *Mailer
}

func (w *WelcomeSender) Send(to string) error {
    body := w.buildMessage()

    return w.mailer.Send(to, body)
}
```

We've made the `*Mailer` private to ensure proper encapsulation of the internals of the class. We can inject the `*Mailer` dependency by defining it as a parameter to our constructor, as shown in the following code:

```
func NewWelcomeSender(in *Mailer) (*WelcomeSender, error) {
    // guard clause
    if in == nil {
        return nil, errors.New("programmer error: mailer must not provided")
    }

    return &WelcomeSender{
        mailer: in,
    }, nil
}
```

In the previous example, we have included a guard clause. The purpose of this is to ensure that the supplied dependency is not `nil`. This is not necessary, and whether or not it is included depends mainly on personal style; it's perfectly acceptable to do this instead:

```
func NewWelcomeSenderNoGuard(in *Mailer) *WelcomeSender {
    return &WelcomeSender{
        mailer: in,
    }
}
```

You might be tempted to think that we are done. After all, we are injecting the dependency, `Mailer`, into `WelcomeSender`.

Sadly, we are not quite there yet. In fact, we are missing the real purpose of DI. No, it's not testing, although we will get to that. The real purpose of DI is decoupling.

At this point, our `WelcomeSender` cannot work without an instance of `Mailer`. They are tightly coupled. So, let's decouple them by applying the *Dependency Inversion Principle* section from Chapter 2, *SOLID Design Principles for Go*.

First, let's look at the `Mailer` struct:

```
// Mailer sends and receives emails
type Mailer struct{
    Host string
    Port string
    Username string
    Password string
}

func (m *Mailer) Send(to string, body string) error {
    // send email
    return nil
}

func (m *Mailer) Receive(address string) (string, error) {
    // receive email
    return "", nil
}
```

We can introduce an abstraction by converting this into an interface based on the method signatures:

```
// Mailer sends and receives emails
type MailerInterface interface {
    Send(to string, body string) error
    Receive(address string) (string, error)
}
```

Hang on, we only need to send emails. Let's apply the *interface segregation principle* and reduce the interface to only the methods we use and update our constructor. Now, we have this:

```
type Sender interface {
    Send(to string, body string) error
}

func NewWelcomeSenderV2(in Sender) *WelcomeSenderV2 {
    return &WelcomeSenderV2{
        sender: in,
    }
}
```

With this one small change, a few handy things have happened. Firstly, our code is now entirely self-contained. This means any bugs, extensions, tests, or other changes will only involve this package. Second, we can use mocks or stubs to test our code, stopping us from spamming ourselves with emails and requiring a working email server for our tests to pass. Lastly, we are no longer tied to the `Mailer` class. If we wanted to change from a welcome email to an SMS or tweet, we could change our input parameter to a different `Sender` and be done.

By defining our dependency as an abstraction (as a local interface) and passing that dependency into our constructor, we have explicitly defined our requirements and given us greater freedom in our testing and extensions.

Addressing the duck in the room

Before we dive too deep into constructor injection, we should spend a moment to talk about duck typing.

We have previously mentioned Go's support for implicit interfaces and how we can leverage it to perform dependency inversion and decouple objects. To those of you familiar with Python or Ruby, this may have felt like duck typing. For everyone else, what is duck typing? It's described as follows:

If it looks like a duck, and it quacks like a duck, then it is a duck

Or, put more technically:

At runtime, dynamically determine an object's suitability based only on the parts of that object that are accessed

Let's look at a Go example to see if it supports duck typing:

```
type Talker interface {
    Speak() string
    Shout() string
}

type Dog struct{}

func (d Dog) Speak() string {
    return "Woof!"
}

func (d Dog) Shout() string {
    return "WOOF!"
}

func SpeakExample() {
    var talker Talker
    talker = Dog{}

    fmt.Print(talker.Speak())
}
```

As you can see, our `Dog` type does not declare that it implements the `Talker` interface, as we might expect from Java or C#, and yet we are able to use it as a `Talker`.

From our example, it looks like Go might support duck typing, but there are a couple of problems:

- In duck typing, compatibility is determined at runtime; Go will check our `Dog` type implements `Talker` at compile time.
- In duck typing, suitability is only based on the parts of the object accessed. In the previous example, only the `Speak()` method is actually used. However, if our `Dog` type did not implement the `Shout()` method, then it would fail to compile.

So if it's not duck typing, what is it? Something somewhat similar called **structural typing**. Structural typing is a static typing system that determines suitability at compile time based on the type's structure. Don't let the less fancy name fool you; structural typing is immensely powerful and extremely useful. Go provides the safety of compile-time checking without the enforced formality of explicitly having to state the interfaces implemented.

Advantages of constructor injection

For many programmers and programming languages, constructor injection is their default method for DI. It is perhaps no surprise therefore that it has numerous advantages.

Separation from the dependency life cycle—Constructor injection, like most DI methods, separates the life cycle management of the dependency from the object that it's being injected into. By doing this, the object becomes more straightforward and easier to understand.

Easy to implement—As we saw in our previous examples, it's easy to take this:

```go
// WelcomeSender sends a Welcome email to new users
type WelcomeSender struct {
    Mailer *Mailer
}

func (w *WelcomeSender) Send(to string) error {
    body := w.buildMessage()

    return w.Mailer.Send(to, body)
}
```

And change it to this:

```go
func NewWelcomeSender(mailer *Mailer) *WelcomeSender {
    return &WelcomeSender{
        mailer: mailer,
    }
}

// WelcomeSender sends a Welcome email to new users
type WelcomeSender struct {
    mailer *Mailer
}

func (w *WelcomeSender) Send(to string) error {
```

```
    body := w.buildMessage()

    return w.mailer.Send(to, body)
}
```

Predictable and concise—By moving the assignment of the dependency to the constructor, we are not only being explicit about our requirements, but we are also ensuring that the dependency is set and available to our methods. This is particularly true if we include a guard clause in the constructor. Without the constructor, each method might have to include a guard clause (as shown in the following example) or risk throwing a nil pointer exception:

```go
type Car struct {
    Engine Engine
}

func (c *Car) Drive() error {
    if c.Engine == nil {
        return errors.New("engine ie missing")
    }

    // use the engine
    c.Engine.Start()
    c.Engine.IncreasePower()

    return nil
}

func (c *Car) Stop() error {
    if c.Engine == nil {

        return errors.New("engine ie missing")
    }

    // use the engine
    c.Engine.DecreasePower()
    c.Engine.Stop()

    return nil
}
```

Instead of the following, which is much more concise:

```go
func NewCar(engine Engine) (*Car, error) {
  if engine == nil {
    return nil, errors.New("invalid engine supplied")
  }

  return &Car{
    engine: engine,
  }, nil
}

type Car struct {
  engine Engine
}

func (c *Car) Drive() error {
  // use the engine
  c.engine.Start()
  c.engine.IncreasePower()

  return nil
}

func (c *Car) Stop() error {
  // use the engine
  c.engine.DecreasePower()
  c.engine.Stop()

  return nil
}
```

By extension, methods can also assume that our dependency is in a good, ready state when accessing the dependency, thus removing the need to handle initialization delays or configuration issues anywhere outside the constructor. Additionally, there are no data races associated with accessing the dependency. It is set during construction and never changed.

Encapsulation—Constructor injection provides a high degree of encapsulation regarding how the object uses the dependency. Consider what happens if we extend our previous Car example by adding a FillPetrolTank() method, as shown in the following code:

```go
func (c *Car) FillPetrolTank() error {
  // use the engine
  if c.engine.IsRunning() {
    return errors.New("cannot fill the tank while the engine is running")
  }
```

```
    // fill the tank!
    return c.fill()
}
```

What happens to the previous code if we assumed that *filling the petrol tank* had nothing to do with the `Engine` and didn't populate one before calling this method?

Without constructor injection ensuring that we supply an `Engine`, this method would crash will a nil pointer exception. Alternatively, this method could have been written without constructor injection, as shown in the following code:

```
func (c *Car) FillPetrolTank(engine Engine) error {
    // use the engine
    if engine.IsRunning() {
        return errors.New("cannot fill the tank while the engine is running")
    }

    // fill the tank!
    return c.fill()
}
```

However, this version now leaks the implementation detail that the method requires `Engine` to work.

Helps to uncover code smells—It's an easy trap to add *just one more* feature to an existing struct or interface. As we saw during our earlier discussions of the *single responsibility principle*, we should resist this urge and keep our objects and interfaces as small as possible. One easy way to spot when an object has too many responsibilities is to count its dependencies. Typically, the more responsibilities an object has, the more dependencies it will accumulate. Therefore with all the dependencies clearly listed in one place, the constructor, it's easy to get a whiff that something might not be quite right.

Applying constructor injection

Let's apply constructor injection to our ACME registration service. This time we will be refactoring the REST package, starting with the `Register` endpoint. You may remember that `Register` is one of three endpoints in our service, the others being `Get` and `List`. The `Register` endpoint has three responsibilities:

- Validate the registration is complete and valid
- Call the currency conversion service to convert the registration price to the currency requested in the registration
- Save the registration and the converted registration price into the database

The code for our `Register` endpoint currently looks as shown in the following code:

```go
// RegisterHandler is the HTTP handler for the "Register" endpoint
// In this simplified example we are assuming all possible errors
// are user errors and returning "bad request" HTTP 400.
// There are some programmer errors possible but hopefully these
// will be caught in testing.
type RegisterHandler struct {
}

// ServeHTTP implements http.Handler
func (h *RegisterHandler) ServeHTTP(response http.ResponseWriter, request
*http.Request) {
   // extract payload from request
   requestPayload, err := h.extractPayload(request)
   if err != nil {
      // output error
      response.WriteHeader(http.StatusBadRequest)
      return
   }

   // register person
   id, err := h.register(requestPayload)
   if err != nil {
      // not need to log here as we can expect other layers to do so
      response.WriteHeader(http.StatusBadRequest)
      return
   }

   // happy path
   response.Header().Add("Location", fmt.Sprintf("/person/%d/", id))
   response.WriteHeader(http.StatusCreated)
}

// extract payload from request
func (h *RegisterHandler) extractPayload(request *http.Request)
(*registerRequest, error) {
   requestPayload := &registerRequest{}

   decoder := json.NewDecoder(request.Body)
   err := decoder.Decode(requestPayload)
   if err != nil {
      return nil, err
   }

   return requestPayload, nil
}
```

```
// call the logic layer
func (h *RegisterHandler) register(requestPayload *registerRequest) (int,
error) {
    person := &data.Person{
        FullName: requestPayload.FullName,
        Phone:    requestPayload.Phone,
        Currency: requestPayload.Currency,
    }

    registerer := &register.Registerer{}
    return registerer.Do(person)
}
```

Disappointingly, we currently only have one test on this function, and it breaks way too easily. It requires both the database and our downstream exchange rate service to be accessible and configured.

While we can ensure our that local database is working, and any changes to it do not affect anyone but us, the downstream exchange rate service is on the internet and is rate limited. We have no control over it or when it works.

This means that even though we only have one test, that test has a high potential to be annoying to run and maintain because it can break at any time for reasons outside our control.

Fortunately, we can not only remove these dependencies but also use mocks to create situations that we could not otherwise. For example, with mocks, we can test our error handling code for when the exchange rate service is down or out of quota.

Decoupling from the dependency

The first step is to identify the dependency we wish to inject. For our handler, this is not the database or the exchange rate call. We wish to inject the next software layer, which in this case is the model layer.

Specifically, we want to inject this line from our `register` method:

```
registerer := &register.Registerer{}
```

Following the same process we used easier, we first promote the object to a member variable, as shown in the following code:

```
// RegisterHandler is the HTTP handler for the "Register" endpoint
type RegisterHandler struct {
   registerer *register.Registerer
}
```

As this does nothing to decouple our code from the dependency, we then define our requirements as a local interface and update the member variable, as shown in the following code:

```
// RegisterModel will validate and save a registration
type RegisterModel interface {
   Do(in *data.Person) (int, error)
}

// RegisterHandler is the HTTP handler for the "Register" endpoint
type RegisterHandler struct {
   registerer RegisterModel
}
```

Building the constructor

Now that `RegisterHandler` requires an abstract dependency, we need to ensure that the dependency has been set by applying constructor injection, as shown in the following code:

```
// NewRegisterHandler is the constructor for RegisterHandler
func NewRegisterHandler(model RegisterModel) *RegisterHandler {
   return &RegisterHandler{
      registerer: model,
   }
}
```

With constructor injection applied, our `RegisterHandler` is less coupled to the model layer and our external resources (database and upstream service). We can leverage this looser coupling to improve and extend the test of our `RegisterHandler`.

Improving test scenario coverage

The first thing we will do is break the dependence on the upstream currency service in the test. Then, we will proceed to add tests to cover additional scenarios that we couldn't cover before. This is what our test currently looks like:

```
func TestRegisterHandler_ServeHTTP(t *testing.T) {
    // ensure the test always fails by giving it a timeout
    ctx, cancel := context.WithTimeout(context.Background(), 5*time.Second)
    defer cancel()

    // Create and start a server
    // With out current implementation, we cannot test this handler without
    // a full server as we need the mux.
    address, err := startServer(ctx)
    require.NoError(t, err)

    // build inputs
    validRequest := buildValidRequest()
    response, err := http.Post("http://"+address+"/person/register",
"application/json", validRequest)

    // validate outputs
    require.NoError(t, err)
    require.Equal(t, http.StatusCreated, response.StatusCode)
    defer response.Body.Close()

    // call should output the location to the new person
    headerLocation := response.Header.Get("Location")
    assert.Contains(t, headerLocation, "/person/")
}
```

We are currently starting our entire HTTP server; this seems excessive, so let's reduce the test scope to just `RegisterHandler`.

This reduction in test scope will also improve the tests by eliminating other peripheral concerns, such as the HTTP router.

As we know that we are going to have multiple similar scenarios to test, let's start by adding a skeleton for a table-driven test:

```
func TestRegisterHandler_ServeHTTP(t *testing.T) {
    scenarios := []struct {
        desc           string
        inRequest      func() *http.Request
        inModelMock    func() *MockRegisterModel
        expectedStatus int
        expectedHeader string
    }{
        // scenarios go here
    }

    for _, s := range scenarios {
        scenario := s
```

```
        t.Run(scenario.desc, func(t *testing.T) {
            // test goes here
        })
    }
}
```

From the original test, we can see that our inputs are an `*http.Request` and `*MockRegisterModel`. Both are a little complicated to create and configure, so we have chosen to build them with a function. Also, from the original test, we can see that the outputs of the test are an HTTP response code and the `Location` header.

These four objects, `*http.Request`, `*MockRegistrationModel`, the HTTP status code, and the `Location` header, will make up the configuration for our test scenarios, as seen in the previous code.

To complete our table-driven test, we copy the contents of the original test into the test loop and replace the inputs and outputs, as shown in the following code:

```
for _, s := range scenarios {
    scenario := s
    t.Run(scenario.desc, func(t *testing.T) {
        // define model layer mock
        mockRegisterModel := scenario.inModelMock()

        // build handler
        handler := &RegisterHandler{
            registerer: mockRegisterModel,
        }

        // perform request
        response := httptest.NewRecorder()
        handler.ServeHTTP(response, scenario.inRequest())

        // validate outputs
        require.Equal(t, scenario.expectedStatus, response.Code)

        // call should output the location to the new person
        resultHeader := response.Header().Get("Location")
        assert.Equal(t, scenario.expectedHeader, resultHeader)

        // validate the mock was used as we expected
        assert.True(t, mockRegisterModel.AssertExpectations(t))
    })
}
```

Now that we have all of the pieces in place, we write our tests scenarios, starting with the happy path:

```
{
    desc: "Happy Path",
    inRequest: func() *http.Request {
        validRequest := buildValidRegisterRequest()
        request, err := http.NewRequest("POST", "/person/register",
validRequest)
        require.NoError(t, err)

        return request
    },
    inModelMock: func() *MockRegisterModel {
        // valid downstream configuration
        resultID := 1234
        var resultErr error

        mockRegisterModel := &MockRegisterModel{}
        mockRegisterModel.On("Do", mock.Anything).Return(resultID,
resultErr).Once()

        return mockRegisterModel
    },
    expectedStatus: http.StatusCreated,
    expectedHeader: "/person/1234/",
},
```

Next, we need to test whether our code handles errors well. So what kinds of errors can we expect? We could examine the code and look for code that looks like `if err != nil`. That might feel like a useful shortcut, but consider this. If our tests mirror the current implementation, what happens when the implementation changes?

A better angle is to consider not the implementation but the feature itself and the situation or use of it. There are two answers that almost always apply. *User errors,* such as incorrect inputs, and *errors returned from dependencies.*

Our *user error* scenario looks as shown in the following code:

```
{
    desc: "Bad Input / User Error",
    inRequest: func() *http.Request {
        invalidRequest := bytes.NewBufferString(`this is not valid JSON`)
        request, err := http.NewRequest("POST", "/person/register",
invalidRequest)
        require.NoError(t, err)
```

```
            return request
        },
        inModelMock: func() *MockRegisterModel {
            // Dependency should not be called
            mockRegisterModel := &MockRegisterModel{}
            return mockRegisterModel
        },
        expectedStatus: http.StatusBadRequest,
        expectedHeader: "",
    },
```

And our *errors returned from dependencies* is shown in the following code:

```
    {
        desc: "Dependency Failure",
        inRequest: func() *http.Request {
            validRequest := buildValidRegisterRequest()
            request, err := http.NewRequest("POST", "/person/register",
    validRequest)
            require.NoError(t, err)

            return request
        },
        inModelMock: func() *MockRegisterModel {
            // call to the dependency failed
            resultErr := errors.New("something failed")

            mockRegisterModel := &MockRegisterModel{}
            mockRegisterModel.On("Do", mock.Anything).Return(0, resultErr).Once()

            return mockRegisterModel
        },
        expectedStatus: http.StatusInternalServerError,
        expectedHeader: "",
    },
```

With those three tests in place we have reasonable test scenario coverage, but we have stumbled over a problem. Our *errors returned from dependencies* scenario results in an HTTP status code of 400 (Bad Request) instead of the expected HTTP 500 (Internal Server Error). After looking into the implementation of the model layer, it becomes evident that the 400 error is intentional and is supposed to indicate that the request was incomplete and therefore failed validation.

Our first instinct is likely to want to move the validation into the HTTP layer. But consider this: what happens if we add another server type, such as gRPC? This validation would still need to be performed. So how can we separate user errors from system errors?

Another option would be to return a named error from the model for validation errors and a different one for other errors. It would be easy to detect and handle the responses separately. This would, however, cause our code to remain tightly coupled with the `model` package.

Another option is to split our call to the model package into two calls, perhaps `Validate()` and `Do()`, but this detracts from the UX of our `model` package. I will leave it to you to decide whether these or another option works for you.

After making these changes to `RegisterHandler` and the other handlers in this package, we can use Go's test coverage tool to see if we missed any obvious scenarios.

 For Unix/Linux users, I have included the script in the source code for this chapter that I use to generate the coverage in HTML. The steps should be similar to other platforms. The script can be found at `https://github. com/PacktPublishing/Hands-On-Dependency-Injection-in-Go/blob/ master/ch06/pcov-html`.

Please note, the test coverage percentage is not significant here. The critical thing to look at is what code has not been executed by any tests and decide whether that indicates an error that could reasonably occur and therefore a scenario that we need to add.

Now that our `RegisterHandler` is in much better shape, we can apply constructor injection in the same way to the other handlers in the `REST` package.

The results of these changes can be seen in the source code for this chapter at `https:// github.com/PacktPublishing/Hands-On-Dependency-Injection-in-Go/tree/master/ ch06/acme/internal/rest`.

Validating our improvements with the dependency graph

Before we wrap up our work on the `REST` package, let's take stock of where we started, and where we are now. When we started, our handlers were tightly coupled with their matching `model` packages and poorly tested. Both of these problems have been resolved.

Let's see whether our dependency graph is showing any signs of improvement:

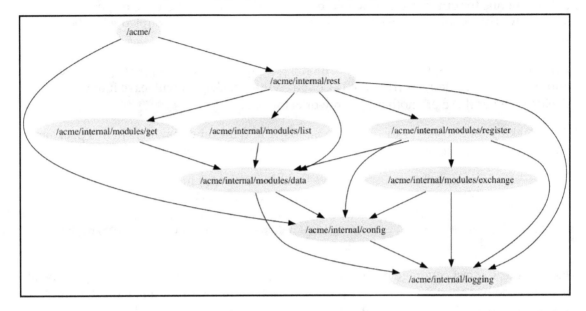

Sadly, it still looks the same as before. After digging into the code, we find the culprit:

```
// New will create and initialize the server
func New(address string) *Server {
    return &Server{
        address:         address,
        handlerGet:      NewGetHandler(&get.Getter{}),
        handlerList:     NewListHandler(&list.Lister{}),
        handlerNotFound: notFoundHandler,
        handlerRegister: NewRegisterHandler(&register.Registerer{}),
    }
}
```

We are instantiating our model layer objects inside the constructor for our `Server` (part of the `REST` package). The fix is easy and hopefully obvious. We push the dependencies up one level, as shown in the following code:

```
// New will create and initialize the server
func New(address string,
    getModel GetModel,
    listModel ListModel,
    registerModel RegisterModel) *Server {

    return &Server{
```

```
    address:          address,
    handlerGet:       NewGetHandler(getModel),
    handlerList:      NewListHandler(listModel),
    handlerNotFound:  notFoundHandler,
    handlerRegister:  NewRegisterHandler(registerModel),
  }
}
```

Checking our dependency graph again, it finally now shows some improvement:

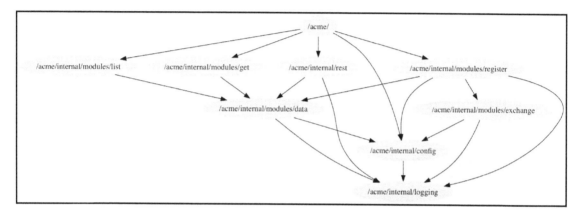

As you can see, it's flatter; the `REST` package has no dependence on the module layer (the `list`, `get`, and `register` packages).

There is still way too much dependence on the `data` and the `config` packages, but we will deal with that in later chapters.

Disadvantages of constructor injection

When it comes to DI, sadly there is no silver bullet. Despite the utility of constructor injection, it cannot be used in all cases. This section covers the disadvantages and limitations of constructor injection.

Can cause lots of changes—When applying constructor injection to existing code, it can result in a lot of changes. This is particularly true if the code was initially written as functions.

Consider the following code:

```
// Dealer will shuffle a deck of cards and deal them to the players
func DealCards() (player1 []Card, player2 []Card) {
    // create a new deck of cards
    cards := newDeck()

    // shuffle the cards
    shuffler := &myShuffler{}
    shuffler.Shuffle(cards)

    // deal
    player1 = append(player1, cards[0])
    player2 = append(player2, cards[1])

    player1 = append(player1, cards[2])
    player2 = append(player2, cards[3])
    return
}
```

As we saw in the previous section, to convert this to use constructor injection, we will have to do the following:

- Convert from a function to a struct
- Convert the dependency on *myShuffler to something abstract by defining an interface
- Create a constructor
- Update all current usage of the function to use the constructor and to inject the dependency

Of all the changes, the one that is most concerning is the last. Changes that occur locally, that is, in the same package, are easier to make and therefore less risky, but alterations to external packages, especially code that belongs to another team, are significantly more dangerous.

Other than being very careful, the best way to mitigate the risk is with tests. If the code has very little or no tests before the refactoring, it is beneficial to create some first before starting any refactoring.

DI with monkey patching might be an attractive candidate to swap out any dependencies in those tests. Yes, these tests will need to be refactored or removed after changing to constructor injection, but there is nothing wrong with that. Having tests will ensure that the code is working before the refactor, and those tests will continue to be informative during the refactoring. Or to put it a different way, the tests will help make the refactoring safer.

Can cause initialization issues—When discussing the advantages of constructor injection, we mentioned separating the object from the life cycle of its dependencies. This code and the complexity still exist, they've just been pushed higher up the call graph. While being able to work on these concerns separately is definitely an advantage, it does create a secondary problem: object initialization order. Consider our ACME registration service. It has three layers, presentation, model, and data.

Before the presentation layer can work, we need to have a working model layer.
Before the model layer can work, we need to have a working data layer.
Before the data layer can work properly, we must create a pool of database connections.

For a simple service, this has already become somewhat complicated. This complexity has led to the creation of many a DI framework, and we will investigate one such framework, Google's Wire, in Chapter 10, *Off-the-Shelf Injection*.

Another potential issue here is the sheer volume of objects that will be created at application start. While this does result in a slightly slower app start, once that initial *cost* has been paid, the application will no longer be delayed by dependency creation.

The last initialization issue to consider here is debugging. When the creation of a dependency and its users are in the same part of the code, it is easier to understand and debug their life cycles and relationships.

The dangers of overuse—Given that this technique is so easy to understand and use, it is also very easy to overuse. The most obvious sign of overuse is excessive constructor parameters. Excessive constructor parameters can indicate that the object has too many responsibilities, but it can also be a symptom of extracting and abstracting too many dependencies.

Before extracting a dependency, think about encapsulation. What information do users of this object need to be aware of? The more information related to the implementation we can hide, the greater the flexibility we have to refactor.

Another aspect to consider is this: does the dependency need to be extracted, or can we leave it to configuration? Consider the following code:

```go
// FetchRates rates from downstream service
type FetchRates struct{}

func (f *FetchRates) Fetch() ([]Rate, error) {
    // build the URL from which to fetch the rates
    url := downstreamServer + "/rates"

    // build request
    request, err := http.NewRequest("GET", url, nil)
```

```
        if err != nil {
            return nil, err
        }

        // fetch rates
        response, err := http.DefaultClient.Do(request)
        if err != nil {
            return nil, err
        }
        defer response.Body.Close()

        // read the content of the response
        data, err := ioutil.ReadAll(response.Body)
        if err != nil {
            return nil, err
        }

        // convert JSON bytes to Go structs
        out := &downstreamResponse{}
        err = json.Unmarshal(data, out)
        if err != nil {
            return nil, err
        }

        return out.Rates, nil
    }
```

It is possible to abstract and inject `*http.Client`, but is that really necessary? In fact, the only aspect that really needs to change is the base URI. We will explore this approach further in Chapter 8, *Dependency Injection by Config*.

Non-obvious requirement—The use of a constructor in Go is not a required pattern. In some teams, it's not even a standard pattern. As such, users might not even realize that the constructor exists and that they must use it. Given the code will likely crash rather spectacularly without the dependencies injected, this is unlikely to cause production issues, but it can be somewhat annoying.

Some teams have attempted to solve this problem by making the object private and only exporting the constructor and an interface, as shown in the following code:

```
    // NewClient creates and initialises the client
    func NewClient(service DepService) Client {
        return &clientImpl{
            service: service,
        }
    }
```

```
// Client is the exported API
type Client interface {
   DoSomethingUseful() (bool, error)
}

// implement Client
type clientImpl struct {
   service DepService
}

func (c *clientImpl) DoSomethingUseful() (bool, error) {
   // this function does something useful
   return false, errors.New("not implemented")
}
```

This approach does ensure that the constructor is used, but it does have some costs. Firstly, we now have to keep the interface and the struct in sync. Not hard, but it is extra work and can get annoying.

Secondly, some users are tempted to use the interface rather than defining their own locally. This results in tight coupling between the user and the exported interface. This coupling can make it more difficult to make additions to the exported API.

Consider using the previous example in another package, as shown in the following code:

```
package other

// StubClient is a stub implementation of sdk.Client interface
type StubClient struct{}

// DoSomethingUseful implements sdk.Client
func (s *StubClient) DoSomethingUseful() (bool, error) {
   return true, nil
}
```

Now, if we add another method to the Client interface, the aforementioned code will be broken.

Constructors are not inherited—Unlike methods and *method injection*, which we will examine in the next chapter, constructors are not included when performing the composition; instead, we are required to remember the constructor exists and to use them.

Another factor to consider when performing composition is that any parameter to the inner struct's constructor will have to be added to the outer struct's constructor, as shown in the following code:

```go
type InnerService struct {
    innerDep Dependency
}

func NewInnerService(innerDep Dependency) *InnerService {
    return &InnerService{
        innerDep: innerDep,
    }
}

type OuterService struct {
    // composition
    innerService *InnerService

    outerDep Dependency
}

func NewOuterService(outerDep Dependency, innerDep Dependency)
*OuterService {
    return &OuterService{
        innerService: NewInnerService(innerDep),
        outerDep:     outerDep,
    }
}
```

A relationship like the preceding one would severely discourage us from changing `InnerService` because we would be forced to make matching changes to `OuterService`.

Summary

In this chapter, we have examined DI with constructor injection. We have seen how easy it is to understand and apply. This is why it is the default choice for many programmers and in many situations.

We have seen how constructor injection brings a level of predictability to the relationship between an object and its dependencies, especially when we use guard clauses.

By applying constructor injection to our REST package, we were left with a collection of loosely coupled and easy-to-follow objects. Because of this, we were able to extend our test scenario coverage easily. We can also expect that any subsequent changes to the model layer are now unlikely to unduly affect our REST package.

In the next chapter, we will introduce DI with method injection, which (among other things) is a very convenient way to handle optional dependencies.

Questions

1. What are the steps we used to adopt constructor injection?
2. What is a guard clause and when would you use it?
3. How does constructor injection affect the life cycle of the dependency?
4. What are the ideal use cases for constructor injection?

7
Dependency Injection with Method Injection

In the previous chapter, we used a constructor to inject our dependencies. Doing so simplified our object and the life cycle of its dependencies. But what happens when our dependency is different for every request? This is where method injection comes in.

The following topics will be covered in this chapter:

- Method injection
- Advantages of method injection
- Applying method injection
- Disadvantages of method injection

Technical requirements

It would be beneficial to be familiar with the code for our service, as introduced in Chapter 4, *Introduction to the ACME Registration Service*.

You might also find it useful to read and run the full versions of the code for this chapter, available at https://github.com/PacktPublishing/Hands-On-Dependency-Injection-in-Go/tree/master/ch07.

Instructions on how to obtain the code and configure the sample service are available in the README file, found at https://github.com/PacktPublishing/Hands-On-Dependency-Injection-in-Go/.

You can find the code for our service, with the changes from this chapter already applied, in ch07/acme.

Method injection

Method injection is everywhere. You probably use it every day and you don't even realize it. Have you ever written code like this?:

```
fmt.Fprint(os.Stdout, "Hello World")
```

How about this?:

```
req, err := http.NewRequest("POST", "/login", body)
```

This is method injection—the passing in of the dependency as a parameter to the request.

Let's examine the previous examples in more detail. The function signature for Fprint() is as follows:

```
// Fprint formats using the default formats for its operands and writes
// to w. It returns the number of bytes written and any write error
// encountered.
func Fprint(w io.Writer, a ...interface{}) (n int, err error)
```

As you can see, the first parameter, io.Writer, is a dependency for this function. What makes this different from any other function call is the fact that the dependency provides an invocation context or data to the function call.

In the first example, the dependency was required, as it is being used as the output destination. However, dependencies used in method injection are not always required. Sometimes the dependency is optional, as we can see in the following example:

```
func NewRequest(method, url string, body io.Reader) (*http.Request, error)
{
    // validate method
    m, err := validateMethod(method)
    if err != nil {
        return nil, err
    }

    // validate URL
    u, err := validateURL(url)
    if err != nil {
        return nil, err
    }

    // process body (if exists)
    var b io.ReadCloser
    if body != nil {
        // read body
```

```
      b = ioutil.NopCloser(body)
   }

   // build Request and return
   req := &http.Request{
      URL:    u,
      Method: m,
      Body:   b,
   }

   return req, nil
}
```

This is not the actual implementation from the standard library; I have simplified it to highlight the critical parts. In the preceding example, io.Reader is optional, and as such, is protected by a guard clause.

When applying method injection, the dependencies are specific to the current invocation, and we will frequently find ourselves needing guard clauses. To help us decide whether or not to include guard clauses, let's dive a little deeper into our examples.

In the fmt.Fprint() standard library implementation, there is no guard clause on io.Writer, meaning that supplying nil will cause the function to panic. This is because, without io.Writer, there is nowhere for the output to go.

However, in the http.NewRequest() implementation, there is a guard clause because it is possible to make an HTTP request that does not contain a request body.

So, what does that mean for the functions that we write? In most cases, we should avoid writing code that can cause a crash with a panic. Let's implement a function whose purpose is similar to Fprint() and see whether we can avoid panics. Here is the first rough implementation (with panic):

```
// TimeStampWriterV1 will output the supplied message to
//writer preceded with a timestamp
func TimeStampWriterV1(writer io.Writer, message string) {
   timestamp := time.Now().Format(time.RFC3339)
   fmt.Fprintf(writer, "%s -> %s", timestamp, message)
}
```

What's the first thing that comes to mind to avoid the panic caused by a nil writer?

We could add a guard clause and return an error when `io.Writer` is not supplied, as shown in the following code:

```
// TimeStampWriterV2 will output the supplied message to
//writer preceded with a timestamp
func TimeStampWriterV2(writer io.Writer, message string) error {
    if writer == nil {
        return errors.New("writer cannot be nil")
    }

    timestamp := time.Now().Format(time.RFC3339)
    fmt.Fprintf(writer,"%s -> %s", timestamp, message)

    return nil
}
```

While this still looks and feels like regular, valid Go code, we now have an error that only happens when we, the programmer, make a mistake. A much better option would be a *reasonable default,* as shown in the following code:

```
// TimeStampWriterV3 will output the supplied message to
//writer preceded with a timestamp
func TimeStampWriterV3(writer io.Writer, message string) {
    if writer == nil {
        // default to Standard Out
        writer = os.Stdout
    }

    timestamp := time.Now().Format(time.RFC3339)
    fmt.Fprintf(writer,"%s -> %s", timestamp, message)
}
```

This technique is called **defensive coding**. The central concept is that *it's better to continue working, even with a degraded experience, than to crash.*

Although these examples have all been functions, method injection can be used with structs in precisely the same way. There is one caveat—do not save the injected dependency as a member variable. We are using method injection because the dependency provides function invocation context or data. Saving the dependency as a member variable causes it to be shared between calls, effectively leaking this context between requests.

Advantages of method injection

As we saw in the previous section, method injection is used extensively in the standard library. It is also extremely useful when you want to write your own shared libraries or frameworks. Its usefulness does not stop there.

It is excellent with functions—Everybody loves a good function, particularly those that follow the *Single responsibility principle* section, as discussed in Chapter 2, *SOLID Design Principles for Go*. They're simple, stateless, and can be highly reusable. Adding method injection to a function will increase its reusability by converting the dependency into an abstraction. Consider the following HTTP handler:

```go
func HandlerV1(response http.ResponseWriter, request *http.Request) {
   garfield := &Animal{
      Type: "Cat",
      Name: "Garfield",
   }

   // encode as JSON and output
   encoder := json.NewEncoder(response)
   err := encoder.Encode(garfield)
   if err != nil {
      response.WriteHeader(http.StatusInternalServerError)
      return
   }

   response.WriteHeader(http.StatusOK)
}
```

Nice and simple. It builds a Go object and then writes the contents of the object to the response as JSON. It's not hard to imagine that the next HTTP handler we write would also have the same final nine lines. So, let's extract them to a function instead of copying and pasting:

```go
func outputAnimal(response http.ResponseWriter, animal *Animal) {
   encoder := json.NewEncoder(response)
   err := encoder.Encode(animal)
   if err != nil {
      response.WriteHeader(http.StatusInternalServerError)
      return
   }

   // Happy Path
   response.WriteHeader(http.StatusOK)
}
```

Now let's examine the inputs to the function; how can we make these more generic or abstract?

While the JSON encoder only needs io.Writer and not the full http.ResponseWriter, we are also outputting the HTTP status codes. So, that is as good as we can do, short of defining our own interface. The second parameter is *Animal. In our function, what is the minimum we actually need?

We are only using *Animal as an input to the JSON encoder, and its function signature is Encode(v interface{}) error. So, we can reduce our param to match, giving us the following:

```
func outputJSON(response http.ResponseWriter, data interface{}) {
    encoder := json.NewEncoder(response)
    err := encoder.Encode(data)
    if err != nil {
        response.WriteHeader(http.StatusInternalServerError)
        return
    }

    // Happy Path
    response.WriteHeader(http.StatusOK)
}
```

Generally, I avoid using interface{} as its use leads to the code becoming littered with type casts and statements that make it harder to read. In this case, however, it's the best (and only) choice.

Similar to other *interface segregation principle*-based examples in other chapters, it's often best to define the minimal possible interface alongside the function or method; alternatively if possible, use the appropriate minimalistic interface from the standard library (such as io.Writer).

Dependencies act as data—Because method injection requires the user to pass in the dependency with each call, this has some interesting side-effect on the relationship between the dependency and the usage. The dependency becomes part of the data in the request and can drastically change the results of the call. Consider the following code:

```
func WriteLog(writer io.Writer, message string) error {
    _, err := writer.Write([]byte(message))
    return err
}
```

A very innocuous and straightforward function, but see what happens when we supply a few different dependencies:

```
// Write to console
WriteLog(os.Stdout, "Hello World!")

// Write to file
file, _ := os.Create("my-log.log")
WriteLog(file, "Hello World!")

// Write to TCP connection
tcpPipe, _ := net.Dial("tcp", "127.0.0.1:1234")
WriteLog(tcpPipe, "Hello World!")
```

Dependencies are request-scoped—These dependencies, by definition, are being created and destroyed all of the time. Therefore, they are not good candidates for constructor injection or even monkey patching. We could, of course, create the object that uses the dependency every request too, but that would neither be performant nor always necessary.

Let's look at an HTTP request handler:

```
// LoadOrderHandler is a HTTP handler that loads orders based on the
current user and supplied user ID
type LoadOrderHandler struct {
    loader OrderLoader
}

// ServeHTTP implements http.Handler
func (l *LoadOrderHandler) ServeHTTP(response http.ResponseWriter, request
*http.Request) {
    // extract user from supplied authentication credentials
    currentUser, err := l.authenticateUser(request)
    if err != nil {
        response.WriteHeader(http.StatusUnauthorized)
        return
    }

    // extract order ID from request
    orderID, err := l.extractOrderID(request)
    if err != nil {
        response.WriteHeader(http.StatusBadRequest)
        return
    }

    // load order using the current user as a request-scoped dependency
    // (with method injection)
    order, err := l.loader.loadOrder(currentUser, orderID)
```

```
    if err != nil {
        response.WriteHeader(http.StatusInternalServerError)
        return
    }

    // output order
    encoder := json.NewEncoder(response)
    err = encoder.Encode(order)
    if err != nil {
        response.WriteHeader(http.StatusInternalServerError)
        return
    }

    response.WriteHeader(http.StatusOK)
}
```

As an HTTP handler, the `ServeHTTP()` method will be called once for every incoming HTTP request. `LoadOrderHandler` depends on `OrderLoader`, in which we will inject our implementation `AuthenticatedLoader` using constructor injection.

The implementation of `AuthenticatedLoader` can be seen in the following code:

```
// AuthenticatedLoader will load orders for based on the supplied owner
type AuthenticatedLoader struct {
    // This pool is expensive to create.
    // We will want to create it once and then reuse it.
    db *sql.DB
}

// load the order from the database based on owner and order ID
func (a *AuthenticatedLoader) loadByOwner(owner Owner, orderID int)
(*Order, error) {
    order, err := a.load(orderID)
    if err != nil {
        return nil, err
    }

    if order.OwnerID != owner.ID() {
        // Return not found so we do not leak information to hackers
        return nil, errNotFound
    }

    // happy path
    return order, nil
}
```

As you can see, `AuthenticatedLoader` depends on a database connection pool; this is expensive to create, so we do not want to recreate it with every request.

The `loadByOwner()` function accepts `Owner` using method injection. We are using method injection here as we expect `Owner` to vary with each request.

This example uses constructor injection for long-lived dependencies and method injection for request-scoped ones. In this way, we are not unnecessarily creating and destroying objects.

Assists with immutability, statelessness, and concurrency—You might accuse me of overselling a little bit here, but after writing some very concurrent Go systems, I have found that objects that are stateless and/or immutable are less prone to concurrency-related problems. Method injection does not grant these features by itself but does make achieving them easier. By passing around the dependency, the ownership and scope of use are much clearer. Additionally, we do not need to concern ourselves with concurrent access to the dependency, as we would if it was a member variable.

Applying method injection

In this section, we are going to improve our ACME registration service by applying method injection with perhaps my favorite package in the entire Go standard library, the context package. Central to this package is the `Context` interface, which describes itself as follows:

A context carries a deadline, cancellation signal, and request-scoped values across API boundaries. Its methods are safe for simultaneous use by multiple goroutines

So, why do I love it so much? By applying method injection, with context as the dependency, I am able to build my processing logic in such a way that it can all be automatically canceled and cleaned up.

A quick recap

Before we dive into the changes, let's take a more in-depth look at the registration function provided by our sample service, and its interactions with external resources. The following diagram outlines the steps that are performed during a single call to the register endpoint:

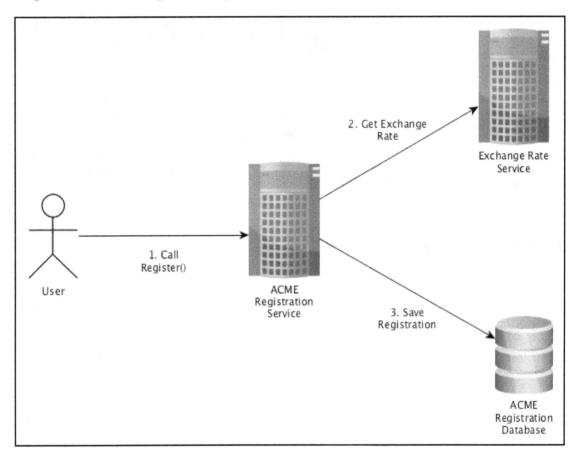

These interactions are as follows:

1. User calls the register endpoint.
2. Our service calls the **Exchange Rate Service**.
3. Our service saves the registration into the database.

Now let's consider how these interactions could go wrong. Ask yourself the following:

- What can fail or become slow?
- How do I want to react or recover from that failure?
- How are my users going to react to my failure?

Considering the interactions in our function, two problems immediately come to mind:

- **Calls to the database can fail or become slow:** How can we recover from this? We could perform retries, but we have to be very careful about this. Databases tend to be more of a finite resource than a web service. As such, retrying requests could, in fact, degrade the performance of the database even further.
- **Calls to the exchange rate service can fail or become slow:** How can we recover from this? We could automatically retry failed requests. This will reduce the occasions where we cannot load an exchange rate. Assuming the business approves, we could set up some default rates to use, instead of entirely failing the registration.

The best change we could make to improve the stability of the system might surprise you.

We could simply not make the request at all. If we were able to change the registration process so that the exchange rate was not needed in this part of the processing, then it could never cause us problems.

Let's assume that none of the aforementioned solutions are available to us in our (contrived) example. The only option we are left with is failure. What happens if loading the exchange rate takes so long that the user gives up and cancels their request? They are likely to assume the registration failed and hopefully try again.

With this in mind, our best course of action is to give up waiting for the exchange rate and not to process the registration any further. This is a process known as **stopping short**.

Stopping short

Stopping short is the process of discontinuing the processing request (before it would otherwise finish) based on an external signal.

In our case, that external signal will be the cancelation of the user's HTTP request. In Go, the `http.Request` object includes a `Context()` method; the following is an extract of the documentation for that method:

For incoming server requests, the context is canceled when the client's connection closes, the request is canceled (with HTTP/2), or when the ServeHTTP method returns

What does it mean when the request is canceled? Most importantly for us, it means that no one is waiting for the response.

If the user has given up listening to the response, it is likely they will consider the request failed and will hopefully try again.

How we should react to this situation depends on the feature we are implementing, but in many cases, mainly features related to loading or fetching data, the most effective response is to stop processing the request.

For the register endpoint of our service, this is the option we have chosen. We are going to pass `Context` from the request through all of the layers of our code using method injection. If the user cancels their request, we will immediately stop processing the request.

Now that we are clear on what we are trying to achieve, let's apply method injection to the layers of our service *from the inside out*. We need to start from the inside to ensure that our code and tests stay running during the refactor.

Applying method injection to the data package

A quick reminder, the `data` package is a **data access layer** (DAL) that provides simplified and abstracted access to the underlying MySQL database.

The following is the current code for the `Save()` function:

```
// Save will save the supplied person and return the ID of the newly
// created person or an error.
// Errors returned are caused by the underlying database or our
// connection to it.
func Save(in *Person) (int, error) {
    db, err := getDB()
    if err != nil {
        logging.L.Error("failed to get DB connection. err: %s", err)
        return defaultPersonID, err
    }

    // perform DB insert
    result, err := db.Exec(sqlInsert, in.FullName, in.Phone, in.Currency,
```

```
in.Price)
   if err != nil {
      logging.L.Error("failed to save person into DB. err: %s", err)
      return defaultPersonID, err
   }

   // retrieve and return the ID of the person created
   id, err := result.LastInsertId()
   if err != nil {
      logging.L.Error("failed to retrieve id of last saved person. err:
%s", err)
      return defaultPersonID, err
   }

   return int(id), nil
}
```

By applying method injection, we get the following:

```
// Save will save the supplied person and return the ID of the newly
// created person or an error.
// Errors returned are caused by the underlying database or our
// connection to it.
func Save(ctx context.Context, in *Person) (int, error) {
   db, err := getDB()
   if err != nil {
      logging.L.Error("failed to get DB connection. err: %s", err)
      return defaultPersonID, err
   }

   // perform DB insert
   result, err := db.ExecContext(ctx, sqlInsert, in.FullName, in.Phone,
in.Currency, in.Price)
   if err != nil {
      logging.L.Error("failed to save person into DB. err: %s", err)
      return defaultPersonID, err
   }

   // retrieve and return the ID of the person created
   id, err := result.LastInsertId()
   if err != nil {
      logging.L.Error("failed to retrieve id of last saved person. err:
%s", err)
      return defaultPersonID, err
   }

   return int(id), nil
}
```

As you can see, we swapped the `Exec()` call for `ExecContext()` but have otherwise changed nothing. Because we have changed the function signature, we are also going to need to update our usage of this package to the following:

```
// save the registration
func (r *Registerer) save(in *data.Person, price float64) (int, error) {
    person := &data.Person{
        FullName: in.FullName,
        Phone:    in.Phone,
        Currency: in.Currency,
        Price:    price,
    }
    return saver(context.TODO(), person)
}

// this function as a variable allows us to Monkey Patch during testing
var saver = data.Save
```

You will notice our use of `context.TODO()`; it is used here as a placeholder until we can refactor the `save()` method to use method injection as well. After updating the tests we broke with the refactor, we can proceed with the next package.

Applying method injection to the exchange package

The exchange package is responsible for loading the current currency exchange rate (for example, Malaysian Ringgit to Australian Dollars) from an upstream service. Similar to the data package, it provides simplified and abstracted access to this data.

The following are the relevant parts of the current code:

```
// Converter will convert the base price to the currency supplied
type Converter struct{}

// Do will perform the load
func (c *Converter) Do(basePrice float64, currency string) (float64, error)
{
    // load rate from the external API
    response, err := c.loadRateFromServer(currency)
    if err != nil {
        return defaultPrice, err
    }

    // extract rate from response
    rate, err := c.extractRate(response, currency)
    if err != nil {
        return defaultPrice, err
```

```
    }

    // apply rate and round to 2 decimal places
    return math.Floor((basePrice/rate)*100) / 100, nil
}

// load rate from the external API
func (c *Converter) loadRateFromServer(currency string) (*http.Response,
error) {
    // build the request
    url := fmt.Sprintf(urlFormat,
        config.App.ExchangeRateBaseURL,
        config.App.ExchangeRateAPIKey,
        currency)

    // perform request
    response, err := http.Get(url)
    if err != nil {
        logging.L.Warn("[exchange] failed to load. err: %s", err)
        return nil, err
    }

    if response.StatusCode != http.StatusOK {
        err = fmt.Errorf("request failed with code %d", response.StatusCode)
        logging.L.Warn("[exchange] %s", err)
        return nil, err
    }

    return response, nil
}
```

The first change is the same as the previous ones. Simple method injection on the `Do()` and `loadRateFromServer()` methods, changing these method signatures to the following:

```
// Converter will convert the base price to the currency supplied
type Converter struct{}

// Do will perform the load
func (c *Converter) Do(ctx context.Context, basePrice float64, currency
string) (float64, error) {

}

// load rate from the external API
func (c *Converter) loadRateFromServer(ctx context.Context, currency
string) (*http.Response, error) {

}
```

Unfortunately, there is no `http.GetWithContext()` method, so we will need to build the request and set the context a slightly more verbose way, giving us the following:

```
// load rate from the external API
func (c *Converter) loadRateFromServer(ctx context.Context, currency
string) (*http.Response, error) {
    // build the request
    url := fmt.Sprintf(urlFormat,
        config.App.ExchangeRateBaseURL,
        config.App.ExchangeRateAPIKey,
        currency)

    // perform request
    req, err := http.NewRequest("GET", url, nil)
    if err != nil {
        logging.L.Warn("[exchange] failed to create request. err: %s", err)
        return nil, err
    }

    // replace the default context with our custom one
    req = req.WithContext(ctx)

    // perform the HTTP request
    response, err := http.DefaultClient.Do(req)
    if err != nil {
        logging.L.Warn("[exchange] failed to load. err: %s", err)
        return nil, err
    }

    if response.StatusCode != http.StatusOK {
        err = fmt.Errorf("request failed with code %d", response.StatusCode)
        logging.L.Warn("[exchange] %s", err)
        return nil, err
    }

    return response, nil
}
```

As we did previously, we will also need to use `context.TODO()` in the model layer that calls the `exchange` package until we have a chance to change them to method injection. With the two *bottom* software layers (the `data` and `exchange` packages) complete, we can move on to the next software layer, business layer, or model layer.

Applying method injection to the model layer (the Get, List, and Register packages)

Previously, in places where we called the `data` or `exchange` packages, we used
`context.TODO()` to ensure the code could still compile and that our tests continued to do
their job. It's now time to apply method injection to the model layer and replace the
`context.TODO()` calls with injected context. First, we change the `getPrice()` and `save()`
methods to accept a context:

```
// get price in the requested currency
func (r *Registerer) getPrice(ctx context.Context, currency string)
(float64, error) {
   converter := &exchange.Converter{}
   price, err := converter.Do(ctx, config.App.BasePrice, currency)
   if err != nil {
      logging.L.Warn("failed to convert the price. err: %s", err)
      return defaultPersonID, err
   }

   return price, nil
}

// save the registration
func (r *Registerer) save(ctx context.Context, in *data.Person, price
float64) (int, error) {
   person := &data.Person{
      FullName: in.FullName,
      Phone:    in.Phone,
      Currency: in.Currency,
      Price:    price,
   }
   return saver(ctx, person)
}
```

Then we can update the package's public API function, `Do()`:

```
type Registerer struct {}

func (r *Registerer) Do(ctx context.Context, in *data.Person) (int, error)
{
   // validate the request
   err := r.validateInput(in)
   if err != nil {
      logging.L.Warn("input validation failed with err: %s", err)
      return defaultPersonID, err
   }
```

```
    // get price in the requested currency
    price, err := r.getPrice(ctx, in.Currency)
    if err != nil {
        return defaultPersonID, err
    }

    // save registration
    id, err := r.save(ctx, in, price)
    if err != nil {
        // no need to log here as we expect the data layer to do so
        return defaultPersonID, err
    }

    return id, nil
}
```

We have *rolled up* the Context objects passed into the data and exchange package into a single, injected dependency; a dependency that we can extract from the http.Request in the REST package.

Applying the method injection of context to the REST package

Finally, now for the key changes. First, we extract the context from the request:

```
// ServeHTTP implements http.Handler
func (h *RegisterHandler) ServeHTTP(response http.ResponseWriter, request
*http.Request) {
    // extract payload from request
    requestPayload, err := h.extractPayload(request)
    if err != nil {
        // output error
        response.WriteHeader(http.StatusBadRequest)
        return
    }

    // call the business logic using the request data and context
    id, err := h.register(request.Context(), requestPayload)
    if err != nil {
        // not need to log here as we can expect other layers to do so
        response.WriteHeader(http.StatusBadRequest)
        return
    }

    // happy path
    response.Header().Add("Location", fmt.Sprintf("/person/%d/", id))
```

```
    response.WriteHeader(http.StatusCreated)
}
```

Then we pass it down to the model:

```
// call the logic layer
func (h *RegisterHandler) register(ctx context.Context, requestPayload
*registerRequest) (int, error) {
    person := &data.Person{
        FullName: requestPayload.FullName,
        Phone:    requestPayload.Phone,
        Currency: requestPayload.Currency,
    }

    return h.registerer.Do(ctx, person)
}
```

After what feels like a lot of *too simple* changes, we are done applying method injection to all of the layers in our register endpoint.

Let's examine what we have achieved. Our processing is now tied to the execution context of the request. Therefore, when the request is canceled, we will immediately stop processing the request.

But why is this important? There are two reasons; the first and most important is user expectations. If the user canceled the request, either manually or via a timeout, they will see an error. They will conclude that the processing has failed. If we continue to process the request and manage to complete it, this will go against their expectations.

The second reason is more pragmatic; when we stop processing the request, we reduce the load on our server and our upstream. This freed-up capacity can then be used to handle other requests.

When it comes to meeting user expectations, there is actually more we can do with the context package. We can add latency budgets.

Latency budgets

As with a lot of IT terms, latency budgets can be used in a multitude of ways. In this case, we refer to the maximum time allowed for a call.

Translating that into our current refactoring, it refers to two things:

- The maximum time allowed for the upstream (database or exchange rate service) call to complete
- The maximum time allowed for our register API to complete

You can see how these two things are related. Let's look at how our API response time is made up:

API response time = (exchange rate service call + database call + our code)

Assuming the performance of *our code* is mainly consistent, then our service quality is directly dependent on the speed of the upstream calls. This is not a very comfortable position to be in, so what can we do?

In the previous section, we examined these failures and some options, and decided that for the moment, we want to fail the request. What is the best failure we can offer our user? One that is both timely and informative.

To achieve this, we are going to use another feature of the context.Context interface: WithTimeout(parent Context, timeout time.Duration) (Context, CancelFunc)

As you might have guessed, this method sets a timeout on the context. This timeout will act as a timer, causing the context to cancel should the latency budget (timeout) be exceeded. Then, because we have our stop short already in place, our request will cease processing and exit.

First, let's apply this to our database call. In the next example, we will create a *sub-context* from the original context and give it a timeout. As contexts are hierarchical, the timeout we are applying will only apply to the sub-context and any contexts we create from it.

In our case, we have decided that the latency budget for calls to the database will be 1 second, as follows:

```
// Save will save the supplied person and return the ID of the newly
// created person or an error.
// Errors returned are caused by the underlying database or our
// connection to it.
func Save(ctx context.Context, in *Person) (int, error) {
    db, err := getDB()
    if err != nil {
        logging.L.Error("failed to get DB connection. err: %s", err)
        return defaultPersonID, err
    }
```

```
    // set latency budget for the database call
    subCtx, cancel := context.WithTimeout(ctx, 1*time.Second)
    defer cancel()

    // perform DB insert
    result, err := db.ExecContext(subCtx, sqlInsert, in.FullName, in.Phone,
in.Currency, in.Price)
    if err != nil {
        logging.L.Error("failed to save person into DB. err: %s", err)
        return defaultPersonID, err
    }

    // retrieve and return the ID of the person created
    id, err := result.LastInsertId()
    if err != nil {
        logging.L.Error("failed to retrieve id of last saved person. err:
%s", err)
        return defaultPersonID, err
    }

    return int(id), nil
}
```

Now, let's apply a latency budget to the exchange service call. To do this, we are going to use another feature of the `http.Request`, `Context()` method, documented as follows:

For outgoing client requests, the context controls cancellation

To set the latency budget on our outgoing HTTP request, we will create another sub-context, as we did for the database, and then set that context into the request with the `WithRequest()` method. After these changes, our code looks like this:

```
    // load rate from the external API
    func (c *Converter) loadRateFromServer(ctx context.Context, currency
string) (*http.Response, error) {
        // build the request
        url := fmt.Sprintf(urlFormat,
            config.App.ExchangeRateBaseURL,
            config.App.ExchangeRateAPIKey,
            currency)

        // perform request
        req, err := http.NewRequest("GET", url, nil)
        if err != nil {
            logging.L.Warn("[exchange] failed to create request. err: %s", err)
            return nil, err
        }
```

```
            // set latency budget for the upstream call
            subCtx, cancel := context.WithTimeout(ctx, 1*time.Second)
            defer cancel()

            // replace the default context with our custom one
            req = req.WithContext(subCtx)

            // perform the HTTP request
            response, err := http.DefaultClient.Do(req)
            if err != nil {
                logging.L.Warn("[exchange] failed to load. err: %s", err)
                return nil, err
            }

            if response.StatusCode != http.StatusOK {
                err = fmt.Errorf("request failed with code %d", response.StatusCode)
                logging.L.Warn("[exchange] %s", err)
                return nil, err
            }

            return response, nil
    }
```

With these changes in place, let's revisit our API response time formula and consider the worst-case scenario – both calls take a fraction under 1 second but successfully complete, giving us this:

API response time = (~1 second + ~ 1 second + our code)

This gives us a maximum execution time of about 2 seconds. But what if we decide that the maximum response time we will allow ourselves is 1.5 seconds?

Thankfully, we can easily do this too. Earlier, I mentioned that contexts are hierarchical. All of our contexts are currently derived from the context in the request. While we cannot change the context that is part of the request, we can derive a context from it with our API's latency budget and then pass that down to the data and exchange packages. The updated parts of the handler look like the following:

```
    // ServeHTTP implements http.Handler
    func (h *RegisterHandler) ServeHTTP(response http.ResponseWriter, request
    *http.Request) {
        // set latency budget for this API
        subCtx, cancel := context.WithTimeout(request.Context(), 1500
    *time.Millisecond)
        defer cancel()

        // extract payload from request
```

```
   requestPayload, err := h.extractPayload(request)
   if err != nil {
      // output error
      response.WriteHeader(http.StatusBadRequest)
      return
   }

   // register person
   id, err := h.register(subCtx, requestPayload)
   if err != nil {
      // not need to log here as we can expect other layers to do so
      response.WriteHeader(http.StatusBadRequest)
      return
   }

   // happy path
   response.Header().Add("Location", fmt.Sprintf("/person/%d/", id))
   response.WriteHeader(http.StatusCreated)
}
```

After a few simple changes, we have far more control over how our API performs, thanks to the context package and a little bit of method injection.

Disadvantages of method injection

I do not have a long list of disadvantages for you; in fact, I have only two.

Adding parameters detracts from the UX—This is a rather big one. Adding parameters to a method or function detracts from the UX of the function. As we saw in `Chapter 3`, *Coding for User Experience,* a bad UX for a function can negatively impact its usability.

Consider the following struct:

```
// Load people from the database
type PersonLoader struct {
}

func (d *PersonLoader) Load(db *sql.DB, ID int) (*Person, error) {
   return nil, errors.New("not implemented")
}

func (d *PersonLoader) LoadAll(db *sql.DB) ([]*Person, error) {
   return nil, errors.New("not implemented")
}
```

This code works; it gets the job done. But it's annoying to have to pass in the database every time. Beyond that, there is no guarantee that the code that calls `Load()` also maintains the database pool.

Another aspect to consider is encapsulation. Does the user of these functions need to know that they depend on a database? Put yourself in the place of the user of the `Load()` function for a moment. What do you want to do and what do you know?

You want to load a person, and you know the ID of that person. You do not know (or care) where the data comes from. If you were designing the function for yourself, what would it look like:

```
type MyPersonLoader interface {
    Load(ID int) (*Person, error)
}
```

It's succinct and easy to use, and none of the implementation details are leaking.

Let's look at another example:

```
type Generator struct{}

func (g *Generator) Generate(storage Storage, template io.Reader,
destination io.Writer, renderer Renderer, formatter Formatter, params
...interface{}) {

}
```

In this case, we have so many parameters, it's hard to separate the data from the non-request-scoped dependencies. If we extract those dependencies, we get the following:

```
func NewGeneratorV2(storage Storage, renderer Renderer, formatter
Formatter) *GeneratorV2 {
    return &GeneratorV2{
        storage:   storage,
        renderer:  renderer,
        formatter: formatter,
    }
}

type GeneratorV2 struct {
    storage    Storage
    renderer   Renderer
    formatter  Formatter
}

func (g *GeneratorV2) Generate(template io.Reader, destination io.Writer,
```

```
params ...interface{}) {

}
```

While the UX is better in the second example, it's still rather cumbersome. The code could benefit from a different approach, such as composition.

Limited applicability—As we have seen in this chapter, method injection is excellent with functions and request-scoped dependencies. While this use case does frequently crop up, method injection does not apply well to non-request-scoped dependencies, which is the bulk of use cases where we want to use **dependency injection (DI)**.

Summary

In this chapter, we have examined DI with method injection, perhaps the most ubiquitous of all forms of DI.

When it comes to extracting dependencies from existing code, for the purposes of testing, it might be the method that first comes to mind. Please be careful with this, we do not want to introduce *test-induced damage*.

Adding parameters to an exported API function for the sole purpose of testing undoubtedly damages UX code. Thankfully, there are some tricks available to us to avoid damaging our API. We can define member functions that only exist in test code. We can also use **Just-In-Time (JIT)** dependency injection, which we will examine in Chapter 9, *Just-in-Time Dependency Injection*.

In this chapter, we have looked at the fantastic and powerful context package. You might be surprised to learn that there is even more value we can extract from this package. I encourage you to check out the Go blog (https://blog.golang.org/context) and investigate this package for yourself.

In the next chapter, we are going to apply a specific form of both constructor injection and method injection called **DI by config**. With it, we will finally untangle the config package from being depended on by just about every other package in our service, making our packages far more decoupled and increasing their reusability potential considerably.

Questions

1. What are the ideal use cases for method injection?
2. Why is it important not to save dependencies injected with method injection?
3. What happens if we use method injection too much?
4. Why is *stopping short* useful to the system as a whole?
5. How can latency budgets improve the UX for our users?

Dependency Injection by Config

8

In this chapter, we will be looking at **dependency injection** (**DI**) by config. Config injection is not a completely different method but an extension of both constructor injection and method injection.

It intends to address potential issues with those methods, such as excessive or repeated injected dependencies, without sacrificing the UX of our code.

The following topics will be covered in this chapter:

- Config injection
- Advantages of config injection
- Applying config injection
- Disadvantages of config injection

Technical requirements

It would be beneficial to be familiar with the code for our service as we introduced in Chapter 4, *Introduction to ACME Registration Service*. This chapter also assumes that you have read Chapter 6, *Dependency Injection with Constructor Injection*, and Chapter 7, *Dependency Injection with Method Injection*.

You might also find it useful to read and run the full versions of the code for this chapter, which is available at https://github.com/PacktPublishing/Hands-On-Dependency-Injection-in-Go/tree/master/ch08.

Instructions to obtain the code and configure the sample service are available in the README here: https://github.com/PacktPublishing/Hands-On-Dependency-Injection-in-Go/

You can find the code for our service, with the changes from this chapter already applied, in ch08/acme.

Config injection

Config injection is a specific implementation of method and parameter injection. With config injection, we combine multiple dependencies and system-level config and merge them into a `config` interface.

Consider the following constructor:

```
// NewLongConstructor is the constructor for MyStruct
func NewLongConstructor(logger Logger, stats Instrumentation, limiter
RateLimiter, cache Cache, timeout time.Duration, workers int) *MyStruct {
 return &MyStruct{
 // code removed
 }
}
```

As you can see, we are injecting multiple dependencies, including a logger, instrumentation, rate limiter, cache, and some configuration.

It is safe to assume that we would be likely to inject at least the logger and the instrumentation into most of our objects in this same project. This results in a minimum of two parameters for every constructor. Across an entire system, this adds up to a lot of extra typing. It also detracts from the UX of our constructors by making them harder to read, and this potentially hides the significant parameters among the common ones.

Consider for a moment—where are the values for timeout and the number of workers that are likely to be defined? They are probably defined from some central source, such as a `config` file.

By applying config injection, our example becomes the following:

```
// NewByConfigConstructor is the constructor for MyStruct
func NewByConfigConstructor(cfg MyConfig, limiter RateLimiter, cache Cache)
*MyStruct {
    return &MyStruct{
        // code removed
    }
}
```

We have merged the common concerns and the configuration together into the config definition but left the significant parameters intact. In this manner, the function parameters are still informative without having to read the `config` interface definition. In a way, we have hidden or encapsulated the common concerns.

There is another usability aspect to consider—the config is now an interface. We should think about what kind of object would implement such an interface. Does such an object already exist? What are its responsibilities?

Often config comes from a single source and its responsibilities are to load the config and provide access to it. Even though we are introducing the config interface to decouple from the actual config management, leveraging the fact that it's a single source is still convenient.

Consider the following code:

```
myFetcher := NewFetcher(cfg, cfg.URL(), cfg.Timeout())
```

This code indicates that all of the parameters are coming from the same place. This is a good indication that they can be merged.

If you come from an object-oriented background, you may be familiar with the concept of a service locator. Config injection is intentionally very similar. Unlike typical service locator usage, however, we are only extracting configuration and a few shared dependencies.

Config injection takes this approach to avoid the service locator's *God object* and inherent coupling between usage and the God object.

Advantages of config injection

Given that config injection is an expanded form of constructor and method injections, the advantages of the other methods also apply here. In this section, we will discuss only the additional benefits that are specific to this method.

It's excellent for decoupling from a config package—When we have a `config` package that loads from a single place, such as a file, then this package tends to become a dependency for many of the other packages in the system. When considering the *Single responsibility principle* section from `Chapter 2`, *SOLID Design Principles for Go*, we recognize that the more users a package or object has, the more resistant and/or difficult it is to change.

With config injection, we are also defining our requirements in a local interface and leveraging Go's implicit interfaces and the **dependency inversion principle (DIP)** to keep the packages decoupled.

These steps also make it significantly easier to test our structs. Consider the following code:

```go
func TestInjectedConfig(t *testing.T) {
    // load test config
    cfg, err := config.LoadFromFile(testConfigLocation)
    require.NoError(t, err)

    // build and use object
    obj := NewMyObject(cfg)
    result, resultErr := obj.Do()

    // validate
    assert.NotNil(t, result)
    assert.NoError(t, resultErr)
}
```

Now, see the same code with config injection:

```go
func TestConfigInjection(t *testing.T) {
    // build test config
    cfg := &TestConfig{}

    // build and use object
    obj := NewMyObject(cfg)
    result, resultErr := obj.Do()

    // validate
    assert.NotNil(t, result)
    assert.NoError(t, resultErr)
}

// Simple implementation of the Config interface
type TestConfig struct {
    logger *logging.Logger
    stats  *stats.Collector
}

func (t *TestConfig) Logger() *logging.Logger {
    return t.logger
}

func (t *TestConfig) Stats() *stats.Collector {
    return t.stats
}
```

Yes, the amount of code is greater. However, we no longer have to manage test configuration files, which can often be a pain. Our tests are entirely self-contained and should have no concurrency problems, as they might with a global config object.

It eases the burden of injecting common concerns—In the previous example, we are using config injection to inject the logging and instrumentation objects. Common concerns such as this are an excellent use for config injection as they are frequently needed but are not informative regarding the purpose of the function itself. They can be considered environmental dependencies. Due to their shared nature, another approach would be to turn them into global singletons instead of injecting them. Personally, I prefer to inject them as this gives me the opportunity to validate their usage. This in itself might feel weird, but in many cases, we build system monitoring and alerts from the existence or lack of instrumentation data, thereby making instrumentation part of the features or contract of our code and something we might want to protect from regression with tests.

It improves usability by reducing parameters—Similar to the previous advantage, applying config injection can enhance the usability of methods, particularly constructors, but reduce the number of parameters. Consider the following constructor:

```
func NewLongConstructor(logger Logger, stats Instrumentation, limiter
RateLimiter, cache Cache, url string, credentials string) *MyStruct {
    return &MyStruct{
        // code removed
    }
}
```

Now. take a look at the same constructor with config injection:

```
func NewByConfigConstructor(cfg MyConfig, url string, credentials string)
*MyStruct {
    return &MyStruct{
        // code removed
    }
}
```

With the environmental dependencies removed from the constructor definition, we are left with significantly fewer parameters. Even more than that, the only parameters that remain are those that are specific to the purpose, hence making the method simpler to understand and use.

Dependency creation can be deferred until use—Have you ever tried to inject a dependency, only to find that it didn't exist or wasn't ready yet? Have you ever had a dependency that was so expensive to start or run that you wanted to create it only when it was absolutely necessary?

With config injection, dependency creation, and access only need to be resolved at the point of usage and not during injection.

Applying config injection

Previously, I mentioned there were a couple of issues that I really wanted us to fix with our ACME registration service. In this section, we are going to use config injection to deal with two of them.

The first is the fact that many of our packages depend on the `config` and `logging` packages, and other than being a substantial single responsibility principle violation, this coupling is likely to cause circular dependency problems.

The second is our inability to test our calls to the exchange rate without actually calling the upstream service. So far, we have avoided adding any tests to this package for fear that our tests would then be affected (in terms of speed and stability) by that service.

First, let's examine where we are. Our dependency graph currently looks as shown in the following diagram:

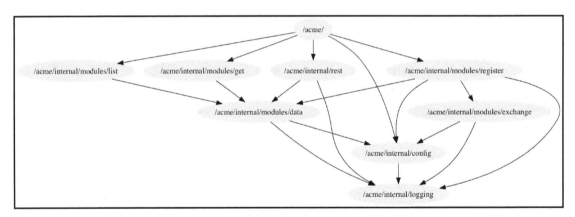

As you can see, we have four packages (`data`, `register`, `exchange`, and `main`) depending on the `config` package and five (`data`, `register`, `exchange`, `rest`, and `config`) that rely on the `logging` package. What is perhaps worse is how these packages depend on the `config` and `logging` packages. Currently, they directly access public singletons. This means that when we want to test our logger usage or swap out some configuration during testing, we would have to monkey patch and this would cause a data race instability in the tests.

To address this, we are going to define one config for each of our objects. Each config will include the logger and any other configuration that it needs. Then, we replace any direct links to the global variables with references to the injected config.

This will result in a bit of shotgun surgery (a lot of little changes), but the code will be a lot better for it.

We will go through only one set of changes here; if you wish to see all of them, please review the source code for this chapter.

Applying config injection to the model layer

Revisiting our `register` package, we see that it has references to both config and logging:

```
// Registerer validates the supplied person, calculates the price in
// the requested currency and saves the result.
// It will return an error when:
// -the person object does not include all the fields
// -the currency is invalid
// -the exchange rate cannot be loaded
// -the data layer throws an error.
type Registerer struct {
}

// get price in the requested currency
func (r *Registerer) getPrice(ctx context.Context, currency string)
(float64, error) {
  converter := &exchange.Converter{}
  price, err := converter.Do(ctx, config.App.BasePrice, currency)
  if err != nil {
    logging.L.Warn("failed to convert the price. err: %s", err)
    return defaultPersonID, err
  }

  return price, nil
}
```

Our first step is to define an interface that will supply the dependencies we need:

```
// Config is the configuration for the Registerer
type Config interface {
  Logger() *logging.LoggerStdOut
  BasePrice() float64
}
```

Do you see anything wrong with this? The first thing that jumps out is the fact that our `Logger()` method returns a pointer to a logger implementation. This will work, but it's not very future proof or testable. We could define a `logging` interface locally and decouple ourselves entirely from the `logging` package. This would mean, however, that we would have to define a `logging` interface in most of our packages. Theoretically, this is the best option, but it is not very practical. Instead, we could define one `logging` interface and have all of the packages depend upon that. While this will mean that we still remained coupled to the `logging` package, we will rely on an interface that seldom changes, rather than an implementation that is far more likely to change.

The second potential issue is the naming of the other method, `BasePrice()`, because it's somewhat generic, and a potential source of confusion later on. It is also the name of the field in the `Config` struct but Go will not allow us to have a member variable and method with the same name, so we will need to change that.

After updating our `config` interface, we have the following:

```
// Config is the configuration for the Registerer
type Config interface {
  Logger() logging.Logger
  RegistrationBasePrice() float64
}
```

We can now apply config injection to our `Registerer`, giving us the following:

```
// NewRegisterer creates and initializes a Registerer
func NewRegisterer(cfg Config) *Registerer {
    return &Registerer{
        cfg: cfg,
    }
}

// Config is the configuration for the Registerer
type Config interface {
    Logger() logging.Logger
    RegistrationBasePrice() float64
}

// Registerer validates the supplied person, calculates the price in
// the requested currency and saves the result.
// It will return an error when:
// -the person object does not include all the fields
// -the currency is invalid
// -the exchange rate cannot be loaded
// -the data layer throws an error.
```

```go
type Registerer struct {
    cfg Config
}

// get price in the requested currency
func (r *Registerer) getPrice(ctx context.Context, currency string)
(float64, error) {
    converter := &exchange.Converter{}
    price, err := converter.Do(ctx, r.cfg.RegistrationBasePrice(), currency)
    if err != nil {
        r.logger().Warn("failed to convert the price. err: %s", err)
        return defaultPersonID, err
    }

    return price, nil
}

func (r *Registerer) logger() logging.Logger {
    return r.cfg.Logger()
}
```

I have also added a convenience method, `logger()`, to reduce the code from
`r.cfg.Logger()` to just `r.logger()`. Our service and tests are currently broken, so we
have more changes to make.

To get the tests going again, we need to define a test configuration and update our tests. For
our test configuration, we could use mockery and create a mock implementation, but we
are not interested in validating our config usage or adding extra code to all of the tests in
this package to configure the mock. Instead, we are going to use a stub implementation that
returns predictable values. Here is our stub test config:

```go
// Stub implementation of Config
type testConfig struct{}

// Logger implement Config
func (t *testConfig) Logger() logging.Logger {
    return &logging.LoggerStdOut{}
}

// RegistrationBasePrice implement Config
func (t *testConfig) RegistrationBasePrice() float64 {
    return 12.34
}
```

And add this test config to all of our `Registerer` tests, as shown in the following code:

```
registerer := &Registerer{
    cfg: &testConfig{},
}
```

Our tests are running again, but strangely, while our service compiles, it would crash with a `nil` pointer exception if we were to run it. We need to update the creation of our `Registerer` from the following:

```
registerModel := &register.Registerer{}
```

We change it to this:

```
registerModel := register.NewRegisterer(config.App)
```

This leads us to the next problem. The `config.App` struct does not implement the methods we need. Adding these methods to `config`, we get the following:

```
// Logger returns a reference to the singleton logger
func (c *Config) Logger() logging.Logger {
    if c.logger == nil {
        c.logger = &logging.LoggerStdOut{}
    }

    return c.logger
}

// RegistrationBasePrice returns the base price for registrations
func (c *Config) RegistrationBasePrice() float64 {
    return c.BasePrice
}
```

With these changes, we have severed the dependency link between the `registration` package and the `config` package. In the `Logger()` method we have illustrated previously, you can see we are still using the logger as a singleton, but instead of being a global public variable, which would be prone to data races, it's now inside the `config` object. On the surface, this might not seem like it made any difference; however, the data races we were primarily concerned about were during testing. Our object now relies on an injected version of the logger and is not required to use the global public variable.

Here, we examine our updated dependency graph to see where to go next:

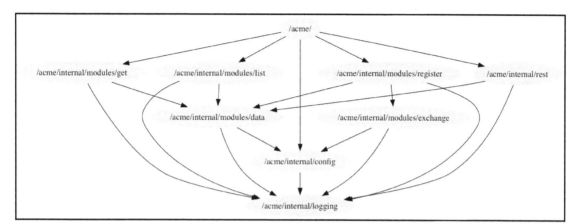

We are down to three links into the config package; that is, those from the main, data, and exchange packages. The link from the main package cannot be removed, hence, we can ignore that. So, let's look into the data package.

Applying config injection to the data package

Our data package is currently based on functions, and as such, the changes are going to be a little different compared to the previous ones. Here is a typical function from the data package:

```
// Load will attempt to load and return a person.
// It will return ErrNotFound when the requested person does not exist.
// Any other errors returned are caused by the underlying database
// or our connection to it.
func Load(ctx context.Context, ID int) (*Person, error) {
    db, err := getDB()
    if err != nil {
        logging.L.Error("failed to get DB connection. err: %s", err)
        return nil, err
    }

    // set latency budget for the database call
    subCtx, cancel := context.WithTimeout(ctx, 1*time.Second)
    defer cancel()

    // perform DB select
    row := db.QueryRowContext(subCtx, sqlLoadByID, ID)
```

```
    // retrieve columns and populate the person object
    out, err := populatePerson(row.Scan)
    if err != nil {
        if err == sql.ErrNoRows {
            logging.L.Warn("failed to load requested person '%d'. err: %s",
ID, err)
            return nil, ErrNotFound
        }

        logging.L.Error("failed to convert query result. err: %s", err)
        return nil, err
    }
    return out, nil
}
```

In this function, we have references to the logger which we want to remove, and one configuration that we really need to extract. The config is required by the first line of the function from the previous code. Here is the getDB() function:

```
var getDB = func() (*sql.DB, error) {
    if db == nil {
        if config.App == nil {
            return nil, errors.New("config is not initialized")
        }

        var err error
        db, err = sql.Open("mysql", config.App.DSN)
        if err != nil {
            // if the DB cannot be accessed we are dead
            panic(err.Error())
        }
    }

    return db, nil
}
```

We have a reference to the DSN to create the database pool. So, what do you think our first step should be?

As with the previous change, let's first define an interface that includes all of the dependencies and configuration that we want to inject:

```
// Config is the configuration for the data package
type Config interface {
    // Logger returns a reference to the logger
    Logger() logging.Logger

    // DataDSN returns the data source name
```

```
      DataDSN() string
}
```

Now, let's update our functions to inject the `config` interface:

```go
// Load will attempt to load and return a person.
// It will return ErrNotFound when the requested person does not exist.
// Any other errors returned are caused by the underlying database
// or our connection to it.
func Load(ctx context.Context, cfg Config, ID int) (*Person, error) {
   db, err := getDB(cfg)
   if err != nil {
      cfg.Logger().Error("failed to get DB connection. err: %s", err)
      return nil, err
   }

   // set latency budget for the database call
   subCtx, cancel := context.WithTimeout(ctx, 1*time.Second)
   defer cancel()

   // perform DB select
   row := db.QueryRowContext(subCtx, sqlLoadByID, ID)

   // retrieve columns and populate the person object
   out, err := populatePerson(row.Scan)
   if err != nil {
      if err == sql.ErrNoRows {
         cfg.Logger().Warn("failed to load requested person '%d'. err: %s",
ID, err)
         return nil, ErrNotFound
      }

      cfg.Logger().Error("failed to convert query result. err: %s", err)
      return nil, err
   }
   return out, nil
}

var getDB = func(cfg Config) (*sql.DB, error) {
   if db == nil {
      var err error
      db, err = sql.Open("mysql", cfg.DataDSN())
      if err != nil {
         // if the DB cannot be accessed we are dead
         panic(err.Error())
      }
   }
```

```
        return db, nil
    }
```

Unfortunately, this change is going to break a lot of things as `getDB()` is called by all of the public functions in the `data` package, which are in turn called by the model layer packages. Thankfully, we have enough unit tests to help prevent regression while working through the changes.

I'd like to ask you to stop for a moment and consider this: we are attempting to make what should be an insignificant change, but it's causing a mass of small changes. Additionally, we are being forced to add one parameter to every public function in this package. How does this make you feel about the decision to build this package based on functions? Refactoring away from functions would be no small task, but do you think it would be worth it?

The changes to the model layer are small, but interesting, thanks to the fact that we have already updated the model layer with config injection.

There are only have two small changes to make:

- We will add the `DataDSN()` method to our config
- We need to pass the config down to data package via the `loader()` call

Here is the code with the changes applied:

```go
// Config is the configuration for Getter
type Config interface {
    Logger() logging.Logger
    DataDSN() string
}

// Getter will attempt to load a person.
// It can return an error caused by the data layer or when the
// requested person is not found
type Getter struct {
    cfg Config
}

// Do will perform the get
func (g *Getter) Do(ID int) (*data.Person, error) {
    // load person from the data layer
    person, err := loader(context.TODO(), g.cfg, ID)
    if err != nil {
        if err == data.ErrNotFound {
            // By converting the error we are hiding the implementation
            // details from our users.
```

```
        return nil, errPersonNotFound
    }
    return nil, err
}

return person, err
}

// this function as a variable allows us to Monkey Patch during testing
var loader = data.Load
```

Sadly, we need to make these small changes in all of our model layer packages. After that is done, our dependency graph now looks as shown in the following diagram:

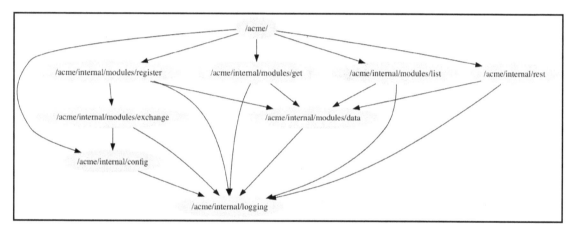

Fantastic. There is only one unnecessary connection to the config package left, and it comes from the exchange package.

Applying config injection to the exchange package

We can apply config injection to the exchange package as we have with the other packages, using the following steps:

1. Define an interface that includes the dependencies and config that we want to inject
2. Define/update the constructor to accept the config interface
3. Save the injected config as a member variable

4. Change the references (for example, to `config` and `logger`) to point to the member variable
5. Update the other layer `config` interfaces to include anything new

After we have applied config injection to the `exchange` package, an unusual situation emerges. Our dependency graph shows that we have removed the link from the `exchange` to `config` packages, as can be seen in the following diagram:

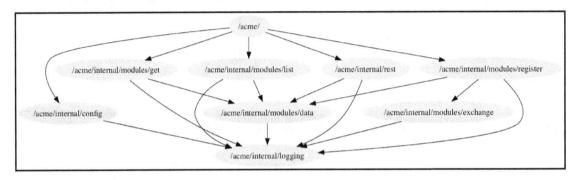

For our tests to remain working, however, we still need to reference the config, as shown in the following code:

```
type testConfig struct{}

// ExchangeBaseURL implements Config
func (t *testConfig) ExchangeBaseURL() string {
    return config.App.ExchangeRateBaseURL
}

// ExchangeAPIKey implements Config
func (t *testConfig) ExchangeAPIKey() string {
    return config.App.ExchangeRateAPIKey
}
```

Stepping back for a moment, we notice that the tests we are referring to are not tests on the `exchange` package, but for its user, the `register` package. This is quite the red flag. We can quickly fix the first part of this problem by applying constructor injection to the relationship between these two packages. We can then mock or stub the calls to the exchanger.

We can also undo some of our earlier changes to the register `Config` interface, removing the `exchange` package related methods and bringing us back to this:

```
// Config is the configuration for the Registerer
type Config interface {
    Logger() logging.Logger
    RegistrationBasePrice() float64
    DataDSN() string
}
```

This finally allows us to remove the link from our `register` tests to the `config` package and, perhaps more importantly, allows us to decouple our test from the external exchange rate service.

When we started this section, we defined two goals. Firstly, to decouple from the `config` package and the `logging` package, and secondly, to be able to test without calling the external service. So far, we have managed to decouple from the `config` package completely. We have removed the usage of the global public logger from all packages except the `config` package, and we have also removed our dependence on the external exchange rate service.

Our service still depends on that external service, however, and we have absolutely no tests that verify that we call it correctly or that prove the service responds as we expect it to. These tests are called **boundary tests**.

Boundary tests

Boundary tests come in two forms, each with their own goal—internal-facing and external-facing.

Internal-facing boundary tests are designed to validate two things:

- That our code calls the external service in the way that we expect it to
- That our code reacts to all responses, happy path and errors, from the external service in the way that we expect it to

As such, internal-facing boundary tests do not interact with the external service, but rather with a mock or stub implementation of the external service.

External-facing boundary tests are the opposite. They interact with the external service and verify that the external service performs as we need it to. Please note that they do not validate the external service's API contract, nor does the service act as its owner expects it to. Instead, however, they focus only on our requirements. External boundary tests are, by nature, going to be slower and less reliable than unit tests. As such, we may prefer not to run them all the time. We can use Go's build flags to achieve this.

Let's start by adding external facing boundary tests to our service. We could write a test that contains HTTP calls to the external service in the format suggested by the service's documentation and then validates the responses. If we were unfamiliar with this service and had not yet built the code that calls the service, this is also an excellent way to learn about the external service.

In our case, however, we have already written the code, so the faster option is to call that code with *live* config. Doing that returns a JSON payload that looks similar to the following:

```
{
    "success":true,
    "historical":true,
    "date":"2010-11-09",
    "timestamp":1289347199,
    "source":"USD",
    "quotes":{
        "USDAUD":0.989981
    }
}
```

While the format of the response is predictable, the `timestamp` and `quotes` values will change. So, what can we test? Perhaps, more importantly, what parts of the response do we depend on? After closer examination of our code, we realize that out of all of the fields in the response, the only one we use is the `quotes` map. Additionally, the only thing we require from the external service is that the currency we requested exists in that map and the value is of the `float64` type. Therefore, by only testing for these specific attributes, our tests will be as resilient to changes as possible.

This gives us a test that looks like the following code:

```
func TestExternalBoundaryTest(t *testing.T) {
    // define the config
    cfg := &testConfig{
        baseURL: config.App.ExchangeRateBaseURL,
        apiKey:  config.App.ExchangeRateAPIKey,
    }

    // create a converter to test
```

```
converter := NewConverter(cfg)

// fetch from the server
response, err := converter.loadRateFromServer(context.Background(),
"AUD")
require.NotNil(t, response)
require.NoError(t, err)

// parse the response
resultRate, err := converter.extractRate(response, "AUD")
require.NoError(t, err)

// validate the result
assert.True(t, resultRate > 0)
}
```

To ensure that this test only runs when we want it to, we put the following build tag at the top of the file:

```
// +build external
```

Now, that let's look at internal facing boundary tests. The first step is to make ourselves a mock implementation of the external service. We have the resulting payload, as mentioned previously. To do this, we will use the httptest package to create an HTTP server that returns our test payload, like this:

```
type happyExchangeRateService struct{}

// ServeHTTP implements http.Handler
func (*happyExchangeRateService) ServeHTTP(response http.ResponseWriter,
request *http.Request) {
  payload := []byte(`
{
    "success":true,
    "historical":true,
    "date":"2010-11-09",
    "timestamp":1289347199,
    "source":"USD",
    "quotes":{
        "USDAUD":0.989981
    }
}`)
  response.Write(payload)
}
```

For now, it returns a fixed response and does nothing to validate the request. We can now build our internal-facing boundary test. Unlike the external-facing boundary test, the result is now entirely controlled by us and is therefore predictable. We can, therefore, test the exact result, as shown in the following code:

```
func TestInternalBoundaryTest(t *testing.T) {
    // start our test server
    server := httptest.NewServer(&happyExchangeRateService{})
    defer server.Close()

    // define the config
    cfg := &testConfig{
        baseURL: server.URL,
        apiKey:  "",
    }

    // create a converter to test
    converter := NewConverter(cfg)
    resultRate, resultErr := converter.Exchange(context.Background(),
100.00, "AUD")

    // validate the result
    assert.Equal(t, 101.01, resultRate)
    assert.NoError(t, resultErr)
}
```

We now have a basic internal facing boundary test. We are able to verify, without depending on the external service, that the external service returns the payload we expect and we are able to extract and use the result correctly. We can further extend our tests to cover more scenarios, including the following:

- A test that verifies our code and returns a sensible error when the external service is down or slow
- A test that proves our code returns a sensible error when the external service returns an empty or invalid response
- A test that validates the HTTP request that our code performs

With our internal-facing boundary tests in place, we finally have tests on our exchange rate code. We have managed to ensure that our code works as intended, with tests that are reliable and entirely controlled by us. Additionally, we have external boundary tests that we can occasionally run to inform us of any changes to the external service that will break our service.

Disadvantages of config injection

As we have seen, config injection can be used with both constructors and functions, It is, therefore, possible to build a system with only config injection. Unfortunately, config injection does have some disadvantages.

Passing config instead of abstract dependencies leaks implementation details—Consider the following code:

```
type PeopleFilterConfig interface {
   DSN() string
}

func PeopleFilter(cfg PeopleFilterConfig, filter string) ([]Person, error)
{
   // load people
   loader := &PersonLoader{}
   people, err := loader.LoadAll(cfg)
   if err != nil {
      return nil, err
   }

   // filter people
   out := []Person{}
   for _, person := range people {
      if strings.Contains(person.Name, filter) {
         out = append(out, person)
      }
   }

   return out, nil
}

type PersonLoaderConfig interface {
   DSN() string
}

type PersonLoader struct{}

func (p *PersonLoader) LoadAll(cfg PersonLoaderConfig) ([]Person, error) {
   return nil, errors.New("not implemented")
}
```

In this example, the `PeopleFilter` function is aware of the fact that `PersonLoader` is a database. This might not seem like a big deal, and if the implementation strategy never changes, it will have no adverse impact. Should we shift from a database to an external service or anything else, however, we would then have to change our `PersonLoader` database as well. A more future-proof implementation would be as follows:

```
type Loader interface {
    LoadAll() ([]Person, error)
}

func PeopleFilter(loader Loader, filter string) ([]Person, error) {
    // load people
    people, err := loader.LoadAll()
    if err != nil {
        return nil, err
    }

    // filter people
    out := []Person{}
    for _, person := range people {
        if strings.Contains(person.Name, filter) {
            out = append(out, person)
        }
    }

    return out, nil
}
```

This implementation is unlikely to require changes should we change where our data is loaded from.

Dependency life cycles are less predictable—In the advantages, we stated that dependency creation can be deferred until use. Your inner critic may have rebelled against that assertion, and for a good reason. It is an advantage, but it also makes the life cycle of the dependency less predictable. When using constructor injection or method injection, the dependency must exist before it is injected. Due to this, any issues with the creation or initialization of the dependency surfaces at this earlier time. When the dependency is initialized at some unknown later point, a couple of issues can arise.

Firstly, if the issue is unrecoverable or causes the system to panic, this would mean the system initially seems healthy and then becomes unhealthy or crashes unpredictably. This unpredictability can lead to issues that are extremely hard to debug.

Secondly, if the initialization of the dependency includes the possibility of a delay, we have to be aware of, and account for, any such delay. Consider the following code:

```
func DoJob(pool WorkerPool, job Job) error {
    // wait for pool
    ready := pool.IsReady()

    select {
    case <-ready:
        // happy path

    case <-time.After(1 * time.Second):
        return errors.New("timeout waiting for worker pool")
    }

    worker := pool.GetWorker()
    return worker.Do(job)
}
```

Now compare this to an implementation that assumes the pool is ready before injection:

```
func DoJobUpdated(pool WorkerPool, job Job) error {
    worker := pool.GetWorker()
    return worker.Do(job)
}
```

What would happen if this function were a part of an endpoint with a latency budget? If the startup delay is greater than the latency budget, then the first request would always fail.

Over-use degrades the UX—While I strongly recommended that you only use this pattern for configuration and environmental dependencies such as instrumentation, it is possible to apply this pattern in many other places. By pushing the dependencies into a config interface, however, they become less apparent, and we have a larger interface to implement. Let's re-examine an earlier example:

```
// NewByConfigConstructor is the constructor for MyStruct
func NewByConfigConstructor(cfg MyConfig, limiter RateLimiter, cache Cache)
*MyStruct {
    return &MyStruct{
    // code removed
    }
}
```

Consider the rate limiter dependency. What happens if we merge that into the Config interface? It becomes less apparent that this object uses and relies on a rate limiter. If every similar function has rate limiting, then this will be less of a problem as its usage becomes more environmental.

The other less visible aspect is configuration. The configuration of the rate limiter is likely not consistent across all usages. This is a problem when all of the other dependencies and config are coming from a shared object. We could compose the config object and customize the rate limiter returned, but this feels like over-engineering.

Changes can ripple through the software layers - This issue only applies when the config passed through the layers. Consider the following example:

```go
func NewLayer1Object(config Layer1Config) *Layer1Object {
    return &Layer1Object{
        MyConfig:      config,
        MyDependency: NewLayer2Object(config),
    }
}

// Configuration for the Layer 1 Object
type Layer1Config interface {
    Logger() Logger
}

// Layer 1 Object
type Layer1Object struct {
    MyConfig     Layer1Config
    MyDependency *Layer2Object
}

// Configuration for the Layer 2 Object
type Layer2Config interface {
    Logger() Logger
}

// Layer 2 Object
type Layer2Object struct {
    MyConfig Layer2Config
}

func NewLayer2Object(config Layer2Config) *Layer2Object {
    return &Layer2Object{
        MyConfig: config,
    }
}
```

With this structure, when we need to add a new configuration or dependency to the `Layer2Config` interface, we would also be forced to add it to the `Layer1Config` interface. `Layer1Config` would then be in violation of the interface segregation principle as discussed in `Chapter 2`, *SOLID Design Principles for Go*, which indicates that we might have a problem. Additionally, depending on the code's layering and level of reuse, the number of changes could be significant. In this case, a better option would be to apply constructor injection to inject `Layer2Object` into `Layer1Object`. This would completely decouple the objects and remove the need for the layered changes.

Summary

In this chapter, we have leveraged config injection, an extended version of constructor and method injection, to improve the UX of our code, primarily by handling the environmental dependencies and config separately from the contextually significant dependencies.

While applying config injection to our sample service, we have decoupled all possible packages from the `config` package, giving it more freedom to evolve over time. We also switched most of the logger usage from a global public variable to an injected abstract dependency by removing any possibility of a data race relating to the logger instance and enabling us to test logger usage without any messy monkey patching.

In the next chapter, we will examine another unusual form of dependency injection, called **Just-in-time (JIT) dependency injection**. With this technique, we will reduce the burden associated with dependency creation and injection between the layers without sacrificing our ability to test with mocks and stubs.

Questions

1. How does config injection differ from method or constructor injection?
2. How do we decide what parameters to move to config injection?
3. Why don't we inject all dependencies via config injection?
4. Why do we want to inject environmental dependencies (such as loggers) instead of using a global public variable?
5. Why are boundary tests important?
6. What are the ideal use cases for config injection?

Just-in-Time Dependency Injection

9

With *traditional* **dependency injection** (**DI**) methods, the parent or calling object supplies the dependencies to the child class. However, there are many cases where the dependencies have a single implementation. In these cases, a pragmatic approach would be to ask yourself, why inject the dependency at all? In this chapter, we will examine **just-in-time** (**JIT**) dependency injection, a strategy that gives us many of the benefits of DI, like decoupling and testability, without adding parameters to our constructors or methods.

The following topics will be covered in this chapter:

- JIT injection
- Advantages of JIT injection
- Applying JIT injection
- Disadvantages of JIT injection

Technical requirements

It would be beneficial to be familiar with the code for our service we introduced in `Chapter 4`, *Introduction to the ACME Registration Service*. This chapter also assumes that you have read `Chapter 6`, *Dependency Injection with Constructor Injection*, and, to a lesser extent, `Chapter 5`, *Dependency Injection with Monkey Patching*.

You might also find it useful to read and run the full version of the code for this chapter, which is available at `https://github.com/PacktPublishing/Hands-On-Dependency-Injection-in-Go/tree/master/ch09`.

Instructions to obtain the code and configure the sample service are available in the README section here: `https://github.com/PacktPublishing/Hands-On-Dependency-Injection-in-Go/`.

You can find the code for our service, with the changes from this chapter already applied, in `ch09/acme`.

In this chapter, we will be using mockery (`https://github.com/vektra/mockery`) to generate mock implementations of our interfaces and also introducing a new tool called **package coverage** (`https://github.com/corsc/go-tools/tree/master/package-coverage`).

JIT injection

Have you ever written an object and injected a dependency that you knew was only going to have one implementation? Perhaps you have injected the database handling code into the business logic layer, as shown in the following code:

```go
func NewMyLoadPersonLogic(ds DataSource) *MyLoadPersonLogic {
    return &MyLoadPersonLogic{
        dataSource: ds,
    }
}

type MyLoadPersonLogic struct {
    dataSource DataSource
}

// Load person by supplied ID
func (m *MyLoadPersonLogic) Load(ID int) (Person, error) {
    return m.dataSource.Load(ID)
}
```

Have you ever added a dependency to your constructor for the sole purpose of mocking it out during testing? This is shown in the following code:

```go
func NewLoadPersonHandler(logic LoadPersonLogic) *LoadPersonHandler {
    return &LoadPersonHandler{
        businessLogic: logic,
    }
}

type LoadPersonHandler struct {
    businessLogic LoadPersonLogic
}

func (h *LoadPersonHandler) ServeHTTP(response http.ResponseWriter, request
*http.Request) {
    requestedID, err := h.extractInputFromRequest(request)
```

```
    output, err := h.businessLogic.Load(requestedID)
    if err != nil {
        response.WriteHeader(http.StatusInternalServerError)
        return
    }

    h.writeOutput(response, output)
}
```

These kinds of things can feel like unnecessary extra work, and they definitely degrade the UX of the code. JIT injection allows us a comfortable middle ground. JIT injection is perhaps best explained by working through some examples. Let's take a look at our first example with JIT injection applied:

```
type MyLoadPersonLogicJIT struct {
    dataSource DataSourceJIT
}

// Load person by supplied ID
func (m *MyLoadPersonLogicJIT) Load(ID int) (Person, error) {
    return m.getDataSource().Load(ID)
}

func (m *MyLoadPersonLogicJIT) getDataSource() DataSourceJIT {
    if m.dataSource == nil {
        m.dataSource = NewMyDataSourceJIT()
    }

    return m.dataSource
}
```

As you can see, we have changed the direct references from `m.dataSource` to `m.getDataSource()` by adding a `getter` function, `getDataSource()`. In `getDataSource()`, we are performing a simple and efficient check to see whether the dependency already exists and when it doesn't, we create it. This is where we get the name *just-in-time injection*.

So, if we are not going to inject the dependency, then why do we need the injection? The simple answer is testing.

In our original example, we were able to *swap out* our dependency with a mock implementation during testing, as shown in the following code:

```
func TestMyLoadPersonLogic(t *testing.T) {
    // setup the mock db
    mockDB := &mockDB{
        out: Person{Name: "Fred"},
```

```
    }

    // call the object we are testing
    testObj := NewMyLoadPersonLogic(mockDB)
    result, resultErr := testObj.Load(123)

    // validate expectations
    assert.Equal(t, Person{Name: "Fred"}, result)
    assert.Nil(t, resultErr)
}
```

With JIT injection, we can still supply a mock implementation, but instead of supplying it via the constructor, we inject it directly into the private member variable, like this:

```
func TestMyLoadPersonLogicJIT(t *testing.T) {
    // setup the mock db
    mockDB := &mockDB{
        out: Person{Name: "Fred"},
    }

    // call the object we are testing
    testObj := MyLoadPersonLogicJIT{
        dataSource: mockDB,
    }
    result, resultErr := testObj.Load(123)

    // validate expectations
    assert.Equal(t, Person{Name: "Fred"}, result)
    assert.Nil(t, resultErr)
}
```

You may have also noticed that in this example we dropped the use of a constructor. This is not necessary and will not always be the case. Applying JIT injection improves the usability of the object by reducing the number of parameters. In our example, there were no parameters left so dropping the constructor seemed appropriate as well.

JIT injection has allowed us to bend the traditional rules of DI by giving the object the ability to create its own dependencies when needed. While this is strictly speaking a violation of the *Single responsibility principle* section, as discussed in Chapter 2, *SOLID Design Principles for Go,* the improvements in usability are significant.

Advantages of JIT injection

This method was designed to address some of the pain points of traditional DI. The advantages listed here are specific to this method and in contrast to other forms of dependency injection. Benefits specific to this method include the following.

Better User Experience (UX) due to fewer inputs—I know I have raised this point a lot, but code that is easier to understand is also easier to maintain and extend. When a function has fewer parameters, it's inherently easier to understand. Compare the constructor:

```
func NewGenerator(storage Storage, renderer Renderer, template io.Reader)
*Generator {
    return &Generator{
        storage:  storage,
        renderer: renderer,
        template: template,
    }
}
```

With this one:

```
func NewGenerator(template io.Reader) *Generator {
    return &Generator{
        template: template,
    }
}
```

In this example, we removed all of the dependencies that had only one live implementation and replaced them with JIT injection. Now, users of this function just need to supply the one dependency that can change.

It's perfect for optional dependencies—Similar to the previous point regarding UX, optional dependencies can bloat a function's parameter list. Additionally, it is not immediately apparent that the dependency is optional. Moving the dependency to a public member variable allows users to supply it only when needed. Applying JIT injection then allows the object to instantiate a copy of the default dependency. This simplifies the code inside the object significantly.

Consider the following code, which does not use JIT injection:

```
func (l *LoaderWithoutJIT) Load(ID int) (*Animal, error) {
    var output *Animal
    var err error

    // attempt to load from cache
    if l.OptionalCache != nil {
```

```
        output = l.OptionalCache.Get(ID)
        if output != nil {
            // return cached value
            return output, nil
        }
    }

    // load from data store
    output, err = l.datastore.Load(ID)
    if err != nil {
        return nil, err
    }

    // cache the loaded value
    if l.OptionalCache != nil {
        l.OptionalCache.Put(ID, output)
    }

    // output the result
    return output, nil
}
```

Applying JIT injection, this becomes the following:

```
func (l *LoaderWithJIT) Load(ID int) (*Animal, error) {
    // attempt to load from cache
    output := l.cache().Get(ID)
    if output != nil {
        // return cached value
        return output, nil
    }

    // load from data store
    output, err := l.datastore.Load(ID)
    if err != nil {
        return nil, err
    }

    // cache the loaded value
    l.cache().Put(ID, output)

    // output the result
    return output, nil
}
```

The function is now more concise and more straightforward to read. We will discuss using JIT injection with optional dependencies more in the next section.

Better encapsulation of the implementation details—One of the counter-arguments to typical DI (that is, constructor or parameter injection) is that by exposing one object's dependence on another, you are leaking implementation details. Consider the following constructor:

```
func NewLoader(ds Datastore, cache Cache) *MyLoader {
    return &MyLoader{
        ds:    ds,
        cache: cache,
    }
}
```

Now, put yourself in the position of the user of `MyLoader`, without knowing its implementation. Does it matter to you that `MyLoader` uses a database or a cache? If you don't have multiple implementations or configurations to use, would it be easier just to let the author of `MyLoader` handle it for you?

Reduction in test-induced damage—Another frequent complaint of those against DI is that dependencies are added to the constructor for the sole purpose of replacing them during testing. This position is well-founded; it's something you will see quite often and one of the more common forms of test-induced damage. JIT injection alleviates this by changing the relationship to a private member variable and removing it from the public API. This still allows us to replace the dependency during testing, but with no public damage.

In case you were wondering, the choice of a private member variable and not public is intentional and intentionally limiting. Being private, we are able to access and replace the dependency only during testing within the same package. Tests outside the package intentionally have no access. The first reason for this is encapsulation. We want to hide the implementation details from other packages so that they do not become coupled with our package. Any such coupling would make it harder to make changes to our implementation. The second reason is API pollution. If we made the member variable public, it would be accessible not only to the tests but to everyone, thereby opening the possibility of unexpected, invalid, or dangerous use of our internals.

It's a great alternative to monkey patching—As you may remember from `Chapter 5`, *Dependency Injection with Monkey Patching*, one of the most significant problems with monkey patching is concurrency during testing. By patching the single global variable to suit the current test, any other test that is using that variable will be impacted and likely broken. It is possible to use JIT injection to avoid this problem. Consider the following code:

```
// Global singleton of connections to our data store
var storage UserStorage

type Saver struct {
```

```
   }

func (s *Saver) Do(in *User) error {
   err := s.validate(in)
   if err != nil {
      return err
   }

   return storage.Save(in)
}
```

As is, the global variable storage is going to need to be monkey patched during testing. But look what happens when we apply JIT injection:

```
// Global singleton of connections to our data store
var storage UserStorage

type Saver struct {
   storage UserStorage
}

func (s *Saver) Do(in *User) error {
   err := s.validate(in)
   if err != nil {
      return err
   }

   return s.getStorage().Save(in)
}

// Just-in-time DI
func (s *Saver) getStorage() UserStorage {
   if s.storage == nil {
      s.storage = storage
   }

   return s.storage
}
```

With all access to the global variable now going via getStorage(), we are able to use JIT injection to *swap out* the storage member variable instead of monkey patching the global (and shared) variable, as seen in this example:

```
func TestSaver_Do(t *testing.T) {
   // input
   carol := &User{
      Name:     "Carol",
      Password: "IamKing",
```

```
    }

    // mocks/stubs
    stubStorage := &StubUserStorage{}

    // do call
    saver := &Saver{
        storage: stubStorage,
    }
    resultErr := saver.Do(carol)

    // validate
    assert.NotEqual(t, resultErr, "unexpected error")
}
```

In the aforementioned test, there are no more data races on the global variable.

It's excellent for layering code—When applying dependency injection to an entire project, it is not uncommon to see a large swath of objects being created early on in the application's execution. For example, our minimal example service already has four objects being built in main(). Four might not sound like a lot, but we haven't applied DI to all our packages, and so far we only have three endpoints.

For our service, we have three layers of code, REST, business logic, and data. The relationships between the layers are straightforward. One object in the REST layer calls its partner object in the business logic layer, which in turns calls the data layer. Other than for testing, we are always injecting the same dependencies. Applying JIT injection would allow us to remove these dependencies from the constructors and make the code more comfortable to use.

Implementation cost is low—As we saw in the previous monkey patching example, applying JIT injection is very easy. Additionally, the changes are confined to a tiny area.

Similarly, applying JIT injection to code that does not already have any form of DI is also cheap. Consider the following code:

```
type Car struct {
    engine Engine
}

func (c *Car) Drive() {
    c.engine.Start()
    defer c.engine.Stop()

    c.engine.Drive()
}
```

If we decide to decouple `Car` from `Engine` then we will only need to define the abstracted interaction as an interface and then change all direct access to `c.engine` to use a `getter` function, as shown in the following code:

```go
type Car struct {
    engine Engine
}

func (c *Car) Drive() {
    engine := c.getEngine()

    engine.Start()
    defer engine.Stop()

    engine.Drive()
}

func (c *Car) getEngine() Engine {
    if c.engine == nil {
        c.engine = newEngine()
    }

    return c.engine
}
```

Consider what the process would have been to apply constructor injection. In what kinds of places would we have had to make changes?

Applying JIT injection

In previous sections, I alluded to the fact that JIT injection can be used with private and public dependencies, two very different use cases. In this section, we will apply both options to achieve very different results.

Private dependencies

There are many places we could improve our service by applying JIT injection. So, how do we decide? Let's see what our dependency graph has to say:

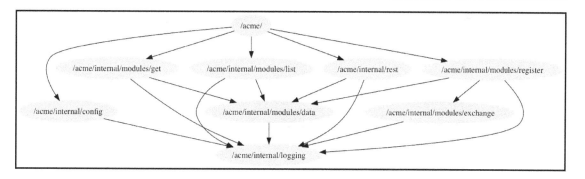

There are lots of connections going into the logging package. But we have already decoupled that a reasonable amount in Chapter 8, *Dependency Injection by Config*.

The next package with the most users is the data package. We worked on that back in Chapter 5, *Dependency Injection with Monkey Patching*, but maybe it's time to revisit it and see if we can improve it even more.

Before we decide, I will introduce you to another way to get a sense of the health of the code and where our efforts might be best spent: unit test coverage. Like the dependency graph, it cannot provide a definitive indicator, but only give you a hint.

Unit test coverage

In Go, test coverage is calculated by adding a -cover flag along with a call to a regular call to go test. As this only works for one package at a time, I find this inconvenient. So we are going to use a tool that recursively calculates test coverage for all the packages in a directory tree. This tool is called **package-coverage** and is available from GitHub (https:// github.com/corsc/go-tools/tree/master/package-coverage).

To calculate the coverage using package-coverage, we use the following commands:

```
$ cd $GOPATH/src/github.com/PacktPublishing/Hands-On-Dependency-Injection-
in-Go/ch08/

$ export ACME_CONFIG=$GOPATH/src/github.com/PacktPublishing/Hands-On-
Dependency-Injection-in-Go/config.json

$ package-coverage -a -prefix $(go list)/ ./acme/
```

Note: I have intentionally used the code from Chapter 8, *Dependency Injection by Config,* so the coverage numbers are before any changes we might make in this chapter.

This gives us the following:

```
-------------------------------------------------------------------------------
|    Branch      |       Dir        |                                         |
|  Cov%  | Stmts |  Cov%  | Stmts | Package                                   |
-------------------------------------------------------------------------------
|  65.66 |   265 |  0.00  |     7 | acme/                                     |
|  47.83 |    23 | 47.83  |    23 | acme/internal/config/                     |
|   0.00 |     4 |  0.00  |     4 | acme/internal/logging/                    |
|  73.77 |    61 | 73.77  |    61 | acme/internal/modules/data/               |
|  61.70 |    47 | 61.70  |    47 | acme/internal/modules/exchange/           |
|  85.71 |     7 | 85.71  |     7 | acme/internal/modules/get/                |
|  46.15 |    13 | 46.15  |    13 | acme/internal/modules/list/               |
|  62.07 |    29 | 62.07  |    29 | acme/internal/modules/register/           |
|  79.73 |    74 | 79.73  |    74 | acme/internal/rest/                       |
-------------------------------------------------------------------------------
```

So, what can we infer from these numbers?

1. The code coverage is reasonable. It could be better but other than the big fat 0 on the logging package, almost all the packages have 50% plus.
2. The statement (stmts) counts are interesting. Statements are roughly equivalent to *lines of code,* and therefore the numbers indicate which packages have more or less code. We can see that the rest, data, and exchange packages are the largest.
3. We can infer from the amount of code in a package that the more code a package has, the more responsibilities and more complexity it has. By extension, the more risk this package poses.

Given that the two largest, riskiest packages, rest and data, both have good test coverage, we still have nothing that indicates it needs urgent attention. But what happens if we consider the test coverage and dependency graph together?

Coverage and dependency graph

The dependency graph told us that the data package had lots of users. The test coverage told us that it was also one of the biggest packages we had. We can, therefore, infer that if we wanted to make improvements, this might be the right place to start.

As you may remember from earlier chapters, the data package uses functions and a global singleton pool, both of which caused us inconvenience. So, let's see if we can use JIT injection to get rid of these pain points.

Chasing away the monkeys

Here is how the get package currently uses the data package:

```
// Do will perform the get
func (g *Getter) Do(ID int) (*data.Person, error) {
   // load person from the data layer
   person, err := loader(context.TODO(), g.cfg, ID)
   if err != nil {
      if err == data.ErrNotFound {
         // By converting the error we are hiding the implementation
         // details from our users.
         return nil, errPersonNotFound
      }
      return nil, err
   }

   return person, err
}

// this function as a variable allows us to Monkey Patch during testing
var loader = data.Load
```

Our first change will be to define an interface that will replace our loader function:

```
//go:generate mockery -name=myLoader -case underscore -testonly -inpkg
type myLoader interface {
   Load(ctx context.Context, ID int) (*data.Person, error)
}
```

You may have noticed we dropped the config parameter. By the time we are done, we will not have to pass this in with every call. I have also added a go generate comment, which will create a mock that we will use later.

Next, we add this dependency as a private member variable and update our Do() method to use JIT injection:

```
// Do will perform the get
func (g *Getter) Do(ID int) (*data.Person, error) {
   // load person from the data layer
   person, err := g.getLoader().Load(context.TODO(), ID)
   if err != nil {
```

```
        if err == data.ErrNotFound {
            // By converting the error we are hiding the implementation
            // details from our users.
            return nil, errPersonNotFound
        }
        return nil, err
    }

    return person, err
}
```

But what will our JIT injection `getter` method look like? The basic structure will be standard, as shown in the following code:

```
func (g *Getter) getLoader() myLoader {
    if g.data == nil {
        // To be determined
    }

    return g.data
}
```

Because the `data` package was implemented as functions, we currently don't have anything that implements our `loader` interface. Our code and unit tests are now broken, so we are going to have to fly blind for a little bit while we get them working again.

The shortest path to getting our code working again is to define ourselves a **data access object** (**DAO**). This will replace the functions in our `data` package with a struct and give us something that implements our `myLoader` interface. To make the minimum number of changes, we will have the DAO methods call the existing functions as shown in the following code:

```
// NewDAO will initialize the database connection pool (if not already
// done) and return a data access object which can be used to interact
// with the database
func NewDAO(cfg Config) *DAO {
    // initialize the db connection pool
    _, _ = getDB(cfg)

    return &DAO{
        cfg: cfg,
    }
}

type DAO struct {
    cfg Config
}
```

```
// Load will attempt to load and return a person.
func (d *DAO) Load(ctx context.Context, ID int) (*Person, error) {
    return Load(ctx, d.cfg, ID)
}
```

Even after adding the DAO into our getLoader() function, our tests are still not restored. Our tests are still using monkey patching so we will need to remove that code and replace it with a mock, giving us the following:

```
func TestGetter_Do_happyPath(t *testing.T) {
    // inputs
    ID := 1234

    // configure the mock loader
    mockResult := &data.Person{
        ID:       1234,
        FullName: "Doug",
    }
    mockLoader := &mockMyLoader{}
    mockLoader.On("Load", mock.Anything, ID).Return(mockResult, nil).Once()

    // call method
    getter := &Getter{
        data: mockLoader,
    }
    person, err := getter.Do(ID)

    // validate expectations
    require.NoError(t, err)
    assert.Equal(t, ID, person.ID)
    assert.Equal(t, "Doug", person.FullName)
    assert.True(t, mockLoader.AssertExpectations(t))
}
```

Finally, our tests are working again. With these refactorings, we have also achieved a few other improvements:

- Our get package tests no longer use monkey patching; this means we can be sure there are no monkey patching related concurrency issues
- Other than the data struct (data.Person), the get package tests no longer use the data package
- Perhaps most significantly, the get package tests no longer require the database to be configured

With our planned changes to the get package complete, we can move over to the data package.

Earlier, we defined a DAO where our `Load()` method called the existing `Load()` function. As there are no more users of the `Load()` function, we can simply copy the code over and update the corresponding tests.

After repeating this simple process for the rest of the `data` package and its users, we are able to successfully migrate away from a function-based package to an object-based one.

Optional public dependencies

So far, we've applied JIT dependency injection to private dependencies with the goal of reducing the parameters and making our `data` package more straightforward to use.

There is another way to use JIT injection—optional public dependencies. These dependencies are public as we want users to be able to change them but we do not make them, part of the constructor because they are optional. Doing so would detract from the UX, especially in cases where the optional dependency is seldom used.

Imagine we were having a performance problem with the *Load all registrations* endpoint of our service and we suspected the problem was related to the responsiveness of the database.

Faced with such a problem, we decide that we need to track how long these queries took by adding some instrumentation. To ensure that we are able to turn this tracker on and off easily, we could make it an optional dependency.

Our first step would be to define our `tracker` interface:

```
// QueryTracker is an interface to track query timing
type QueryTracker interface {
    // Track will record/out the time a query took by calculating
    // time.Now().Sub(start)
    Track(key string, start time.Time)
}
```

We have a decision to make. The use of `QueryTracker` is optional, and this means that users are not guaranteed to have injected the dependency.

To avoid guard clauses wherever `QueryTracker` is used, we are going to introduce a NO-OP implementation that can be used when the user did not supply one. A NO-OP implementation, sometimes called a **null object**, is an object that implements an interface but where all the methods intentionally do nothing.

Here is the NO-OP implementation of `QueryTracker`:

```
// NO-OP implementation of QueryTracker
type noopTracker struct{}

// Track implements QueryTracker
func (_ *noopTracker) Track(_ string, _ time.Time) {
    // intentionally does nothing
}
```

Now, we can introduce it to our DAO as a public member variable:

```
// DAO is a data access object that provides an abstraction over
// our database interactions.
type DAO struct {
    cfg Config

    // Tracker is an optional query timer
    Tracker QueryTracker
}
```

And we can use JIT injection to access the tracker, which defaults to the NO-OP version:

```
func (d *DAO) getTracker() QueryTracker {
    if d.Tracker == nil {
        d.Tracker = &noopTracker{}
    }

    return d.Tracker
}
```

Now that everything is in place, we can add the following lines to the beginning of any method we want to track:

```
// track processing time
defer d.getTracker().Track("LoadAll", time.Now())
```

An interesting thing to note here is the use of `defer`. Basically, `defer` has two significant features that we are using here. Firstly, it will be called whenever the function exits, allowing us to add the tracker once, instead of next to every return statement. Secondly, the parameters of `defer` are determined at the time the line is encountered, and not the time they are executed. This means the value of `time.Now()` will be called at the start of the function we are tracking and not when the `Track()` function returns.

For our tracker to be of use, we need to provide an implementation other than the NO-OP. We could push these values to an external system like StatsD or Graphite, but for simplicity we will output the results to the log. The code for this is as follows:

```
// NewLogTracker returns a Tracker that outputs tracking data to log
func NewLogTracker(logger logging.Logger) *LogTracker {
    return &LogTracker{
        logger: logger,
    }
}

// LogTracker implements QueryTracker and outputs to the supplied logger
type LogTracker struct {
    logger logging.Logger
}

// Track implements QueryTracker
func (l *LogTracker) Track(key string, start time.Time) {
    l.logger.Info("[%s] Timing: %s\n", key, time.Now().Sub(start).String())
}
```

Now, we can temporarily update our DAO usage from this:

```
func (l *Lister) getLoader() myLoader {
    if l.data == nil {
        l.data = data.NewDAO(l.cfg)
    }

    return l.data
}
```

And update it to this:

```
func (l *Lister) getLoader() myLoader {
    if l.data == nil {
        l.data = data.NewDAO(l.cfg)

        // temporarily add a log tracker
        l.data.(*data.DAO).Tracker = data.NewLogTracker(l.cfg.Logger())
    }

    return l.data
}
```

Yes, the line is kind of ugly, but luckily it's only temporary. If we decided to make our QueryTracker permanent or found ourselves using it most of the time, then we could switch over to constructor injection pretty easily.

Disadvantages of JIT injection

While JIT injection can be handy, it cannot be used in all scenarios, and there are a few gotchas to be wary of. These include the following:

Can only be applied to static dependencies—The first and perhaps most significant disadvantage is that this method can only be applied to dependencies that only change during testing. We cannot use it to replace parameter injection or config injection. This is caused by the fact that dependency instantiation happens inside a private method and only on the first attempt to access the variable.

Dependency and user life cycles are not separated—When using constructor injection or parameter injection, it's often safe to assume the dependency being injected is fully initialized and ready for use. Any costs or delays, like those related to creating resource pools or preloading data, will have already been paid. With JIT injection, the dependency is created immediately before the first use. As such, any initialization cost has to be paid by that first request. The following diagram shows a typical interaction between three objects (a caller, a callee, and a data store):

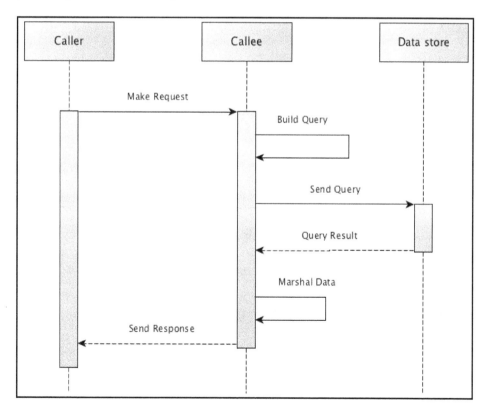

Now, compare that with the interaction when the data store object is created during the call:

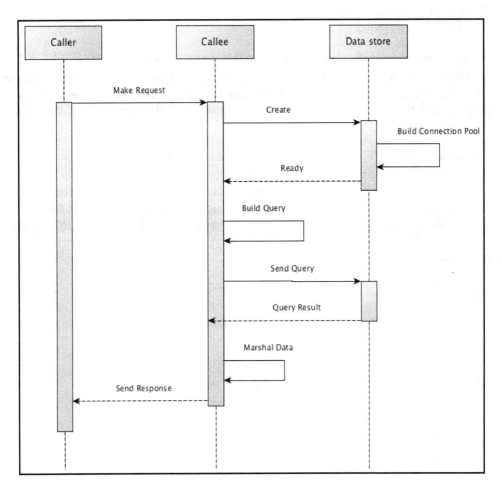

You can see the additional time (cost) that is incurred in the second diagram. These costs do not happen in most cases as creating objects in Go is fast. However, when they do exist, they can cause some unintended or inconvenient behavior during application startup.

Another downside in cases like the one previously mentioned, where the state of the dependency is uncertain, exists in the resulting code. Consider the following code:

```
func (l *Sender) Send(ctx context.Context, payload []byte) error {
    pool := l.getConnectionPool()

    // ensure pool is ready
```

```
select {
case <-pool.IsReady():
    // happy path

case <-ctx.Done():
    // context timed out or was cancelled
    return errors.New("failed to get connection")
}

// get connection from pool and return afterwards
conn := pool.Get()
defer l.connectionPool.Release(conn)

// send and return
_, err := conn.Write(payload)

return err
}
```

Compare the previous code with the same code where the dependency is guaranteed to be in a *ready* state:

```
func (l *Sender) Send(payload []byte) error {
    pool := l.getConnectionPool()

    // get connection from pool and return afterwards
    conn := pool.Get()
    defer l.connectionPool.Release(conn)

    // send and return
    _, err := conn.Write(payload)

    return err
}
```

This is only a few lines of code, sure, but it's vastly simpler to read and therefore maintain. It was also a lot easier to implement and test.

Potential data and initialization races—Similar to the previous point, this one also revolves around the initialization of the dependency. In this case, however, the issues are related to accessing the dependency itself. Let's return to our earlier example of a connection pool but change how the instantiation occurs:

```
func newConnectionPool() ConnectionPool {
    pool := &myConnectionPool{}

    // initialize the pool
```

```
    pool.init()

    // return a "ready to use pool"
    return pool
}
```

As you can see, this constructor of the connection pool will not return until after the pool is fully initialized. So, what happens when another call to the getConnectionPool() occurs while the initialization is happening?

We could end up creating two connection pools. This diagram shows this interaction:

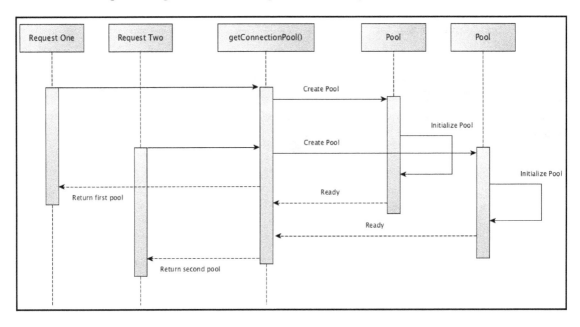

So, what happens to the other connection pool? It will be orphaned. All CPU spent on creating it is wasted, and it's even possible that it does not get cleaned up properly by the garbage collector; so any resources such as memory, file handles, or network ports could be lost.

There is a simple way to ensure that this issue is avoided but it comes with a very minor cost. We can use the sync package from the standard library. There are several nice options from this package, but in this case I recommend Once(). By adding Once() to our getConnectionPool() method, we get this:

```
func (l *Sender) getConnection() ConnectionPool {
    l.initPoolOnce.Do(func() {
        l.connectionPool = newConnectionPool()
    })

    return l.connectionPool
}
```

There are two minor costs associated with this approach. The first is the added complexity to the code; it's minor, but it does exist.

The second is that every call to getConnectionPool(), of which there could be many, will check Once() to see whether it is the first call. This is an incredibly small cost, but, depending on your performance requirements, it could be inconvenient.

Objects are not entirely decoupled—Throughout this book, we've used the dependency graph to identify potential issues, particularly regarding the relationships between packages, and in some cases the over-dependence on particular packages. While we can and should still use the *Dependency inversion principle* section from Chapter 2, *SOLID Design Principles for Go*, and define our dependency as a local interface, by including the dependency's creation in our code, the dependency graph will still show the relationship between our package and the dependency. In a way, our object is still somewhat coupled to our dependency.

Summary

In this chapter, we used JIT injection, a somewhat unusual DI method, to remove some of the monkey patching from earlier chapters.

We also used a different form of JIT injection to add an optional dependency, without detracting from the UX of our code.

Additionally, we examined how JIT injection can also be used to reduce test-induced damage, without sacrificing our ability to use mocks and stubs in our tests.

In the next chapter, we will examine the last DI method in the book, off-the-shelf injection. We will discuss the general advantages and disadvantages of adopting a DI framework, and for our examples we will use Google's Wire framework.

Questions

1. How does JIT injection differ from constructor injection?
2. When working with optional dependencies, why is using a NO-OP implementation important?
3. What are the ideal use cases for JIT injection?

10
Off-the-Shelf Injection

For our final chapter in this section, we are looking at **dependency injection** (**DI**) using a framework. Choosing a DI framework that matches your preferred style can make your life significantly easier. Even if you prefer not to use a framework, examining how it is implemented and the approach it takes can be informative and help you find improvements for your preferred implementation.

While there are many frameworks available to us, including Facebook's Inject (`https://github.com/facebookgo/inject`) and Uber's Dig (`https://godoc.org/go.uber.org/dig`), for our sample service we are going to use Google's Go Cloud Wire (`https://github.com/google/go-cloud/tree/master/wire`).

The following topics will be covered in this chapter:

- Off-the-shelf injection with Wire
- Advantages of off-the-shelf injection
- Applying off-the-shelf injection
- Disadvantages of off-the-shelf injection

Technical requirements

It would be beneficial to be familiar with the code for our service, which we introduced in `Chapter 4`, *Introduction to the ACME Registration Service*. This chapter also assumes that you have read `Chapter 6`, *Dependency Injection with Constructor Injection*.

You might also find it useful to read and run the full versions of the code for this chapter, which is available at `https://github.com/PacktPublishing/Hands-On-Dependency-Injection-in-Go/tree/master/ch10`.

Instructions to obtain the code and configure the sample service are available in the README here: `https://github.com/PacktPublishing/Hands-On-Dependency-Injection-in-Go/`.

You can find the code for our service, with the changes from this chapter already applied, in ch10/acme.

Off-the-shelf injection with Wire

The Go Cloud project is an initiative that intends to make it easier for application developers to deploy cloud applications on any combination of cloud providers seamlessly. The integral part of this project is a code generation-based dependency injection tool called **Wire**.

Wire is a good fit for our example service as it promotes the use of explicit instantiation and discourages the use of global variables; just as we attempted to achieve in our refactoring in previous chapters. Additionally, Wire uses code generation to avoid any performance penalties or code complexity that can result from the use of runtime reflection.

Perhaps the most useful aspect of Wire for us is its simplicity. After we understand a few simple concepts, the code we have to write and the code that is generated is reasonably straightforward.

Introducing providers

The documentation defines a provider as follows:

> *"A function that can produce a value."*

For our purposes, we can put it a different way—a provider returns an instance of a dependency.

The simplest form a provider can take is a *simple no argument function,* as shown in the following code:

```
// Provider
func ProvideFetcher() *Fetcher {
    return &Fetcher{}
}

// Object being "provided"
type Fetcher struct {
}

func (f *Fetcher) GoFetch() (string, error) {
```

```
return "", errors.New("not implemented yet")
}
```

Providers can also indicate that they require dependencies to be injected by having parameters like this:

```
func ProvideFetcher(cache *Cache) *Fetcher {
    return &Fetcher{
        cache: cache,
    }
}
```

The dependencies (parameters) of this provider must be provided by other providers.

Providers can also indicate that they may fail to initialize by returning an error, as shown in the following code:

```
func ProvideCache() (*Cache, error) {
    cache := &Cache{}

    err := cache.Start()
    if err != nil {
        return nil, err
    }

    return cache, nil
}
```

It is important to note that when a provider returns an error, any injector that uses the dependency provided must also return an error.

Understanding injectors

The second concept integral to Wire is injectors. Injectors are where the magic happens. They are functions that we (developers) define that Wire uses as a base for its code generation.

For example, if we want to have a function that can create an instance of our service's REST server, including initializing and injecting all the required dependencies, we can achieve this with the following function:

```
func initializeServer() (*rest.Server, error) {
    wire.Build(wireSet)
    return nil, nil
}
```

That probably feels like a big sell for such a simple function, especially as it does not seem to do anything (that is, `returns nil, nil`). But that is all we need to write; the code generator will turn it into the following:

```
func initializeServer() (*rest.Server, error) {
    configConfig, err := config.Load()
    if err != nil {
        return nil, err
    }
    getter := get.NewGetter(configConfig)
    lister := list.NewLister(configConfig)
    converter := exchange.NewConverter(configConfig)
    registerer := register.NewRegisterer(configConfig, converter)
    server := rest.New(configConfig, getter, lister, registerer)
    return server, nil
}
```

We will go into this in more detail in the *Applying* section, but for now there are three features of the aforementioned function to remember. Firstly, the generator does not care about the implementation of the function, except that the function must include a `wire.Build(wireSet)` call. Secondly, the function must return the concrete type that we are planning to use. And lastly, if we rely on any providers that return an error, then the injector must also return an error.

Adopting provider sets

The last concept that we need to know when using Wire is provider sets. Provider sets offer a way to group providers, and this can be helpful when writing injectors. Their use is optional; for example, earlier we used a provider set called `wireSet`, as shown in the following code:

```
func initializeServer() (*rest.Server, error) {
    wire.Build(wireSet)
    return nil, nil
}
```

However, we could have passed in all the providers individually, as shown in the following code:

```
func initializeServer() (*rest.Server, error) {
    wire.Build(
        // *config.Config
        config.Load,

        // *exchange.Converter
```

```
        wire.Bind(new(exchange.Config), &config.Config{}),
        exchange.NewConverter,

        // *get.Getter
        wire.Bind(new(get.Config), &config.Config{}),
        get.NewGetter,

        // *list.Lister
        wire.Bind(new(list.Config), &config.Config{}),
        list.NewLister,

        // *register.Registerer
        wire.Bind(new(register.Config), &config.Config{}),
        wire.Bind(new(register.Exchanger), &exchange.Converter{}),
        register.NewRegisterer,

        // *rest.Server
        wire.Bind(new(rest.Config), &config.Config{}),
        wire.Bind(new(rest.GetModel), &get.Getter{}),
        wire.Bind(new(rest.ListModel), &list.Lister{}),
        wire.Bind(new(rest.RegisterModel), &register.Registerer{}),
        rest.New,
    )

    return nil, nil
}
```

Sadly, the previous example is not contrived. It's taken from our small example service.

As you might expect, there are plenty more features in Wire, but at this point we have covered enough to get us started.

Advantages of off-the-shelf injection

While we have been talking specifically about Wire so far in this chapter, I would like to take a moment to discuss the advantages of off-the-shelf injection in a more general sense. When evaluating a tool or framework, it's essential to cast a critical eye over the advantages, disadvantages, and effects on your code that it may have.

Some of the possible advantages of off-the-shelf injection include the following.

A reduction in boilerplate code—After applying constructor injection to a program, it's common that the `main()` function becomes bloated with the instantiation of objects. As the project grows, so does `main()`. While this does not impact the performance of the program, it does become inconvenient to maintain.

Many dependency injection frameworks aim to either remove this code or move it elsewhere. As we will see, this is `main()` for our sample service before adopting Google Wire:

```
func main() {
    // bind stop channel to context
    ctx := context.Background()

    // build the exchanger
    exchanger := exchange.NewConverter(config.App)

    // build model layer
    getModel := get.NewGetter(config.App)
    listModel := list.NewLister(config.App)
    registerModel := register.NewRegisterer(config.App, exchanger)

    // start REST server
    server := rest.New(config.App, getModel, listModel, registerModel)
    server.Listen(ctx.Done())
}
```

And this is `main()` after adopting Google Wire:

```
func main() {
    // bind stop channel to context
    ctx := context.Background()

    // start REST server
    server, err := initializeServer()
    if err != nil {
        os.Exit(-1)
    }

    server.Listen(ctx.Done())
}
```

And all of the related objection creation is reduced to this:

```
func initializeServer() (*rest.Server, error) {
    wire.Build(wireSet)
    return nil, nil
}
```

Because Wire is a code generator, we actually end up with more code, but less of it was written or maintained by us. Similarly, if we were to use another popular DI framework called **Dig**, `main()` would become this:

```
func main() {
   // bind stop channel to context
   ctx := context.Background()

   // build DIG container
   container := BuildContainer()

   // start REST server
   err := container.Invoke(func(server *rest.Server) {
      server.Listen(ctx.Done())
   })

   if err != nil {
      os.Exit(-1)
   }
}
```

As you can see, we gain a similar reduction in code.

Automatic instantiation order—Similar to the previous point, as the project grows, so does the complexity of the ordering in which dependencies must be created. As such, much of the *magic* provided by off-the-shelf injection frameworks is focused on removing this complexity. In both the cases of Wire and Dig, providers explicitly define their direct dependencies and ignore any requirements of their dependencies.

Consider the following example. Let's say we have an HTTP handler like this:

```
func NewGetPersonHandler(model *GetPersonModel) *GetPersonHandler {
   return &GetPersonHandler{
      model: model,
   }
}

type GetPersonHandler struct {
   model *GetPersonModel
}

func (g *GetPersonHandler) ServeHTTP(response http.ResponseWriter, request
*http.Request) {
   response.WriteHeader(http.StatusInternalServerError)
   response.Write([]byte(`not implemented yet`))
}
```

As you can see, the handler depends on a model, which looks as shown in the following code:

```
func NewGetPersonModel(db *sql.DB) *GetPersonModel {
    return &GetPersonModel{
        db: db,
    }
}

type GetPersonModel struct {
    db *sql.DB
}

func (g *GetPersonModel) LoadByID(ID int) (*Person, error) {
    return nil, errors.New("not implemented yet")
}

type Person struct {
    Name string
}
```

This model depends on `*sql.DB`. However, when we define the provider for our handler, it defines only that it requires `*GetPersonModel` and has no knowledge of `*sql.DB`, like this:

```
func ProvideHandler(model *GetPersonModel) *GetPersonHandler {
    return &GetPersonHandler{
        model: model,
    }
}
```

Compared to the alternative of creating the database, injecting it into a model, and then injecting the model into the handler, this is much simpler both to write and maintain.

Someone has already done the thinking for you—Perhaps the least obvious but most important advantage a good DI framework can offer is the knowledge of its creators. The act of creating and maintaining a framework is definitely a non-trivial exercise, and it teaches its authors far more about DI than most programmers need to know. This knowledge often results in subtle but useful features appearing in the framework. For example, in the Dig framework, by default, all dependencies are singletons. This design choice results in performance and resource usage improvements as well as a more predictable dependency life cycle.

Applying off-the-shelf injection

As I mentioned in the previous section, by adopting Wire we are hoping to see a significant reduction in the code and complexity in `main()`. We are also hoping to be able to essentially forget about the instantiation order of the dependencies by leaving the framework to handle it for us.

Adopting Google Wire

The first thing we need to do, however, is to get our house in order. Most, if not all, of the objects we are going to let Wire handle use our `*config.Config` object, and currently it exists as a global singleton, as shown in the following code:

```
// App is the application config
var App *Config

// Load returns the config loaded from environment
func init() {
    filename, found := os.LookupEnv(DefaultEnvVar)
    if !found {
        logging.L.Error("failed to locate file specified by %s",
DefaultEnvVar)
        return
    }

    _ = load(filename)
}

func load(filename string) error {
    App = &Config{}
    bytes, err := ioutil.ReadFile(filename)
    if err != nil {
        logging.L.Error("failed to read config file. err: %s", err)
        return err
    }

    err = json.Unmarshal(bytes, App)
    if err != nil {
        logging.L.Error("failed to parse config file. err : %s", err)
        return err
    }

    return nil
}
```

To change this to a form that Wire can use, we need to delete the global instance and change the config loading to a function instead of being triggered by `init()`.

After a quick look at the uses of our global singleton, it shows that only `main()` and a few tests in the `config` package refer to the singleton. Thanks to all our previous work, this change is going to be rather straightforward. Here is the config loader after refactoring:

```go
// Load returns the config loaded from environment
func Load() (*Config, error) {
    filename, found := os.LookupEnv(DefaultEnvVar)
    if !found {
        err := fmt.Errorf("failed to locate file specified by %s",
DefaultEnvVar)
        logging.L.Error(err.Error())
        return nil, err
    }

    cfg, err := load(filename)
    if err != nil {
        logging.L.Error("failed to load config with err %s", err)
        return nil, err
    }

    return cfg, nil
}
```

And here is our updated `main()`:

```go
func main() {
    // bind stop channel to context
    ctx := context.Background()

    // load config
    cfg, err := config.Load(config.DefaultEnvVar)
    if err != nil {
        os.Exit(-1)
    }

    // build the exchanger
    exchanger := exchange.NewConverter(cfg)

    // build model layer
    getModel := get.NewGetter(cfg)
    listModel := list.NewLister(cfg)
    registerModel := register.NewRegisterer(cfg, exchanger)

    // start REST server
```

```
    server := rest.New(cfg, getModel, listModel, registerModel)
    server.Listen(ctx.Done())
}
```

Now that we have removed the config global, we are ready to start adopting Google Wire.

We are going to start by adding a new file; we are naming it `wire.go`. It can be called anything, but we need a separate file because we are going to use Go build tags to separate the code we write in this file from the version generated by Wire.

In case you are not familiar with build tags, in Go they are comments at the top of the file, before the `package` statement, in this form:

```
//+build myTag

package main
```

These tags tell the compiler when or when not to include the file during compilation. For example, the aforementioned tag tells the compiler to include this file only when the build is triggered, like this:

$ go build -tags myTag

We can also use build tags to do the reverse and make a file that is only included when the tag is not specified, like this:

```
//+build !myTag

package main
```

Back to `wire.go`, inside this file we are going to define an injector for the config that uses our config loader as a provider, as shown in the following code:

```
//+build wireinject

package main

import (
    "github.com/PacktPublishing/Hands-On-Dependency-Injection-in-
Go/ch10/acme/internal/config"
    "github.com/google/go-cloud/wire"
)

// The build tag makes sure the stub is not built in the final build.

func initializeConfig() (*config.Config, error) {
    wire.Build(config.Load)
```

```
        return nil, nil
    }
```

Let's break down the injector a little more. The function signature defines a function that returns an instance of `*config.Config` or an error, which is the same as `config.Load()` from earlier.

The first line of the function calls `wire.Build()` and supplies our provider, and the second line returns `nil, nil`. In truth, it does not matter what it returns as long as it is valid Go code. The code generator in Wire will read the function signature and the `wire.Build()` call only.

Next, we open a Terminal and run `wire` in the directory that contains our `wire.go` file. Wire will create a new file for us called `wire_gen.go`, which looks as shown in the following code:

```
// Code generated by Wire. DO NOT EDIT.

//go:generate wire
//+build !wireinject

package main

import (
    "github.com/PacktPublishing/Hands-On-Dependency-Injection-in-
Go/ch10/acme/internal/config"
)

// Injectors from wire.go:

func initializeConfig() (*config.Config, error) {
    configConfig, err := config.Load()
    if err != nil {
        return nil, err
    }
    return configConfig, nil
}
```

You will notice that this file also has a build tag, but it is the opposite of the one that we wrote earlier. Wire has copied our `initializeConfig()` method and *filled in all the details* for us.

So far, the code is pretty simple and likely to be very similar to what we could have written ourselves. You might be tempted to feel like we have not really gained much so far. I agree. By the time we convert the rest of our objects over, the amount of code and complexity Wire will take care of for us will be significantly more.

To complete this set of changes, we update `main()` to use our `initializeConfig()` function like so:

```
func main() {
    // bind stop channel to context
    ctx := context.Background()

    // load config
    cfg, err := initializeConfig()
    if err != nil {
        os.Exit(-1)
    }

    // build the exchanger
    exchanger := exchange.NewConverter(cfg)

    // build model layer
    getModel := get.NewGetter(cfg)
    listModel := list.NewLister(cfg)
    registerModel := register.NewRegisterer(cfg, exchanger)

    // start REST server
    server := rest.New(cfg, getModel, listModel, registerModel)
    server.Listen(ctx.Done())
}
```

With config handled, we can move on to the next object, `*exchange.Converter`. In the previous examples, we did not use a provider set but instead passed our provider directly into the `wire.Build()` call. We are about to add another provider so now it's time to get a little more organized. We will, therefore, add a private global variable to `main.go` and add our `Config` and `Converter` providers to it, as shown in the following code:

```
// List of wire enabled objects
var wireSet = wire.NewSet(
    // *config.Config
    config.Load,

    // *exchange.Converter
    wire.Bind(new(exchange.Config), &config.Config{}),
    exchange.NewConverter,
)
```

As you can see, I have also added a `wire.Bind()` call. Wire requires us to define or map the concrete types that satisfy an interface so that it is able to satisfy them during injection. The constructor for `*exchange.Converter` looks like this:

```
// NewConverter creates and initializes the converter
func NewConverter(cfg Config) *Converter {
    return &Converter{
        cfg: cfg,
    }
}
```

As you might remember, this constructor uses config injection and a locally defined `Config` interface. However, the actual config object that we inject is `*config.Config`. Our `wire.Bind()` call tells Wire that where the `exchange.Config` interface is needed use `*config.Config`.

With our provider set in place, we can now update our config injector and add an injector for the `Converter` as shown in the following code:

```
func initializeConfig() (*config.Config, error) {
    wire.Build(wireSet)
    return nil, nil
}

func initializeExchanger() (*exchange.Converter, error) {
    wire.Build(wireSet)
    return nil, nil
}
```

It is important to note that while `exchange.NewConverter()` does not return an error, our injector must. This is because of our dependence on the config provider, which returns an error. This may sound like a pain to remember but don't worry, Wire helps us get it right.

Moving on down our list of objects, we will need to do the same for our model layer. The injectors are entirely predictable and almost identical to `*exchange.Converter`, as are the changes to our provider set.

Note that `main()` and the provider set after the changes look as shown in the following code:

```
func main() {
    // bind stop channel to context
    ctx := context.Background()

    // load config
    cfg, err := initializeConfig()
```

```
    if err != nil {
        os.Exit(-1)
    }

    // build model layer
    getModel, _ := initializeGetter()
    listModel, _ := initializeLister()
    registerModel, _ := initializeRegisterer()

    // start REST server
    server := rest.New(cfg, getModel, listModel, registerModel)
    server.Listen(ctx.Done())
}

// List of wire enabled objects
var wireSet = wire.NewSet(
    // *config.Config
    config.Load,

    // *exchange.Converter
    wire.Bind(new(exchange.Config), &config.Config{}),
    exchange.NewConverter,

    // *get.Getter
    wire.Bind(new(get.Config), &config.Config{}),
    get.NewGetter,

    // *list.Lister
    wire.Bind(new(list.Config), &config.Config{}),
    list.NewLister,

    // *register.Registerer
    wire.Bind(new(register.Config), &config.Config{}),
    wire.Bind(new(register.Exchanger), &exchange.Converter{}),
    register.NewRegisterer,
)
```

There are a couple of things of importance. Firstly, our provider set is getting rather long. This is probably OK, as the only changes we are making are to add more provider and bind statements.

Secondly, we no longer call `initializeExchanger()`, and we have actually deleted that injector. The reason we don't need this anymore is Wire is handling the injection into the model layer for us.

Lastly, for brevity, I have ignored the errors that could be returned from the model layer injectors. This is a bad practice, but don't worry, we will be deleting these lines soon after our next set of changes.

After a quick run of Wire and our tests to make sure everything is still working as expected, we are ready to move on to our final object, the REST server.

First, we make the following, perhaps predictable, additions to the provider set:

```
// List of wire enabled objects
var wireSet = wire.NewSet(
    // lines omitted

    // *rest.Server
    wire.Bind(new(rest.Config), &config.Config{}),
    wire.Bind(new(rest.GetModel), &get.Getter{}),
    wire.Bind(new(rest.ListModel), &list.Lister{}),
    wire.Bind(new(rest.RegisterModel), &register.Registerer{}),
    rest.New,
)
```

After that, we define the injector for our REST server in `wire.go` like this:

```
func initializeServer() (*rest.Server, error) {
    wire.Build(wireSet)
    return nil, nil
}
```

Now, we can update `main()` to call only the REST server injector like so:

```
func main() {
    // bind stop channel to context
    ctx := context.Background()

    // start REST server
    server, err := initializeServer()
    if err != nil {
        os.Exit(-1)
    }

    server.Listen(ctx.Done())
}
```

With that done, we can delete all of the injectors except `initializeServer()`, then run Wire, and we are done!

Now might be a good time to examine the code that Wire generated for us:

```
func initializeServer() (*rest.Server, error) {
    configConfig, err := config.Load()
    if err != nil {
        return nil, err
    }
    getter := get.NewGetter(configConfig)
    lister := list.NewLister(configConfig)
    converter := exchange.NewConverter(configConfig)
    registerer := register.NewRegisterer(configConfig, converter)
    server := rest.New(configConfig, getter, lister, registerer)
    return server, nil
}
```

Does it look familiar? It's incredibly similar to main() before we adopted wire.

Given that our code was already using constructor injection and our service is rather small, it's easy to feel like we did a lot of work for minimal gain. If we were adopting Wire from the start, this would definitely not feel this way. In our particular case, the benefits are more long term. Now that Wire is handling the constructor injection and all the complexity related to instantiation and instantiation ordering, all extensions to our service will be a whole lot simpler and less prone to human error.

API regression tests

With our conversion to Wire complete, how do we make sure our service still works as we expect?

Our only immediate option is to just run the app and try it. This option might be OK for right now, but I don't like it as a long-term option, so let's see if we can add some automated tests.

The first question we should be asking ourselves is *what are we testing?* We should not need to test Wire itself, we can trust the tool authors to do that. In what other ways can things go wrong?

A typical answer would be our use of Wire. If we had misconfigured Wire, it would have failed to generate, so that is covered. That leaves us with the app itself.

To test the app, we need to run it and then make an HTTP call into it, and then validate the response is as we expected.

The first thing we need to consider is how to start the app, and, perhaps more importantly, how to do it in a way that we can have multiple tests running at the same time.

At the moment, our config (database connection, HTTP port, and so on) are hardcoded in a file on the disk. We could use that, but it includes a fixed HTTP server port. On the other hand, hardcoding database credentials in our tests is way worse.

Let's use a middle ground. First, let's load the standard `config` file:

```
// load the standard config (from the ENV)
cfg, err := config.Load()
require.NoError(t, err)
```

Now, let's find a free TCP port to which we can bind our server. We can use port 0 and allow the system to assign one automatically, as shown in the following code:

```
func getFreePort() (string, error) {
    for attempt := 0; attempt <= 10; attempt++ {
        addr := net.JoinHostPort("", "0")
        listener, err := net.Listen("tcp", addr)
        if err != nil {
            continue
        }

        port, err := getPort(listener.Addr())
        if err != nil {
            continue
        }

        // close/free the port
        tcpListener := listener.(*net.TCPListener)
        cErr := tcpListener.Close()
        if cErr == nil {
            file, fErr := tcpListener.File()
            if fErr == nil {
                // ignore any errors cleaning up the file
                _ = file.Close()
            }
            return port, nil
        }
    }

    return "", errors.New("no free ports")
}
```

We can now use that free port and replace the address in the `config` file with one that uses the free port like so:

```
// get a free port (so tests can run concurrently)
port, err := getFreePort()
require.NoError(t, err)

// override config port with free one
cfg.Address = net.JoinHostPort("0.0.0.0", port)
```

And now we are stuck. Currently, to create an instance of the server, the code looks like this:

```
// start REST server
server, err := initializeServer()
if err != nil {
    os.Exit(-1)
}

server.Listen(ctx.Done())
```

The config is automatically injected, no chance for us to use our custom config. Thankfully, Wire can help with this too.

To be able to inject the config in our tests manually, but not modify `main()`, we need to split our provider set into two parts. The first part is all the dependencies except config:

```
var wireSetWithoutConfig = wire.NewSet(
    // *exchange.Converter
    exchange.NewConverter,

    // *get.Getter
    get.NewGetter,

    // *list.Lister
    list.NewLister,

    // *register.Registerer
    wire.Bind(new(register.Exchanger), &exchange.Converter{}),
    register.NewRegisterer,

    // *rest.Server
    wire.Bind(new(rest.GetModel), &get.Getter{}),
    wire.Bind(new(rest.ListModel), &list.Lister{}),
    wire.Bind(new(rest.RegisterModel), &register.Registerer{}),
    rest.New,
)
```

And the second includes the first and then adds the config and all the related bindings:

```
var wireSet = wire.NewSet(
    wireSetWithoutConfig,

    // *config.Config
    config.Load,

    // *exchange.Converter
    wire.Bind(new(exchange.Config), &config.Config{}),

    // *get.Getter
    wire.Bind(new(get.Config), &config.Config{}),

    // *list.Lister
    wire.Bind(new(list.Config), &config.Config{}),

    // *register.Registerer
    wire.Bind(new(register.Config), &config.Config{}),

    // *rest.Server
    wire.Bind(new(rest.Config), &config.Config{}),
)
```

The next step is to create an injector that takes config as a parameter. In our case, it's a little bit weird as this is caused by our config injection, but it looks like this:

```
func initializeServerCustomConfig(_ exchange.Config, _ get.Config, _
list.Config, _ register.Config, _ rest.Config) *rest.Server {
    wire.Build(wireSetWithoutConfig)
    return nil
}
```

After running Wire, we can now start our test server, as shown in the following code:

```
// start the test server on a random port
go func() {
    // start REST server
    server := initializeServerCustomConfig(cfg, cfg, cfg, cfg, cfg)
    server.Listen(ctx.Done())
}()
```

Putting all of it together, we now have a function that creates a server on a random port and returns the address of the server, so that our test knows where to call. Here is the completed function:

```
func startTestServer(t *testing.T, ctx context.Context) string {
    // load the standard config (from the ENV)
    cfg, err := config.Load()
    require.NoError(t, err)

    // get a free port (so tests can run concurrently)
    port, err := getFreePort()
    require.NoError(t, err)

    // override config port with free one
    cfg.Address = net.JoinHostPort("0.0.0.0", port)

    // start the test server on a random port
    go func() {
        // start REST server
        server := initializeServerCustomConfig(cfg, cfg, cfg, cfg, cfg)
        server.Listen(ctx.Done())
    }()

    // give the server a chance to start
    <-time.After(100 * time.Millisecond)

    // return the address of the test server
    return "http://" + cfg.Address
}
```

Now, let's look at a test. Again, we are going to use the register endpoint as an example. Firstly, our test needs to start a test server. In the following example, you will also notice that we are defining a context with a timeout. When the context is done, via timeout or being canceled, the test server will shut down; therefore, this timeout becomes the *maximum execution time* of our test. Here is the code to start the server:

```
// start a context with a max execution time
ctx, cancel := context.WithTimeout(context.Background(), 5*time.Second)
defer cancel()

// start test server
serverAddress := startTestServer(t, ctx)
```

Next, we need to build and send the request. In this case, we've chosen to hardcode the payload and the URL. This might seem strange, but it's actually somewhat helpful. If the payload or the URL, both of which constitute the API of our service, were to change accidentally, these tests would break. Consider, on the other hand, if for the URL we used a constant that was also used to configure the server. If that constant was changed, the API would change and would break our users. Same goes for the payload, we could use the same Go object that is used internally, but changes there would also not cause the test to break.

Yes, this duplication is more work and does make the tests more brittle, both of which are not good, but it's better for our tests to break than for us to break our users.

The code to build and send the request is as follows:

```
    // build and send request
    payload := bytes.NewBufferString(`
{
    "fullName": "Bob",
    "phone": "0123456789",
    "currency": "AUD"
}
`)

    req, err := http.NewRequest("POST", serverAddress+"/person/register",
payload)
    require.NoError(t, err)

    resp, err := http.DefaultClient.Do(req)
    require.NoError(t, err)
```

Now all that is left is to validate the results. After putting it all together, we have this:

```
func TestRegister(t *testing.T) {
    // start a context with a max execution time
    ctx, cancel := context.WithTimeout(context.Background(), 5*time.Second)
    defer cancel()

    // start test server
    serverAddress := startTestServer(t, ctx)

    // build and send request
    payload := bytes.NewBufferString(`
{
    "fullName": "Bob",
    "phone": "0123456789",
    "currency": "AUD"
}
```

```
`)

    req, err := http.NewRequest("POST", serverAddress+"/person/register",
payload)
    require.NoError(t, err)

    resp, err := http.DefaultClient.Do(req)
    require.NoError(t, err)

    // validate expectations
    assert.Equal(t, http.StatusCreated, resp.StatusCode)
    assert.NotEmpty(t, resp.Header.Get("Location"))
}
```

That's it. We now have an automated test that ensures our app starts, can be called, and responds as we expect. If you are interested, there are tests for the other two endpoints in the code for this chapter.

Disadvantages of off-the-shelf injection

As much as framework authors would love for their work to be a silver bullet, solving all the world's DI problems, this is sadly not the case; there are some costs associated with adopting a framework and reasons that you may choose not to use one. These include the following.

Only supports constructor injection—You may have noticed in this chapter that all of the examples used constructor injection. This is not by accident. Wire, like many frameworks, only supports constructor injection. We did not have to remove our use of other DI methods, but the framework is unable to assist us with it.

Adoption can be costly—As you saw in the previous section, the end result of adopting a framework can be rather good, but our service is small and we were already using DI. If either of these things were not true, we would have been in for a lot more refactoring work. And as we have discussed before, the more changes we make, the more risk we incur.

These costs and this risk can be mitigated with prior experience with the framework and by adopting the framework from early in the project.

Ideological issues—This is not a disadvantage per se but more a reason you might not want to adopt a framework. In the Go community, you will come across a sentiment that frameworks are *not idiomatic* or *in-line with Go's philosophy*. While there has been no official statement or documentation that I could find to support this, I believe this is based on the fact that Go's creators were fans and authors of the Unix philosophy, which states *do trivial things in isolation and then compose to make things useful*.

Frameworks can be seen to violate this ideology, especially if they become a pervasive part of the system as a whole. The frameworks we have mentioned in this chapter have a relatively small scope; so as with everything else, I will leave you to make your own call.

Summary

In this chapter, we discussed using a DI framework in an attempt to lighten the burden of managing and injecting dependencies. We have discussed the advantages and disadvantages commonly found in DI frameworks and applied Google's Wire framework to our sample service.

This was the last DI method we will be discussing, and, in the next chapter, we will be taking a completely different tact and looking at reasons not to use DI. We will also be looking at situations where applying DI actually makes the code worse.

Questions

1. When adopting a DI framework, what can you expect to gain?
2. When evaluating a DI framework, what kinds of issues should you being looking out for?
3. What are the ideal use cases for adopting off-the-shelf injection?
4. Why is it important to protect your service from accidental API changes?

11
Curb Your Enthusiasm

In this chapter, we will examine some of the ways **dependency injection** (**DI**) can go wrong.

As programmers, our enthusiasm towards a new tool or technique can sometimes get the better of us. Hopefully, this chapter will help to ground us and keep us out of trouble.

It's important to remember that DI is a tool and, as such, it should be applied selectively, when it's convenient, and when it's the right tool for the job.

The following topics will be covered in this chapter:

- DI induced damage
- Premature future-proofing
- Mocking HTTP requests
- Unnecessary injection?

Technical requirements

You might also find it useful to read and run the full versions of the code for this chapter, which are available at https://github.com/PacktPublishing/Hands-On-Dependency-Injection-in-Go/tree/master/ch11.

DI induced damage

DI induced damage results from situations where the use of DI makes the code harder to understand, maintain, or otherwise use.

A long constructor parameter list

A long constructor parameter list is perhaps the most common and most often complained about code damage caused by DI. While DI is not the root cause of code damage, it certainly doesn't help.

Consider the following example, which uses constructor injection:

```
func NewMyHandler(logger Logger, stats Instrumentation,
    parser Parser, formatter Formatter,
    limiter RateLimiter,
    cache Cache, db Datastore) *MyHandler {

    return &MyHandler{
        // code removed
    }
}

// MyHandler does something fantastic
type MyHandler struct {
    // code removed
}

func (m *MyHandler) ServeHTTP(response http.ResponseWriter, request
*http.Request) {
    // code removed
}
```

The constructor simply has too many parameters. This makes it unwieldy to use, test, and maintain. So, what is the cause of the problem here? There are actually three different issues.

The first and, perhaps, most common when adopting DI for the first time is incorrect abstractions. Consider the last two parameters of the constructor are `Cache` and `Datastore`. Assuming that the `cache` is used in front of the `datastore` and not to cache the output of `MyHandler`, then these should be combined into a different abstraction. The `MyHandler` code does not need to be intimately aware of where and how the data is stored; it only needs to be prescriptive about what it needs. We should replace these two input values with a more generic abstraction, as shown in the following code:

```
// Loader is responsible for loading the data
type Loader interface {
    Load(ID int) ([]byte, error)
}
```

Incidentally, this would also be a great place for another package/layer.

The second issue is similar to the first, a single responsibility principle violation. Our `MyHandler` has taken on too much responsibility. It is currently decoding the request, loading the data from the datastore and/or cache, and then rendering the response. The best way to address this is to think about the software's layers. The is the top layer, our HTTP handler; it is required to understand and speak HTTP. We, therefore, should look for ways to have that as its primary (and perhaps only) responsibility.

The third problem are the cross-cutting concerns. Our parameters include logging and instrumentation dependencies, which are likely to be used by most of our code and seldom changed outside of a few tests. We have a few options to deal with this; we could apply config injection, thereby collapsing them into one dependency and merging them with any config we might have. Or we could use **just-in-time** (**JIT**) injection to access global singletons.

In this case, we have decided to go with config injection. After applying it, we are left with the following code:

```
func NewMyHandler(config Config,
    parser Parser, formatter Formatter,
    limiter RateLimiter,
    loader Loader) *MyHandler {

    return &MyHandler{
        // code removed
    }
}
```

We are still left with five parameters, which is far better than what we started with, but still rather a lot.

We can reduce this even further using composition. Firstly, let's look at our previous example's constructor, which is demonstrated in the following code:

```
func NewMyHandler(config Config,
    parser Parser, formatter Formatter,
    limiter RateLimiter,
    loader Loader) *MyHandler {

    return &MyHandler{
        config:    config,
        parser:    parser,
        formatter: formatter,
        limiter:   limiter,
        loader:    loader,
    }
}
```

Starting with `MyHandler` as a *base handler*, we can define a new handler that wraps our base handler, as shown in the following code:

```
type FancyFormatHandler struct {
    *MyHandler
}
```

Now we can define a new constructor for our `FancyFormatHandler` in the following way:

```
func NewFancyFormatHandler(config Config,
    parser Parser,
    limiter RateLimiter,
    loader Loader) *FancyFormatHandler {

    return &FancyFormatHandler{
        &MyHandler{
            config:    config,
            formatter: &FancyFormatter{},
            parser:    parser,
            limiter:   limiter,
            loader:    loader,
        },
    }
}
```

And just like that, we have one parameter fewer. The real source of magic here is the anonymous composition; because of that, any calls to `FancyFormatHandler.ServeHTTP()` will actually call `MyHandler.ServeHTTP()`. In this case, we're adding a little bit of code, to improve the UX of the handlers for our users.

Injecting an object when config would do

Often times, your first instinct will be to inject a dependency so that you can test your code in isolation. However, to do so, you are forced to introduce so much abstraction and indirection that the amount of code and complexity increases exponentially.

One widespread occurrence of this is using the common library for accessing external resources, such as network resources, files, or databases. Let's use our sample service's `data` package, for example. If we wanted to abstract our usage of the `sql` package, we would likely start by defining an interface, as shown in the following code:

```
type Connection interface {
    QueryRowContext(ctx context.Context, query string, args ...interface{})
*sql.Row
    QueryContext(ctx context.Context, query string, args ...interface{})
```

```
(*sql.Rows, error)
   ExecContext(ctx context.Context, query string, args ...interface{})
(sql.Result, error)
}
```

Then we realize that `QueryRowContext()` and `QueryContext()` return `*sql.Row` and `*sql.Rows` respectively. Digging into these structs, we find that there is no way for us to populate their internal state from outside of the `sql` package. To get around this, we have to define our own `Row` and `Rows` interfaces, as shown in the following code:

```
type Row interface {
   Scan(dest ...interface{}) error
}

type Rows interface {
   Scan(dest ...interface{}) error
   Close() error
   Next() bool
}

type Result interface {
   LastInsertId() (int64, error)
   RowsAffected() (int64, error)
}
```

We are now fully decoupled from the `sql` package and are able to mock it in our tests. But let's stop for a minute and consider where we're at:

- We've introduced about 60 lines of code, which we haven't yet written any tests for
- We cannot test the new code without using an actual database, which means we'll never be fully decoupled from the database
- We've added another layer of abstraction and a small amount of complexity along with it

Now, compare this with installing a database locally and ensuring it's in a good state. There is complexity here too, but, arguably, an insignificant once-off cost, especially when spread across all of the projects we work on. We would also have to create and maintain the tables in the database. The easiest option for this is an SQL script—a script that could also be used to support the live systems.

For our sample service, we decided to maintain an SQL file and a locally installed database. As a result of this decision, we do not need to mock calls to the database but instead only need to pass in the database configuration to our local database.

This kind of situation appears a lot, especially with low-level packages from trusted sources, such as the standard library. The key to addressing this is to be pragmatic. Ask yourself, do I really need to mock this? Is there some configuration I can pass in that will result in less work?

At the end of the day, we have to make sure we are getting enough return from the extra work, code, and complexity to justify the effort.

Needless indirection

Another way the DI can be misapplied is by introducing abstractions that have limited (or no) purpose. Similar to our earlier discussion on injecting config instead of objects, this extra level of indirection leads to additional work, code, and complexity.

Let's look at an example of a case where you could introduce an abstraction to help with testing, but there is really no need.

In the standard HTTP library, there is a struct called `http.ServeMux`. `ServeMux` is used to build an HTTP router, which is a mapping between URLs and HTTP handlers. Once `ServeMux` is configured, it is then passed into the HTTP server, as shown in the following code:

```
func TestExample(t *testing.T) {
    router := http.NewServeMux()
    router.HandleFunc("/health", func(resp http.ResponseWriter, req
*http.Request) {
        _, _ = resp.Write([]byte(`OK`))
    })

    // start a server
    address := ":8080"
    go func() {
        _ = http.ListenAndServe(address, router)
    }()

    // call the server
    resp, err := http.Get("http://:8080/health")
    require.NoError(t, err)

    // validate the response
    responseBody, err := ioutil.ReadAll(resp.Body)
    assert.Equal(t, []byte(`OK`), responseBody)
}
```

As our service expands, we need to be sure to add more endpoints. To prevent API regression, we've decided to add some tests to ensure our router is configured correctly. Because of our familiarity with DI, we can jump right in and introduce an abstraction of `ServerMux` so that we can add a mock implementation. This is shown in the following example:

```go
type MyMux interface {
    Handle(pattern string, handler http.Handler)
    Handler(req *http.Request) (handler http.Handler, pattern string)
    ServeHTTP(resp http.ResponseWriter, req *http.Request)
}

// build HTTP handler routing
func buildRouter(mux MyMux) {
    mux.Handle("/get", &getEndpoint{})
    mux.Handle("/list", &listEndpoint{})
    mux.Handle("/save", &saveEndpoint{})
}
```

With our abstraction in place, we can define a mock implementation, `MyMux`, and write ourselves a test, as shown in the following example:

```go
func TestBuildRouter(t *testing.T) {
    // build mock
    mockRouter := &MockMyMux{}
    mockRouter.On("Handle", "/get", &getEndpoint{}).Once()
    mockRouter.On("Handle", "/list", &listEndpoint{}).Once()
    mockRouter.On("Handle", "/save", &saveEndpoint{}).Once()

    // call function
    buildRouter(mockRouter)

    // assert expectations
    assert.True(t, mockRouter.AssertExpectations(t))
}
```

This all looks pretty good. The problem, however, is that it wasn't necessary. Our goal was to protect ourselves from accidental API regression by testing the mapping between the endpoints and URLs.

Our goal can be achieved without mocking the `ServeMux`. First, let's go back to our original function before we introduced the `MyMux` interface, as shown in the following example:

```go
// build HTTP handler routing
func buildRouter(mux *http.ServeMux) {
    mux.Handle("/get", &getEndpoint{})
    mux.Handle("/list", &listEndpoint{})
```

```
    mux.Handle("/save", &saveEndpoint{})
}
```

Digging a little deeper into `ServeMux`, we can see that, if we call the `Handler(req *http.Request)` method, it will return the `http.Handler` configured to that URL.

Because we know that we are going to do this once for every endpoint, we should define a function to do just that, as shown in the following example:

```
func extractHandler(router *http.ServeMux, path string) http.Handler {
    req, _ := http.NewRequest("GET", path, nil)
    handler, _ := router.Handler(req)
    return handler
}
```

With our function in place, we can now build a test that validates the expected handler is returned from for each URL, as shown in the following example:

```
func TestBuildRouter(t *testing.T) {
    router := http.NewServeMux()

    // call function
    buildRouter(router)

    // assertions
    assert.IsType(t, &getEndpoint{}, extractHandler(router, "/get"))
    assert.IsType(t, &listEndpoint{}, extractHandler(router, "/list"))
    assert.IsType(t, &saveEndpoint{}, extractHandler(router, "/save"))
}
```

In the previous example, you'll also have noticed that our `buildRouter()` function and our tests are awfully similar. This leaves us to wonder about the efficacy of the tests.

In this case, it would be more effective to ensure we have API regression tests that validate not only the router's configuration but also the input and output formats, just as we did at the end of `Chapter 10`, *Off-the-Shelf Injection*.

Service locator

First, a definition—Service locator is a software design pattern that revolves around an object that acts as a central repository of all dependencies and is able to return them by name. You'll find this pattern in use in many languages and at the heart of some DI frameworks and containers.

Before we dig into why this is DI induced damage, let's look at an example of an overly simplified service locator:

```
func NewServiceLocator() *ServiceLocator {
    return &ServiceLocator{
        deps: map[string]interface{}{},
    }
}

type ServiceLocator struct {
    deps map[string]interface{}
}

// Store or map a dependency to a key
func (s *ServiceLocator) Store(key string, dep interface{}) {
    s.deps[key] = dep
}

// Retrieve a dependency by key
func (s *ServiceLocator) Get(key string) interface{} {
    return s.deps[key]
}
```

In order to use our service locator, we first have to create it and map our dependencies with their names, as shown in the following example:

```
// build a service locator
locator := NewServiceLocator()

// load the dependency mappings
locator.Store("logger", &myLogger{})
locator.Store("converter", &myConverter{})
```

With our service locator built and dependencies set, we can now pass it around and extract dependencies as needed, as shown in the following code:

```
func useServiceLocator(locator *ServiceLocator) {
    // use the locators to get the logger
    logger := locator.Get("logger").(Logger)

    // use the logger
    logger.Info("Hello World!")
}
```

Now, if we wanted to *swap out* the logger for a mock one during testing, then we would only have to construct a new service locator with the mock logger and pass it into our function.

So what is wrong with that? Firstly, our service locator is now a God object (as mentioned in Chapter 1, *Never Stop Aiming for Better*) that we would likely end up passing around all over the place. It might sound like a good thing to only have to pass one object into every function but it leads to the second issue.

The relationship between an object and the dependencies it uses is now completely hidden from the outside. We are no longer able to look at a function or struct definition and immediately know what dependencies are required.

And lastly, we are operating without the protection of Go's type system and compiler. In the previous example, the following line might have caught your attention:

```
logger := locator.Get("logger").(Logger)
```

Because the service locator accepts and returns `interface{}`, every time we need to access a dependency, we are required to cast into the appropriate type. This casting not only makes the code messier, it can cause runtime crash if the value is missing or of the wrong type. We can account for these issues with yet more code, as shown in the following example:

```
// use the locators to get the logger
loggerRetrieved := locator.Get("logger")
if loggerRetrieved == nil {
    return
}
logger, ok := loggerRetrieved.(Logger)
if !ok {
    return
}

// use the logger
logger.Info("Hello World!")
```

With the previous approach, our application will no longer crash, but it's getting rather messy.

Premature future-proofing

Sometimes, the application of DI is not wrong, but just unnecessary. A common manifestation of this is premature future-proofing. Premature future-proofing occurs when we add features to software that we don't yet need, based on the assumption that we might need it one day. As you might expect, this results in unnecessary work and complexity.

Let's look at an example by borrowing from our example service. Currently, we have a Get endpoint, as shown in the following code:

```
// GetHandler is the HTTP handler for the "Get Person" endpoint
type GetHandler struct {
    cfg    GetConfig
    getter GetModel
}

// ServeHTTP implements http.Handler
func (h *GetHandler) ServeHTTP(response http.ResponseWriter, request
*http.Request) {
    // extract person id from request
    id, err := h.extractID(request)
    if err != nil {
        // output error
        response.WriteHeader(http.StatusBadRequest)
        return
    }

    // attempt get
    person, err := h.getter.Do(id)
    if err != nil {
        // not need to log here as we can expect other layers to do so
        response.WriteHeader(http.StatusNotFound)
        return
    }

    // happy path
    err = h.writeJSON(response, person)
    if err != nil {
        response.WriteHeader(http.StatusInternalServerError)
    }
}

// output the supplied person as JSON
func (h *GetHandler) writeJSON(writer io.Writer, person *get.Person) error
{
    output := &getResponseFormat{
        ID:       person.ID,
        FullName: person.FullName,
        Phone:    person.Phone,
        Currency: person.Currency,
        Price:    person.Price,
    }

    return json.NewEncoder(writer).Encode(output)
}
```

It's a simple REST endpoint that returns JSON. If we decided that, one day, we might want to output in a different format, we could move the encoding to a dependency, as shown in the following example:

```
// GetHandler is the HTTP handler for the "Get Person" endpoint
type GetHandler struct {
    cfg        GetConfig
    getter     GetModel
    formatter Formatter
}

// ServeHTTP implements http.Handler
func (h *GetHandler) ServeHTTP(response http.ResponseWriter, request
*http.Request) {
    // no changes to this method
}

// output the supplied person
func (h *GetHandler) buildOutput(writer io.Writer, person *Person) error {
    output := &getResponseFormat{
        ID:        person.ID,
        FullName: person.FullName,
        Phone:    person.Phone,
        Currency: person.Currency,
        Price:    person.Price,
    }

    // build output payload
    payload, err := h.formatter.Marshal(output)
    if err != nil {
        return err
    }

    // write payload to response and return
    _, err = writer.Write(payload)
    return err
}
```

That code looks reasonable. So, where is the problem? Simply put, it's work we didn't need to do.

By extension, it's code that we didn't need to write or maintain. In this simple example, our changes only added a small amount of extra complexity and this is relatively common. This small amount of additional complexity multiplied across the entire system would slow us down.

If this should ever become an actual requirement, then this is absolutely the right way to deliver the feature, but at that point, it's a feature and therefore a burden that we must have.

Mocking HTTP requests

Earlier in this chapter, we talked about how the injection is not the answer to all problems and, in some cases, passing in configuration is far more efficient and a whole lot less code. A frequently occurring example of this occurs when we deal with external services, particularly HTTP services such as the upstream currency conversion service in our sample service.

It is possible to mock an HTTP request to the external service and use the mock to thoroughly test calls to an external service, but it's just not necessary. Let's look at a side-by-side comparison of mocking versus config by using code from our sample service.

The following is the code from our sample service, which calls to the external currency conversion service:

```go
// Converter will convert the base price to the currency supplied
type Converter struct {
   cfg Config
}

// Exchange will perform the conversion
func (c *Converter) Exchange(ctx context.Context, basePrice float64,
currency string) (float64, error) {
   // load rate from the external API
   response, err := c.loadRateFromServer(ctx, currency)
   if err != nil {
      return defaultPrice, err
   }

   // extract rate from response
   rate, err := c.extractRate(response, currency)
   if err != nil {
      return defaultPrice, err
   }

   // apply rate and round to 2 decimal places
   return math.Floor((basePrice/rate)*100) / 100, nil
}

// load rate from the external API
func (c *Converter) loadRateFromServer(ctx context.Context, currency
```

```go
string) (*http.Response, error) {
   // build the request
   url := fmt.Sprintf(urlFormat,
      c.cfg.ExchangeBaseURL(),
      c.cfg.ExchangeAPIKey(),
      currency)

   // perform request
   req, err := http.NewRequest("GET", url, nil)
   if err != nil {
      c.logger().Warn("[exchange] failed to create request. err: %s", err)
      return nil, err
   }

   // set latency budget for the upstream call
   subCtx, cancel := context.WithTimeout(ctx, 1*time.Second)
   defer cancel()

   // replace the default context with our custom one
   req = req.WithContext(subCtx)

   // perform the HTTP request
   response, err := http.DefaultClient.Do(req)
   if err != nil {
      c.logger().Warn("[exchange] failed to load. err: %s", err)
      return nil, err
   }

   if response.StatusCode != http.StatusOK {
      err = fmt.Errorf("request failed with code %d", response.StatusCode)
      c.logger().Warn("[exchange] %s", err)
      return nil, err
   }

   return response, nil
}

func (c *Converter) extractRate(response *http.Response, currency string)
(float64, error) {
   defer func() {
      _ = response.Body.Close()
   }()

   // extract data from response
   data, err := c.extractResponse(response)
   if err != nil {
      return defaultPrice, err
   }
```

```
    // pull rate from response data
    rate, found := data.Quotes["USD"+currency]
    if !found {
        err = fmt.Errorf("response did not include expected currency '%s'",
currency)
        c.logger().Error("[exchange] %s", err)
        return defaultPrice, err
    }

    // happy path
    return rate, nil
}
```

Before we embark on writing the tests, we should first ask ourselves, what do we want to test? Here are the typical test scenarios:

- **Happy path**: The external server returns the data, and we extract it successfully
- **Failed/slow request**: The external server returns an error or does not answer in time
- **Error response**: The external server returns an invalid HTTP response code to indicate it's having issues
- **Invalid response**: The external server returns a payload in a format that we don't expect

We will start our comparison by mocking the HTTP request.

Mocking an HTTP request with DI

If we are going to use DI and mocks, then the cleanest option is to mock the HTTP request so that we can make it return whatever response we need.

To achieve this, the first thing we need to do is abstract building and sending of HTTP requests, as shown in the following code:

```
// Requester builds and sending HTTP requests
//go:generate mockery -name=Requester -case underscore -testonly -inpkg -
note @generated
type Requester interface {
    doRequest(ctx context.Context, url string) (*http.Response, error)
}
```

You can see we have also included a *go generate* comment that will create the mock implementation for us.

We can then update our `Converter` to use the `Requester` abstraction, as shown in the following example:

```go
// NewConverter creates and initializes the converter
func NewConverter(cfg Config, requester Requester) *Converter {
    return &Converter{
        cfg:       cfg,
        requester: requester,
    }
}

// Converter will convert the base price to the currency supplied
type Converter struct {
    cfg       Config
    requester Requester
}

// load rate from the external API
func (c *Converter) loadRateFromServer(ctx context.Context, currency
string) (*http.Response, error) {
    // build the request
    url := fmt.Sprintf(urlFormat,
        c.cfg.ExchangeBaseURL(),
        c.cfg.ExchangeAPIKey(),
        currency)

    // perform request
    response, err := c.requester.doRequest(ctx, url)
    if err != nil {
        c.logger().Warn("[exchange] failed to load. err: %s", err)
        return nil, err
    }

    if response.StatusCode != http.StatusOK {
        err = fmt.Errorf("request failed with code %d", response.StatusCode)
        c.logger().Warn("[exchange] %s", err)
        return nil, err
    }

    return response, nil
}
```

With the `requester` abstraction in place, we can use the mock implementation to test, as shown in the following code:

```
func TestExchange_invalidResponse(t *testing.T) {
    // build response
    response := httptest.NewRecorder()
    _, err := response.WriteString(`invalid payload`)
    require.NoError(t, err)

    // configure mock
    mockRequester := &mockRequester{}
    mockRequester.On("doRequest", mock.Anything,
mock.Anything).Return(response.Result(), nil).Once()

    // inputs
    ctx, cancel := context.WithTimeout(context.Background(), 1*time.Second)
    defer cancel()

    basePrice := 12.34
    currency := "AUD"

    // perform call
    converter := &Converter{
        requester: mockRequester,
        cfg:        &testConfig{},
    }
    result, resultErr := converter.Exchange(ctx, basePrice, currency)

    // validate response
    assert.Equal(t, float64(0), result)
    assert.Error(t, resultErr)
    assert.True(t, mockRequester.AssertExpectations(t))
}
```

In the previous example, our mock requester returns an invalid response instead of calling to the external service. With this, we can ensure that our code behaves appropriately when this happens.

In order to cover the other typical test scenarios, we would only need to copy this test and change the response from the mock and the expectations.

Now let's compare our mock based tests with the config-based equivalent.

Mocking HTTP requests with config

We can test `Converter` without making any code changes at all. The first step is to define an HTTP server that returns the response we need. In the following example, the server is returning the same as the mock in the previous section:

```
server := httptest.NewServer(http.HandlerFunc(func(response
http.ResponseWriter, request *http.Request) {
    payload := []byte(`invalid payload`)
    response.Write(payload)
}))
```

Then we take the URL from the test server and pass it in as a config to `Converter`, as shown in the following example:

```
cfg := &testConfig{
    baseURL: server.URL,
    apiKey:  "",
}

converter := NewConverter(cfg)
```

And now, the following example shows how we can perform the HTTP call and validate the response, as we did in the mock version:

```
result, resultErr := converter.Exchange(ctx, basePrice, currency)

// validate response
assert.Equal(t, float64(0), result)
assert.Error(t, resultErr)
```

With this approach, we can achieve the same level of test scenario coverage as the mock-based version, but with far less code and complexity. Perhaps, more importantly, we do not incur the test-induced damage of an additional constructor parameter.

Unnecessary injection

By now, you are probably thinking, *there are times when using DI is not the best option, but how do I know when?* For this, I would like to offer you another self-survey.

When you are unsure how to proceed, or before you embark on a potentially big refactor, first take a quick run through my DI Survey:

- **Is the dependency an environmental concern (such as logging)?**
  Environmental dependencies are necessary but have a tendency to pollute the UX of the function, particularly a constructor. Injecting them is appropriate, but you should prefer a less obtrusive DI method such as JIT injection or config injection.

- **Are there tests in place to protect us during refactoring?**
  When applying DI to existing code that has low test coverage, adding some monkey patching will be the smallest change you can make and therefore the one that poses the least risk. Once tests are in place, it will be protected for future changes; even if those changes mean the removal of monkey patching.

- **Is the dependency's existence informative?**
  What does the existence of the dependency tell the user about the struct? If the answer is not much or nothing, then the dependency can be merged into any config injection. Similarly, if the dependency does not exist outside the scope of this struct, then you can manage it with JIT injection.

- **How many implementations of the dependency are you going to have?**
  If the answer is more than one, then injecting the dependency is the right option. If the answer is one, then you need to dig a little deeper. Does the dependency ever change? If it has never changed, then injecting it is a waste of effort, and, likely, adds unnecessary complexity.

- **Is the dependency ever changed outside the tests?**
  If it's only changed during testing, then this is a great candidate for JIT injection, after all, we want to avoid test-induced damage.

- **Does the dependency need to change for each execution?**
  If the answer is yes, then you should use method injection. Whenever possible, try to avoid adding any logic to your struct that determines which dependency you are going to use (for example, `switch` statements). Instead, ensure that you either inject the dependency and use it, or inject a factory or locator object that includes the logic for deciding the dependency. This will ensure that your struct stays clear of any single responsibility related issues. It also helps us to avoid making shotgun surgery type changes when we add a new implementation of the dependency.

- **Is the dependency stable?**
  A stable dependency is something that already exists, is unlikely to change (or change in a backward compatible way) and is unlikely to be replaced. Good examples of this are the standard library and well managed, infrequently changed public packages. If the dependency is stable, then injecting it for the purposes of decoupling has less value as the code has not changed and can be trusted.

  You may wish to inject a stable dependency to be able to test how you are using it, as we saw earlier with the SQL package and HTTP client examples. However, to avoid test-induced damage and unnecessary complexity, we should either be adopting JIT injection, to avoid polluting the UX, or avoiding the injection altogether.

- **Is this struct going to have one or multiple usages?**
  If the struct has only a single use, then pressures on that code to be flexible and extendable are low. We can, therefore, favor less injection and more specificity in our implementation; at least until our situation changes. On the other hand, code that is used in many places will have far more considerable pressure to change and, arguably, want to have greater flexibility, to be more useful in more cases. In these cases, you will want to favor injection more to give the users more flexibility. Just be careful not to have so much injection that the UX of the function is terrible.

  With shared code, you should also spend more effort decoupling your code from as many external (non-stable) dependencies as possible. When users adopt your code, they may not want to adopt all of your dependencies.

- **Is this code wrapping the dependency?**
  If we are wrapping a package to make its UX more convenient to insulate us from changes in that package, then injecting that package is unnecessary. The code we are writing is tightly coupled with the code it is wrapping, so introducing an abstraction does not achieve anything significant.

- **Does applying DI make the code better?**
  This is, of course, extraordinarily subjective but perhaps also the most crucial question. Abstraction is useful, but it also adds indirection and complication. Decoupling is important but not always necessary. Decoupling between packages and layers is more important than decoupling between objects within a package.

With experience and repetition, you'll find that many of these questions will become second nature as you develop an intuitive sense of when to apply DI and which method to use.

In the meantime, the following table might help:

Method	Ideal for:
Monkey patching	• Code that relies on a singleton • Code that currently has no tests or existing dependency injection • Decoupling packages without making any changes to the dependent package
Constructor injection	• Dependencies that are required • Dependencies that must be ready before any methods are called • Dependencies that are used by most or all of the methods of an object • Dependencies that don't change between requests • Dependencies that have multiple implementations
Method injection	• Used with functions, frameworks and shared libraries • Request-scoped dependencies • Stateless objects • Dependencies that provide context or data in the request, and, as such, are expected to vary between calls
Config injection	• Replacing constructor or method injection to improve the UX of the code
JIT injection	• Replacing a dependency that would otherwise have been injected into the constructor and of which there is only one production implementation • Providing a layer of indirection or abstraction between an object and a global singleton or environmental dependency. Particularly when we want to swap out the global singleton during testing • Allowing dependencies to be optionally provided by the user
Off-the-shelf injection	• Reducing the cost of adopting constructor injection • Reducing the complexity of maintaining the order in which dependencies are created

Summary

In this chapter, we examined the effects of applying DI unnecessarily or incorrectly. We also discussed some situations where employing DI is not the best tool for the job.

We then wrapped up the chapter with a list of 10 questions that you can ask yourself to determine whether DI is appropriate for your current use case.

In the next chapter, we'll wrap up our examination of DI with a review of everything we've discussed throughout this book. In particular, we'll contrast the state of our sample service now with its original state. We'll also take a quick look at how to start a new service with DI.

Questions

1. What form of DI induced damage do you see most often?
2. Why is it important not to blindly apply DI all of the time?
3. Does adopting a framework, such as Google Wire, eliminate all forms of DI induced damage?

12
Reviewing Our Progress

In this, our final chapter, we will take a look back and compare the state and quality of our sample service now, after applying **dependency injection** (**DI**), with how it was when we started.

We will be taking a look at the improvements we have made, along with one final look at our dependency graph, and will discuss our improvements in test coverage and the testability of the service.

Finally, we will wrap up this chapter with a brief discussion of what we could have done if we had been starting a new service with DI instead of applying it to existing code.

The following topics will be covered in this chapter:

- An overview of the improvements
- A review of the dependency graph
- A review of test coverage and testability
- Starting a new service with DI

Technical requirements

It would be beneficial to be familiar with the code for our service, as introduced in Chapter 4, *Introduction to ACME registration service*. This chapter also assumes that you have read Chapter 5, *Dependency Injection with Monkey Patching*, through to Chapter 10, *Off-the-Shelf Injection*, on the various DI methods and other various improvements we made along the way.

You might also find it useful to read and run the full versions of the code for this chapter, which are available at https://github.com/PacktPublishing/Hands-On-Dependency-Injection-in-Go/tree/master/ch12.

Instructions for obtaining the code and configuring the sample service are available in the README, which can be found at `https://github.com/PacktPublishing/Hands-On-Dependency-Injection-in-Go/`.

You can find the code for our service, with the changes from this chapter already applied, at `https://github.com/PacktPublishing/Hands-On-Dependency-Injection-in-Go/tree/master/ch12/acme`.

Overview of the improvements

Phew, we made it. How do you think we did? Do you think the improvements were worth the effort? Let's see.

To see how far we have come, we should first recap where we started.

In `Chapter 4`, *Introduction to the ACME Registration Service*, we had a small, simple, working service. It got the job done for our users, but it created many inconveniences for those of us that had to maintain and extend it.

Global singletons

One of the biggest pains was undoubtedly the use of global public singletons. At first glance, they seemed to make the code more concise, but they were actually making it much harder for us to test.

The use of `init()` functions to create variables meant that we either had to use the live versions (that is, on the database) or had to monkey patch the globals, which led to potential data races.

We started off with two public globals (`config` and `logger`) and one private global (the database connection pool). In `Chapter 5`, *Dependency Injection with Monkey Patching*, we used monkey patching to give us the ability to test the code that relied on the database connection pool singleton.

In `Chapter 10`, *Off-the-Shelf Injection*, we finally managed to remove the `config` global, after first removing most of the direct access to it during the changes we made in `Chapter 8`, *Dependency Injection by Config*.

By removing direct access and defining local config interfaces, we were able to completely decouple our model and data layers from the config. This means that our code is portable, should we ever want to use it in another application.

Perhaps most importantly, this means that writing tests on this code is now far less work, and our tests can all run independently and concurrently. Without the link to the global instance, we don't have to monkey patch. Without the dependency link, we are left with a smaller, more focused `config` interface, which is much easier to mock, stub, and generally understand.

The global `logger` instance managed to survive our many refactorings, but the only place it is used is during the `config` loading code. So, let's remove it now. Our `config` loading function currently looks like that shown in the following code:

```
// Load returns the config loaded from environment
func Load() (*Config, error) {
   filename, found := os.LookupEnv(DefaultEnvVar)
   if !found {
      err := fmt.Errorf("failed to locate file specified by %s",
DefaultEnvVar)
      logging.L.Error(err.Error())
      return nil, err
   }

   cfg, err := load(filename)
   if err != nil {
      logging.L.Error("failed to load config with err %s", err)
      return nil, err
   }

   return cfg, nil
}
```

It's pretty safe to say that, if we fail to load the config, our service is not going to work. We can, therefore, change our errors to write directly to *standard error* directly. Our updated function looks as follows:

```
// Load returns the config loaded from environment
func Load() (*Config, error) {
   filename, found := os.LookupEnv(DefaultEnvVar)
   if !found {
      err := fmt.Errorf("failed to locate file specified by %s",
DefaultEnvVar)
      fmt.Fprintf(os.Stderr, err.Error())
      return nil, err
   }

   cfg, err := load(filename)
   if err != nil {
      fmt.Fprintf(os.Stderr, "failed to load config with err %s", err)
      return nil, err
```

```
    }

    return cfg, nil
}
```

The logger is otherwise *passed in* using config injection. By using config injection, we were able to forget about common concerns (such as the `logger`) without detracting from the UX of our constructors. We are now also able to easily write tests that validate logging without any data race issues. While such tests might feel weird, consider this—logs are an output of our system, and we will often rely on them when something goes wrong and we need to debug.

As such, there might be cases when it's useful to ensure that we are creating logs as we expect to and continue to do so, despite any future refactoring. This is not something we will want to test often, but when we do, the test itself is as simple as the following:

```
func TestLogging(t *testing.T) {
    // build log recorder
    recorder := &LogRecorder{}

    // Call struct that uses a logger
    calculator := &Calculator{
        logger: recorder,
    }
    result := calculator.divide(10, 0)

    // validate expectations, including that the logger was called
    assert.Equal(t, 0, result)
    require.Equal(t, 1, len(recorder.Logs))
    assert.Equal(t, "cannot divide by 0", recorder.Logs[0])
}

type Calculator struct {
    logger Logger
}

func (c *Calculator) divide(dividend int, divisor int) int {
    if divisor == 0 {
        c.logger.Error("cannot divide by 0")
        return 0
    }

    return dividend / divisor
}

// Logger is our standard interface
type Logger interface {
```

```
    Error(message string, args ...interface{})
}

// LogRecorder implements Logger interface
type LogRecorder struct {
    Logs []string
}

func (l *LogRecorder) Error(message string, args ...interface{}) {
    // build log message
    logMessage := fmt.Sprintf(message, args...)

    // record log message
    l.Logs = append(l.Logs, logMessage)
}
```

Finally, the global instance of the database connection pool also remains; however, unlike `Config` and `Logger`, it is private, so any risks associated with it have a limited scope. In fact, by using **just-in-time** (**JIT**) DI, we were able to decouple our model layer tests from the data package entirely, without detracting from the UX of the model layer packages.

High coupling with the config package

When we started in `Chapter 4`, *Introduction to the ACME Registration Service*, we had not used any interfaces at all, and as a result, all of our packages were very tightly coupled with one another. Because of this, our packages had a high resistance to change; none more so than the `config` package. This was our original `Config` struct and the global singleton:

```
// App is the application config
var App *Config

// Config defines the JSON format for the config file
type Config struct {
    // DSN is the data source name (format:
https://github.com/go-sql-driver/mysql/#dsn-data-source-name)
    DSN string

    // Address is the IP address and port to bind this rest to
    Address string

    // BasePrice is the price of registration
    BasePrice float64

    // ExchangeRateBaseURL is the server and protocol part of the
    // URL from which to load the exchange rate
```

```
    ExchangeRateBaseURL string

    // ExchangeRateAPIKey is the API for the exchange rate API
    ExchangeRateAPIKey string
}
```

With the combination of a global singleton, lack of interfaces, and the fact that almost every package referenced this package, any change we made to the `Config` struct had the potential to break everything. Similarly, if we had decided to change the config format from a flat JSON file to a more complicated structure, we would have been in for some pretty nasty shotgun surgery.

Let's compare our original `Config` struct with what we have now:

```
// Config defines the JSON format for the config file
type Config struct {
    // DSN is the data source name (format:
https://github.com/go-sql-driver/mysql/#dsn-data-source-name)
    DSN string

    // Address is the IP address and port to bind this rest to
    Address string

    // BasePrice is the price of registration
    BasePrice float64

    // ExchangeRateBaseURL is the server and protocol part of the
    // URL from which to load the exchange rate
    ExchangeRateBaseURL string

    // ExchangeRateAPIKey is the API for the exchange rate API
    ExchangeRateAPIKey string

    // environmental dependencies
    logger logging.Logger
}

// Logger returns a reference to the singleton logger
func (c *Config) Logger() logging.Logger {
    if c.logger == nil {
        c.logger = &logging.LoggerStdOut{}
    }

    return c.logger
}

// RegistrationBasePrice returns the base price for registrations
```

```go
func (c *Config) RegistrationBasePrice() float64 {
    return c.BasePrice
}

// DataDSN returns the DSN
func (c *Config) DataDSN() string {
    return c.DSN
}

// ExchangeBaseURL returns the Base URL from which we can load
// exchange rates
func (c *Config) ExchangeBaseURL() string {
    return c.ExchangeRateBaseURL
}

// ExchangeAPIKey returns the DSN
func (c *Config) ExchangeAPIKey() string {
    return c.ExchangeRateAPIKey
}

// BindAddress returns the host and port this service should bind to
func (c *Config) BindAddress() string {
    return c.Address
}
```

As can be seen, we now have a lot more code. However, the extra code mostly comprises getter functions that implement the various config interfaces of the packages. These getter functions give us a layer of indirection that allows us to change how the config is loaded and stored, without having to impact the other packages.

With the introduction of local Config interfaces into many of the packages, we were able to decouple those packages from our config package. While the other packages still indirectly use the config package, we have gained two benefits. Firstly, they can evolve separately. Secondly, the packages all *document* their requirements locally, giving us a smaller scope to work with when we are dealing with the package. This is especially helpful during testing when we are using mocks and stubs.

Removing the dependence on upstream service

In Chapter 6, *Dependency Injection with Constructor Injection,* we used constructor injection to decouple our model layer from the `exchange` package. You may remember that the `exchange` package is a thin abstraction over our upstream currency converter service. Not only did this ensure that our model layer tests no longer required the upstream service to be working in order to pass, but it also gave us the ability to ensure we had adequately handled cases where the service was failing.

In Chapter 8, *Dependency Injection by Config,* we added boundary tests that further removed our dependence on the upstream service by giving us the ability to test the `exchange` package independently of the upstream service. After removing all dependence on the upstream service from our frequently run unit tests, we added an external-facing boundary that tests the external service. However, we protected this test with a build tag, giving us the ability to run it selectively and occasionally, thus providing us with protection from internet and upstream service issues.

Stopping short and latency budgets

In Chapter 7, *Dependency Injection with Method Injection,* we used method injection to introduce the `context` package and request-scoped dependencies. By using `context` as a request-scoped dependency, we were then able to implement latency budgets and *stopping short*. With these in place, we are able to reduce our resource usage during abnormal system behavior. For example, if retrieving data (from the upstream currency conversion service or the database) is taking so long that the client is no longer waiting for a response, we can cancel the request and stop any further processing.

Simplified dependency creation

When we started in Chapter 4, *Introduction to the ACME Registration Service,* our `main()` function looks rather simple, as shown in the following code:

```
func main() {
   // bind stop channel to context
   ctx := context.Background()

   // start REST server
   server := rest.New(config.App.Address)
   server.Listen(ctx.Done())
}
```

After applying several DI methods to our code, by Chapter 9, *Just-in-Time Dependency Injection*, our main() function had become the following:

```
func main() {
    // bind stop channel to context
    ctx := context.Background()

    // build the exchanger
    exchanger := exchange.NewConverter(config.App)

    // build model layer
    getModel := get.NewGetter(config.App)
    listModel := list.NewLister(config.App)
    registerModel := register.NewRegisterer(config.App, exchanger)

    // start REST server
    server := rest.New(config.App, getModel, listModel, registerModel)
    server.Listen(ctx.Done())
}
```

As you can see, it had become longer and more complicated. This is a common complaint regarding DI. So, in Chapter 10, *Off-the-Shelf Injection*, we reduced this cost by letting Wire do it for us. This brings us back to a nice concise main() function, as follows:

```
func main() {
    // bind stop channel to context
    ctx := context.Background()

    // start REST server
    server, err := initializeServer()
    if err != nil {
        os.Exit(-1)
    }

    server.Listen(ctx.Done())
}
```

Similarly, in Chapter 9, *Just-in-Time Dependency Injection*, we recognized the fact that there would only ever be one live implementation of the data layer, and the only time we would inject anything different was during testing. We, therefore, decided not to make the data layer a constructor parameter, but instead to use JIT injection, as shown in the following code:

```
// Getter will attempt to load a person.
type Getter struct {
    cfg  Config
    data myLoader
```

```
    }

    // Do will perform the get
    func (g *Getter) Do(ID int) (*data.Person, error) {
        // load person from the data layer
        person, err := g.getLoader().Load(context.TODO(), ID)
        if err != nil {
            if err == data.ErrNotFound {
                return nil, errPersonNotFound
            }
            return nil, err
        }

        return person, err
    }

    // Use JIT DI to lessen the constructor parameters
    func (g *Getter) getLoader() myLoader {
        if g.data == nil {
            g.data = data.NewDAO(g.cfg)
        }

        return g.data
    }
```

As can be seen here, this gives us simplified, local dependency creation without detracting from the UX of our constructors and without losing our ability to mock the data layer during testing.

Coupling and extensibility

After all our changes, perhaps our most significant win is the decoupling of our packages. Wherever possible, our packages define and depend only on local interfaces. As a result of this, our unit tests are entirely isolated from other packages and validate our usage of our dependencies—the contract between our packages—without any dependence on them. This means a minimal scope of knowledge is required when working on our packages.

Perhaps more importantly, any changes or extensions we might want to make are likely to be contained to a single or small number of packages. For example, if we wanted to add a cache in front of our upstream currency conversion service, all of the changes would be made only to the exchange package. Similarly, if we wanted to reuse this package in another service, we could copy or extract it and use it without changes.

Review of the dependency graph

Throughout this book, we have used the dependency graph as a way to discover potential issues. Here is how it looked when we started:

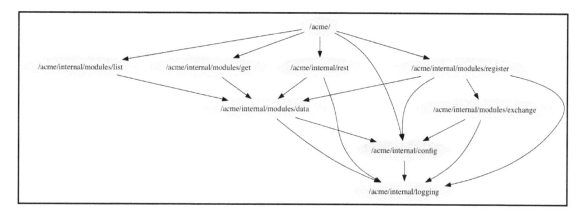

For a small service with only three endpoints, it's kind of complicated. From this graph, we also noticed that there were a lot of arrows pointing to the `data`, `config`, and `logging` packages.

Working under the assumption that more arrows going into or coming out of a package meant the more risk, complexity, and coupling, we set about trying to reduce these relationships.

The highest impact change was our adoption of the config injection, which included the definition of local `config` interfaces (as discussed in the previous section). This removed all of the arrows going into the config package, except for the one from `main()`, which we cannot remove.

Furthermore, during our config injection work, we also removed all the references to the global logging instance, and instead injected the logger. This, however, did not change the graph. This was due to our decision to re-use the `Logger` interface defined in that package.

We could have defined a copy of this interface inside every package and removed this coupling, but decided not to, given that the logger definition was probably not going to change. Copying the interface everywhere would add code for no gain beyond removing arrows from the graph.

After all of our refactoring and decoupling work, our dependency graph looks like the following diagram:

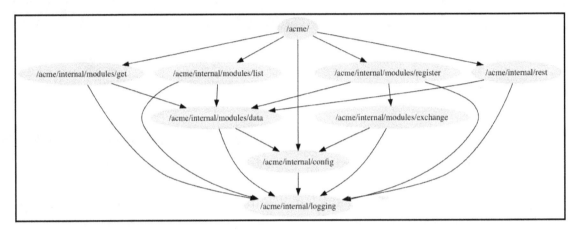

It's better, but sadly, it's still rather messy. To address this and the issue regarding the logging interface that we mentioned earlier, I have one more trick to show you.

So far, we have been generating the graphs with a command like the following:

```
$ BASE_PKG=github.com/PacktPublishing/Hands-On-Dependency-Injection-in-
Go/ch12/acme
godepgraph -s -o $BASE_PKG $BASE_PKG | dot -Tpng -o depgraph.png
```

We can remove the `logging` package from the chart by using Godepgraph's exclusions feature, changing the command to the following form:

```
$ BASE_PKG=github.com/PacktPublishing/Hands-On-Dependency-Injection-in-
Go/ch12/acme
godepgraph -s -o $BASE_PKG -p $BASE_PKG/internal/logging $BASE_PKG | dot -
Tpng -o depgraph.png
```

This finally gives us the nice clear pyramid of a graph that we had been aiming for:

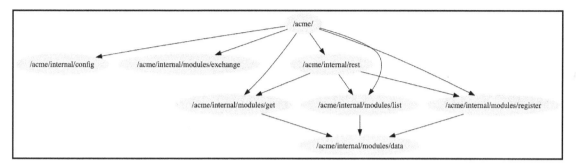

You might be wondering if we can further flatten the graph by removing the links between the REST and model packages (get, list, and register).

We are currently injecting the model code into the REST package; however, the one remaining link between the two is the output format of the model packages. Let's take a look at this now.

Our list model API looks like this:

```
// Lister will attempt to load all people in the database.
// It can return an error caused by the data layer
type Lister struct {
    cfg  Config
    data myLoader
}

// Exchange will load the people from the data layer
func (l *Lister) Do() ([]*data.Person, error) {
    // code removed
}
```

We are returning a slice of the *data.Person type, which forces our local interface in the REST package to be defined as follows:

```
type ListModel interface {
    Do() ([]*data.Person, error)
}
```

Given that data.Person is a **data transfer object** (DTO), I am inclined to be pragmatic and leave it. We could, of course, remove it. To do so, we would need to change our ListModel definition to expect a slice of interface{}, and then define an interface into which we could cast our *data.Person when we need to use it.

There are two major issues with this. Firstly, it's a lot of extra work that only removes one line from the dependency graph, but makes the code messier. Secondly, we are effectively bypassing the type system and creating a way for our code to fail at runtime, should the return type of our model layer become different from the REST package's expectations.

Review of test coverage and testability

When we introduced our sample service, we identified several issues related to testing. The first of these issues was the *lack of isolation*, where tests for one layer were also indirectly testing all the layers below it, as shown in the following code:

```go
func TestGetHandler_ServeHTTP(t *testing.T) {
    // ensure the test always fails by giving it a timeout
    ctx, cancel := context.WithTimeout(context.Background(), 5*time.Second)
    defer cancel()

    // Create and start a server
    // With out current implementation, we cannot test this handler without
    // a full server as we need the mux.
    address, err := startServer(ctx)
    require.NoError(t, err)

    // build inputs
    response, err := http.Get("http://" + address + "/person/1/")

    // validate outputs
    require.NoError(t, err)
    require.Equal(t, http.StatusOK, response.StatusCode)

    expectedPayload :=
[]byte(`{"id":1,"name":"John","phone":"0123456780","currency":"USD","price":100}` + "\n")
    payload, _ := ioutil.ReadAll(response.Body)
    defer response.Body.Close()

    assert.Equal(t, expectedPayload, payload)
}
```

This is a test in the REST layer, but because it calls the actual model, and therefore, the actual data layers, it is effectively testing everything. This makes it a reasonable integration test, as it ensures the layers work together appropriately. But is a poor unit test, because the layers are not isolated.

Our unit test now looks as follows:

```go
func TestGetHandler_ServeHTTP(t *testing.T) {
    scenarios := []struct {
        desc           string
        inRequest      func() *http.Request
        inModelMock    func() *MockGetModel
        expectedStatus  int
        expectedPayload string
    }{
        // scenarios removed
    }

    for _, s := range scenarios {
        scenario := s
        t.Run(scenario.desc, func(t *testing.T) {
            // define model layer mock
            mockGetModel := scenario.inModelMock()

            // build handler
            handler := NewGetHandler(&testConfig{}, mockGetModel)

            // perform request
            response := httptest.NewRecorder()
            handler.ServeHTTP(response, scenario.inRequest())

            // validate outputs
            require.Equal(t, scenario.expectedStatus, response.Code,
scenario.desc)

            payload, _ := ioutil.ReadAll(response.Body)
            assert.Equal(t, scenario.expectedPayload, string(payload),
scenario.desc)
        })
    }
}
```

This test is considered isolated because, instead of relying on the other layers, we are relying on an abstraction—in our case, a mock implementation called *MockGetModel. Let's take a look at a typical mock implementation:

```go
type MockGetModel struct {
    mock.Mock
}

func (_m *MockGetModel) Do(ID int) (*Person, error) {
    outputs := _m.Called(ID)
```

```
if outputs.Get(0) != nil {
    return outputs.Get(0).(*Person), outputs.Error(1)
}

return nil, outputs.Error(1)
}
```

As you can see, the mock implementation is very simple; definitely simpler than the actual implementation of this dependency. Because of this simplicity, we are able to trust that it performs as we expect, and therefore, any problems that arise in the test will be caused by the actual code and not the mock. This trust can be further reinforced by the use of a code generator, such as Mockery (as introduced in `Chapter 3`, *Coding for User Experience*), that generates reliable and consistent code.

The mock has also given us the ability to test other scenarios easily. We now have tests for the following:

- Happy path
- Missing ID in the request
- Invalid ID in the request
- Dependency (model layer or below) failure
- The requested record does not exist

Many of these situations were difficult to reliably test without the changes we made.

Now that our test is isolated from the other layers, the test itself has a much smaller scope. This means we need to know less; all we need to know is the API contract for the layer we are testing.

In our example, this means that we only need to worry about HTTP concerns such as extracting data from the request, outputting the correct status code, and rendering the response payload. Additionally, the manner in which the code we are testing can fail has been reduced. So, we ended up with less test setup, shorter tests, and more scenario coverage.

The second issue related to testing was *duplication of effort*. With the lack of isolation, our original tests were often somewhat superfluous. For example, the model layer test for the Get endpoint looked like this:

```
func TestGetter_Do(t *testing.T) {
    // inputs
    ID := 1

    // call method
```

```
getter := &Getter{}
person, err := getter.Do(ID)

// validate expectations
require.NoError(t, err)
assert.Equal(t, ID, person.ID)
assert.Equal(t, "John", person.FullName)
}
```

This looks alright on the surface, but when we consider the fact that this test scenario has already been covered by our REST package test, we actually gain nothing from this test. On the other hand, let's look at one of the several tests we have now:

```
func TestGetter_Do_noSuchPerson(t *testing.T) {
    // inputs
    ID := 5678

    // configure the mock loader
    mockLoader := &mockMyLoader{}
    mockLoader.On("Load", mock.Anything, ID).Return(nil,
data.ErrNotFound).Once()

    // call method
    getter := &Getter{
        data: mockLoader,
    }
    person, err := getter.Do(ID)

    // validate expectations
    require.Equal(t, errPersonNotFound, err)
    assert.Nil(t, person)
    assert.True(t, mockLoader.AssertExpectations(t))
}
```

This test is now 100% predictable, as it does not rely on the current state of the database. It doesn't test the database, nor how we interact with it, but instead tests how we interact with the *data loader* abstraction. This means that the data layer implementation is free to evolve or change without needing to revisit and update the test. This test also validates that, if we receive an error from the data layer, we appropriately transform this error as our API contract expects.

We still have tests at both layers, as before, but instead of the tests bringing us no value, they now bring significant value.

Thirdly, another issue we encountered when testing was *test verbosity*. One of the many changes we made was the adoption of table-driven tests. The original service test for our register endpoint looked as follows:

```
func TestRegisterHandler_ServeHTTP(t *testing.T) {
    // ensure the test always fails by giving it a timeout
    ctx, cancel := context.WithTimeout(context.Background(), 5*time.Second)
    defer cancel()

    // Create and start a server
    // With out current implementation, we cannot test this handler without
    // a full server as we need the mux.
    address, err := startServer(ctx)
    require.NoError(t, err)

    // build inputs
    validRequest := buildValidRequest()
    response, err := http.Post("http://"+address+"/person/register",
"application/json", validRequest)

    // validate outputs
    require.NoError(t, err)
    require.Equal(t, http.StatusCreated, response.StatusCode)
    defer response.Body.Close()

    // call should output the location to the new person
    headerLocation := response.Header.Get("Location")
    assert.Contains(t, headerLocation, "/person/")
}
```

And now, consider how it looks in the following code block:

```
func TestRegisterHandler_ServeHTTP(t *testing.T) {
    scenarios := []struct {
        desc          string
        inRequest     func() *http.Request
        inModelMock   func() *MockRegisterModel
        expectedStatus int
        expectedHeader string
    }{
        // scenarios removed
    }

    for _, s := range scenarios {
        scenario := s
        t.Run(scenario.desc, func(t *testing.T) {
            // define model layer mock
            mockRegisterModel := scenario.inModelMock()
```

```
    // build handler
    handler := NewRegisterHandler(mockRegisterModel)

    // perform request
    response := httptest.NewRecorder()
    handler.ServeHTTP(response, scenario.inRequest())

    // validate outputs
    require.Equal(t, scenario.expectedStatus, response.Code)

    // call should output the location to the new person
    resultHeader := response.Header().Get("Location")
    assert.Equal(t, scenario.expectedHeader, resultHeader)

    // validate the mock was used as we expected
    assert.True(t, mockRegisterModel.AssertExpectations(t))
    })
  }
}
```

I know what you are thinking, the test became more verbose, not less. Yes, this individual test did. However, in the originals, if we were to test for another scenario, the first step would have been to *copy and paste* almost the entire test, leaving us with approximately 10 lines of duplicated code and only a few lines that were unique to that test scenario.

With our table-driven tests style, we have eight lines of shared code that execute for every scenario and are clearly visible as such. Each scenario is neatly specified as an object in a slice like so:

```
{
    desc: "Happy Path",
    inRequest: func() *http.Request {
        validRequest := buildValidRegisterRequest()
        request, err := http.NewRequest("POST", "/person/register",
validRequest)
        require.NoError(t, err)

        return request
    },
    inModelMock: func() *MockRegisterModel {
        // valid downstream configuration
        resultID := 1234
        var resultErr error

        mockRegisterModel := &MockRegisterModel{}
        mockRegisterModel.On("Do", mock.Anything,
mock.Anything).Return(resultID, resultErr).Once()
```

```
        return mockRegisterModel
   },
   expectedStatus: http.StatusCreated,
   expectedHeader: "/person/1234/",
},
```

For us to add another scenario, all we have to do is add another item to the slice. This is both very simple, and quite neat and tidy.

Lastly, if we ever need to make changes to the tests, perhaps because the API contract changed, we now have only one test to fix, instead of many.

The fourth issue we encountered was *reliance on our upstream service*. This is one of my pet peeves. Tests are supposed to be reliable and predictable, and test failures should be an absolute indicator that there is a problem that needs fixing. When tests rely on a third party and an internet connection, anything could go wrong, and the tests can break for any reason. Thankfully, after our changes in Chapter 8, *Dependency Injection by Config*, all of our tests, except the external-facing boundary tests, now rely on an abstraction and a mock implementation of the upstream service. Not only are our tests reliable, but we can now easily test our error-handling conditions similar to how we discussed earlier.

In the following test, we have removed and mocked calls to the converter package in order to test what happens to our registrations when we fail to load the currency conversion:

```
func TestRegisterer_Do_exchangeError(t *testing.T) {
    // configure the mocks
    mockSaver := &mockMySaver{}
    mockExchanger := &MockExchanger{}
    mockExchanger.
        On("Exchange", mock.Anything, mock.Anything, mock.Anything).
        Return(0.0, errors.New("failed to load conversion")).
        Once()

    // define context and therefore test timeout
    ctx, cancel := context.WithTimeout(context.Background(), 1*time.Second)
    defer cancel()

    // inputs
    in := &Person{
        FullName: "Chang",
        Phone:    "11122233355",
        Currency: "CNY",
    }

    // call method
```

```
registerer := &Registerer{
    cfg:       &testConfig{},
    exchanger: mockExchanger,
    data:      mockSaver,
}
ID, err := registerer.Do(ctx, in)

// validate expectations
require.Error(t, err)
assert.Equal(t, 0, ID)
assert.True(t, mockSaver.AssertExpectations(t))
assert.True(t, mockExchanger.AssertExpectations(t))
}
```

You might remember that we still have tests in our exchange package. In fact, we have two types. We have *internal-facing boundary tests* that call a fake HTTP server that we created. These tests ensure that when the server gives a particular response, our code reacts as we expect, as shown in the following snippet:

```
func TestInternalBoundaryTest(t *testing.T) {
    // start our test server
    server := httptest.NewServer(&happyExchangeRateService{})
    defer server.Close()

    // define the config
    cfg := &testConfig{
        baseURL: server.URL,
        apiKey:  "",
    }

    // create a converter to test
    converter := NewConverter(cfg)
    resultRate, resultErr := converter.Exchange(context.Background(),
100.00, "AUD")

    // validate the result
    assert.Equal(t, 158.79, resultRate)
    assert.NoError(t, resultErr)
}

type happyExchangeRateService struct{}

// ServeHTTP implements http.Handler
func (*happyExchangeRateService) ServeHTTP(response http.ResponseWriter,
request *http.Request) {
    payload := []byte(`
{
  "success":true,
```

```
    "timestamp":1535250248,
    "base":"EUR",
    "date":"2018-08-26",
    "rates": {
     "AUD":1.587884
    }
  }
`)
    response.Write(payload)
}
```

But we also have *external-facing boundary tests*, which still call the upstream service. These tests help us validate that the upstream service performs as we need it to, in concert with our code. However, to ensure our tests are predictable, we do not run the external tests very often. We achieved this by adding a build tag to this file, allowing us an easy way to decide when to include the tests. Typically, I would only run these tests either when something went wrong, or in order to set up a special step in the build pipeline that runs only these tests. We could then decide how to proceed after any failures during these tests.

Test coverage

To talk about raw numbers for a moment, when we started, our service's test coverage looked like this:

```
---------------------------------------------------------------------------------
|      Branch       |      Dir       |                                          |
|  Cov%  |  Stmts  |  Cov%  |  Stmts  |  Package                                 |
---------------------------------------------------------------------------------
|  52.94 |    238  |  0.00  |     3   |  acme/                                   |
|  73.33 |     15  |  73.33 |    15   |  acme/internal/config/                   |
|  0.00  |      4  |  0.00  |     4   |  acme/internal/logging/                  |
|  63.33 |     60  |  63.33 |    60   |  acme/internal/modules/data/             |
|  0.00  |     38  |  0.00  |    38   |  acme/internal/modules/exchange/         |
|  50.00 |      6  |  50.00 |     6   |  acme/internal/modules/get/              |
|  25.00 |     12  |  25.00 |    12   |  acme/internal/modules/list/             |
|  64.29 |     28  |  64.29 |    28   |  acme/internal/modules/register/         |
|  73.61 |     72  |  73.61 |    72   |  acme/internal/rest/                     |
---------------------------------------------------------------------------------
```

As you can see, the test coverage was somewhat low. With the difficulty in writing tests and our inability to mock or stub our dependencies, this is not surprising.

After our changes, our test coverage is improving:

```
---------------------------------------------------------------------
|     Branch     |       Dir      |                                 |
|  Cov%  | Stmts |  Cov%  | Stmts | Package                         |
---------------------------------------------------------------------
|  63.11 |   309 | 30.00  |    20 | acme/                          |
|  28.57 |    28 | 28.57  |    28 | acme/internal/config/          |
|   0.00 |     4 |  0.00  |     4 | acme/internal/logging/         |
|  74.65 |    71 | 74.65  |    71 | acme/internal/modules/data/    |
|  61.70 |    47 | 61.70  |    47 | acme/internal/modules/exchange/|
|  81.82 |    11 | 81.82  |    11 | acme/internal/modules/get/     |
|  38.10 |    21 | 38.10  |    21 | acme/internal/modules/list/    |
|  75.76 |    33 | 75.76  |    33 | acme/internal/modules/register/|
|  77.03 |    74 | 77.03  |    74 | acme/internal/rest/            |
---------------------------------------------------------------------
```

While a lot of the changes we made to our service make it easier to test, we didn't spend that much time on adding additional tests. The bulk of the improvements that we did achieve came from increased scenario coverage, mainly involving being able to test the non-happy path code.

If we wanted to improve the test coverage, the easiest way to find out where more tests are needed is to use the standard go tools to calculate the coverage and display it as HTML. To do this, we run the following commands in a Terminal:

```
# Change directory to the code for this chapter
$ cd $GOPATH/src/github.com/PacktPublishing/Hands-On-Dependency-Injection-
in-Go/ch12/

# Set the config location
$ export ACME_CONFIG=cd $GOPATH/src/github.com/PacktPublishing/Hands-On-
Dependency-Injection-in-Go/config.json

# Calculate coverage
$ go test ./acme/ -coverprofile=coverage.out

# Render as HTML
$ go tool cover -html=coverage.out
```

After running these commands, the coverage will open in your default browser. To find potential places to make improvements we then scanning through the files, look for blocks of red code. Code highlighted in red indicates a line that was not executed during the tests.

It is not pragmatic to remove all the untested lines, especially as some errors are close to impossible to trigger—rather, the key is to examine the code and decide if it represents a scenario that should be tested.

Consider the following example (the lines not covered are bold)—we'll examine it in closer detail now:

```go
// load rate from the external API
func (c *Converter) loadRateFromServer(ctx context.Context, currency
string) (*http.Response, error) {
    // build the request
    url := fmt.Sprintf(urlFormat,
        c.cfg.ExchangeBaseURL(),
        c.cfg.ExchangeAPIKey(),
        currency)

    // perform request
    req, err := http.NewRequest("GET", url, nil)
    if err != nil {
        c.logger().Warn("[exchange] failed to create request. err: %s", err)
        return nil, err
    }

    // set latency budget for the upstream call
    subCtx, cancel := context.WithTimeout(ctx, 1*time.Second)
    defer cancel()

    // replace the default context with our custom one
    req = req.WithContext(subCtx)

    // perform the HTTP request
    response, err := http.DefaultClient.Do(req)
    if err != nil {
        c.logger().Warn("[exchange] failed to load. err: %s", err)
        return nil, err
    }

    if response.StatusCode != http.StatusOK {
        err = fmt.Errorf("request failed with code %d", response.StatusCode)
        c.logger().Warn("[exchange] %s", err)
        return nil, err
    }

    return response, nil
}
```

Firstly, let's talk about these lines:

```
if response.StatusCode != http.StatusOK {
    err = fmt.Errorf("request failed with code %d", response.StatusCode)
    c.logger().Warn("[exchange] %s", err)
    return nil, err
}
```

These lines handle the scenario where the upstream service fails to return HTTP 200 (OK). Given the nature of the internet and HTTP services, the scenario has a high chance of happening. We should, therefore, construct a test that ensures our code handles this situation.

Now, take a look at these lines:

```
req, err := http.NewRequest("GET", url, nil)
if err != nil {
    c.logger().Warn("[exchange] failed to create request. err: %s", err)
    return nil, err
}
```

Do you know how `http.NewRequest()` can fail? After digging around in the standard library, it appears that it can fail if we specify a valid HTTP method or if the URL fails to parse. These are programmer mistakes, and mistakes that we are unlikely to make. Even if we did make them, the results would be obvious and caught by existing tests.

Additionally, adding a test for these conditions would be difficult, and almost certainly detrimental to the cleanliness of our code.

Lastly, our tests so far suffer from a *lack of end-to-end testing*. At the end of Chapter 10, *Off-the-Shelf Injection*, we added a small number of end-to-end tests. We initially used these tests to validate that Google Wire performed as we expected. In the long term, they will serve to protect our API from accidental regression. Changes to our service's public API, whether it's the URL, the inputs or the output payloads, have a high chance of causing our users' code to break. Changes will sometimes be necessary, and in those cases, these tests will also serve a reminder to us that we need to take other actions as well, such as informing our users or versioning the API.

Starting a new service with DI

Throughout this book, we have applied DI to an existing service. While this is by far the most common situation we will find ourselves in, sometimes we will have the honor of starting a new project from scratch.

So, what could we do differently?

The user experience

The first thing we should always do is stop and think about the problem we are trying to solve. Go back to the UX discovery survey (`Chapter 3`, *Coding for User Experience*). Ask yourselves the following:

- Who are our users?
- What do our users want to achieve?
- What are our users capable of?
- How do our users expect to use the system we are going to create?

Imagine that you were starting the ACME registration service, how would you answer these questions?

The answers might be something like the following:

- **Who are our users?**—The users of this service will be the mobile application and web developers responsible for registration frontends.
- **What do our users want to achieve?**—They want to be able to create, view, and manage registrations.
- **What are our users capable of?**—They are familiar with calling HTTP-based REST services. They are familiar with passing in and consuming JSON-encoded data.
- **How do our users expect to use the system we are going to create?**—Given their familiarity with JSON and REST, they expect to do everything via HTTP requests. With the first, most obvious set of users out of the way, we can move onto the second most important group: the development team.
- **Who are the users of our code?**—Myself and the rest of the development team.
- **What do our users want to achieve?**—We want to build a fast, reliable system that is easy to manage and extend.
- **What are our users capable of?**—We are also familiar with HTTP, REST, and JSON. We are also familiar with MySQL and Go. We are also comfortable with the many forms of DI.
- **How do our users expect to use the code we are going to create?**—We would like to use DI to ensure our code is loosely coupled, and easy to test and maintain.

You can see how by considering our users, we have already started to outline our service. We have determined that give that familiarity with HTTP, JSON, and REST from both users that this is the best choice for communications. Given the developers' familiarity with Go and MySQL, these are going to be the best choices concerning implementation technologies.

Code structure

Armed with the framework provided by getting to know our users, we are ready to think about implementation and code structure.

Given we are making a standalone service, we are going to need a `main()` function. After that, the next thing I always add is an `internal` folder directly under `main()`. This adds a clean boundary between the code for this service and any code in the same repository.

When you are publishing a package or SDK for others to use, this is an easy way to ensure your internal implementation packages do not leak into the public API. If your team happens to use a mono-repo or multiple services in one repository, then it's a great way to ensure that you do not have package name collisions with other teams.

The layers we had in our original service were relatively normal, so can reuse them here. These layers are shown in the following diagram:

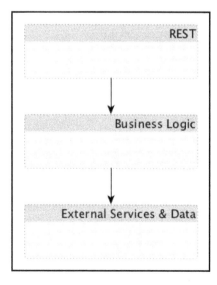

The main advantage of using this particular set of layers is that each layer represents a different aspect required when processing a request. The **REST** layer deals only with HTTP-related concerns; specifically, extracting data from the requests and rendering the responses. The **Business Logic** layer is where the logic from the business resides. It also tends to contain coordination logic related to calling the **External Services and Data** layer. The **External Services and Data** will handle interaction with external services and systems such as databases.

As you can see, each layer has an entirely separate responsibility and perspective. Any system-level changes, such as changing a database or changing from JSON to something else, can be handled entirely in one layer and should cause no changes to the other layers. The dependency contracts between the layers will be defined as interfaces, and this is how we will leverage not only DI, but testing with mocks and stubs.

As the service grows, our layers will likely consist of many small packages, rather than one large package per layer. These small packages will export their own public APIs so that other packages in the layer can use them. This does, however, deteriorate the encapsulation of the layer. Let's look at an example.

Let's assume that we have performance issues with our database and want to add a cache so that we can reduce the number of calls we make to it. It might look something like that shown in the following code:

```go
// DAO is a data access object that provides an abstraction over our
// database interactions.
type DAO struct {
    cfg Config

    db    *sql.DB
    cache *cache.Cache
}

// Load will attempt to load and return a person.
// It will return ErrNotFound when the requested person does not exist.
// Any other errors returned are caused by the underlying database or
// our connection to it.
func (d *DAO) Load(ctx context.Context, ID int) (*Person, error) {
    // load from cache
    out := d.loadFromCache(ID)
    if out != nil {
        return out, nil
    }

    // load from database
    row := d.db.QueryRowContext(ctx, sqlLoadByID, ID)
```

```
    // retrieve columns and populate the person object
    out, err := populatePerson(row.Scan)
    if err != nil {
        if err == sql.ErrNoRows {
            d.cfg.Logger().Warn("failed to load requested person '%d'. err:
%s", ID, err)
            return nil, ErrNotFound
        }

        d.cfg.Logger().Error("failed to convert query result. err: %s", err)
        return nil, err
    }

    // save person into the cache
    d.saveToCache(ID, out)

    return out, nil
}
```

However, there is no need for the existence of this cache to be visible to the **Business Logic** layer. We can make sure that the encapsulation of data layer does not leak the cache package by adding another internal folder under the data folder.

This change might seem unnecessary, and for small projects, that's a good argument. But as the project grows, the little cost of adding an extra internal folder will pay off and ensure that our encapsulation never leaks.

Cross-cutting concerns

We have seen that it's possible to deal with cross-cutting concerns, such as logging and configuration, in many different ways. It's advisable to decide on a strategy upfront and get your team to agree on it. Monkey patching, constructor injection, config injection, and JIT injection are all possible ways to either pass around or access config and logging singletons. The choice is entirely up to you and your preferences.

Designing from outside-in

One of the great things about applying DI from the start of a project is that it gives us the ability to defer decisions until we are better informed to make them.

For example, after deciding to implement a HTTP REST service, we can then proceed to design our endpoints. When designing our Get endpoint, we could describe it like so:

The get endpoint returns a person object in JSON with the form
{"id":1,"name":"John","phone":"0123456789","currency":"USD","price":100}

You might notice that this only describes what the user needs, and does nothing to specify where the data is coming from. We can then actually code our endpoint to achieve this exact goal. And it might even look a lot like this, from Chapter 10, *Off-the-Shelf Injection*:

```go
type GetHandler struct {
    getter GetModel
}

// ServeHTTP implements http.Handler
func (h *GetHandler) ServeHTTP(response http.ResponseWriter, request
*http.Request) {
    // extract person id from request
    id, err := h.extractID(request)
    if err != nil {
        // output error
        response.WriteHeader(http.StatusBadRequest)
        return
    }

    // attempt get
    person, err := h.getter.Do(id)
    if err != nil {
        // not need to log here as we can expect other layers to do so
        response.WriteHeader(http.StatusNotFound)
        return
    }

    // happy path
    err = h.writeJSON(response, person)
    if err != nil {
        // this error should not happen but if it does there is nothing we
        // can do to recover
        response.WriteHeader(http.StatusInternalServerError)
    }
}
```

As GetModel is a locally defined abstraction, it also doesn't describe where or how the data is stored.

The same process could be applied to our implementation of `GetModel` in the business logic layer. It does not need to know how it's being called or where the data is stored, it only needs to know that it needs to coordinate the process and convert any response from the data layer to the format expected by the REST layer.

At each step of the way, the scope of the problem is small. The interactions with layers below depend on abstractions and the implementations of each layer is straightforward.

And when all the layers of a function are implemented, we can use DI to wire it all together.

Summary

In this chapter, we examined the state and quality of our sample service after applying DI, and contrasted that with its original state, thereby reminding ourselves both why we made the changes, and what we gained from making them.

We took one final look at our dependency graph to get a visual perspective on just how well we managed to decouple our packages.

We also saw how our sample service was both significantly easier to test, and that our tests were much more focused after making our changes.

At the end of the chapter, we also discussed how to approach starting a new service and how DI can help with that endeavor too.

With that, we have finished our examination of DI for Go. Thank you for taking the time to read this book—I hope that you have found it both pragmatic and useful.

Happy coding!

Questions

1. What was the most important improvement made to our sample service?
2. In our dependency graph, why isn't the data package under `main`?
3. What would you do differently if you were starting a new service?

Assessment

Many of the questions at the ends of the chapters are intentionally thought-provoking, and as with many things in programming, the answers often depend on the programmer's situation or worldview.

Therefore, the answers following are likely to differ from yours, and that's alright. These are my answers and not necessarily the *right* answers for you.

Chapter 1, Never Stop Aiming for Better

1. What is dependency injection?

During this chapter, I defined dependency injection as coding in such a way that those resources (that is, functions or structs) we depend on are abstractions.

We went on to say that because these dependencies are abstract, changes to them do not necessitate changes to our code. The fancy word for this is **decoupling**.

For me, decoupling is really the essential attribute and goal here. When objects are decoupled, they are just easier to work with. Easier to extend, refactor, reuse, and test. While these are all fantastically important, I also try to be pragmatic. In the end, the software will work just the same if it is not decoupled and does not use dependency injection. But it will become progressively harder to work with and extend.

2. What are the four highlighted advantages of dependency injection?

- **Dependency injection reduces the knowledge required when working on a piece of code by expressing dependencies in an abstract or generic manner.**
  This, for me, is about speed. When I jump into a piece of code, especially in a large project, it's easier to understand what a particular section (such as a struct) is doing when its dependencies are abstract. Typically, this is because the relationship is well described and the interactions clean (in other words, there is no object envy).
- **Dependency injection enables us to test our code in isolation of our dependencies.**
  Similar to the first point, when the dependency is abstract and interactions clean, testing the current piece of code by manipulating its interactions with dependencies is easy to understand and therefore faster.

- **Dependency injection enables us to quickly and reliably test situations that are otherwise difficult or impossible.**
  I know, I focus a lot on testing. I am not actually zealot on this; it's purely self-protection and my idea of professionalism. When I am writing code for someone else, I want it to be as good as possible (within resource constraints). Furthermore, I want it to continue to work the way I intended it to. Tests help me to both clarify and document my intent during construction and in the future.
- **Dependency injection reduces the impact of extensions or changes.**
  Sure, if a method signature changes, its usages will change. When we rely on our own code (such as local interfaces), we at least have a choice in how to react to changes. We can switch to other dependencies; we can add an adapter in between. Regardless of how we deal with it, when our code and tests rely on the unchanged, we can be confident that any problems that arise are in the changed portion or in the features that it provides.

3. What sorts of issues does it address?

The answer to this is essentially the entire section on *code smells,* which include code bloat, resistance to change, wasted effort, and tight coupling.

4. Why is it important to be skeptical?

In our industry, there is almost always more than one way to solve the problem at hand. Similarly, there are almost always many people selling you a *magic bullet* to solve all of your problems. Personally, my answer when asked whether a solution will work is often *it depends*. It might infuriate those that come to me for a simple answer and receive a bunch of questions instead, but there really is seldom a definitive answer. In truth, this is likely what keeps me coming back for more. There is always something new to learn, some new idea to try, some old notion to rediscover. So, I implore you, always listen, always question, and don't be afraid to experiment and fail.

5. What does *idiomatic Go* mean to you?

There is absolutely no correct answer to this. Please don't let anyone tell you otherwise. If you are consistent among the team you are working on, that is enough. If you don't like this style, propose and debate for a better one. While many people are resistant to change, far fewer are against better code.

Chapter 2, SOLID Design Principles for Go

1. How does the single responsibility principle improve Go code?

By applying the single responsibility principle, the complexity of our code is reduced as it is decomposed code into smaller, more concise pieces.

With the smaller, more concise pieces, we gain increases in the potential usability of that same code. These smaller pieces are easier to compose into larger systems, due to their lighter requirements and more generic nature.

The single responsibility principle also makes tests simpler to write and maintain because when a piece of code has only one purpose, there is only much less scope (and therefore complexity) required to test.

2. How does the open/closed principle improve Go code?

The open/closed principle helps reduce the risk of additions and extensions by encouraging us not to change existing code, particularly exported APIs.

The open/closed principle also helps reduce the number of changes needed to add or remove a feature. This is particularly prevalent when moving away from certain code patterns, such as switch statements. Switch statements are great, but they tend to exist in more than one place, and it's easy to miss one instance when adding new features.

Additionally, when problems do arise, they are easier to find, given that they are either in the newly added code or the interactions between it and its usages.

3. How does the Liskov substitution principle improve Go code?

By following the Liskov substitution principle, our code performs consistently regardless of the dependencies we are injecting. Violating the Liskov substitution principle, on the other hand, leads us to violate the open/closed principle. These violations cause our code to have too much knowledge of the implementations, which in turn breaks the abstraction of the injected dependencies.

When implementing interfaces, we can use the Liskov substitution principle's focus on *consistent* behavior as a way of detecting code smells related to incorrect abstractions.

4. How does the interface segregation principle improve Go code?

The interface segregation principle requires us to define thin interfaces and explicit inputs. These features allow us to decouple our code from the implementations that are fulfilling our dependencies.

All of this leads to dependency definitions that are concise, easy to understand, and convenient to use, particularly when using them with mocks and stubs during testing.

5. How does the dependency inversion principle improve Go code?

The dependency inversion principle forces us to focus on the ownership of the abstractions and change their focus from *uses* to *requires*.

It also further decouples our dependency definitions from their implementations. As with the interface segregation principle, the result is code that is more straightforward and separate, particularly from its users.

Chapter 3, Coding for User Experience

1. Why is the usability of code important?

Good UX is not nearly as apparent as bad UX. This is because when UX is good, it *just works*.

Typically, the more complicated, obfuscated, or unusual a piece code is, the harder it is to understand. The harder code is to follow, the harder it is to maintain or extend and the higher the chance of mistakes being made.

2. Who benefits the most from code with great UX?

As programmers, we are both the creators and greatest users of our code; it is, therefore, our colleagues and ourselves that benefit most.

3. How do you construct good UX?

The best UXes are intuitive and natural to their users. The key, therefore, is to try to think as your users do. Chances are that the code you write will make sense and hopefully be natural to you, but can you say the same for the rest of your team?

In this chapter, we defined some aspects to keep in mind:

- Start simple, and get complicated only when you must.
- Apply just enough abstraction.
- Follow industry, team, and language conventions.
- Export only what you must.
- Aggressively apply the single responsibility principle.

We also introduced the *UX Discovery Survey* as a way to *get into the minds* of your users. The survey consisted of four questions:

- Who is the user?
- What are your users capable of?
- Why do users want to use your code?
- How do your users expect to use it?

4. What can unit testing do for you?

In short, many things. It does differ from person to person. Primarily, I use tests to give me the confidence to either *go fast* or *take on the big jobs,* depending on what is needed.

I also find that tests do an excellent job of documenting the intent of the author and are less likely to go stale as comments can.

5. What kind of test scenarios should you consider?

You always want to consider at least three scenarios:

- **The happy path:** Does your function do what you expect it to do?
- **Input errors:** Predictable errors in usage (particularly inputs)
- **Dependency issues:** Does your code behave when the dependencies fail?

6. How do Table-Driven Tests (TDTs) help?

TDTs are great for reducing the duplication caused by multiple test scenarios for the same function.

They are typically more efficient to create than copy/pasting a lot of tests.

7. How can testing damage your software design?

There are many ways that this could happen, and some are quite subjective/personal; but, in this chapter, we outlined a few common causes:

- Parameters, config options, or outputs that only exist because of tests
- Parameters that cause or a caused by leaky abstractions
- Publishing mocks in production code
- Excessive test coverage

Chapter 4, Introduction to the ACME Registration Service

1. Which of the goals defined for our service is most important to you personally?

This is subjective, and as such, there is no right answer. Personally, it would have to be readability or testability. If the code is easy to read, then I can figure it out easier and probably remember more about it as well. On the other hand, if it's more testable, then I can leverage that fact to write more tests. With more tests in place, I won't have to remember as much and can let the tests make sure everything performs as I need it.

2. Which of the issues outlined seems to be most urgent or important?

This is also subjective. It might surprise you, but I would say *lack of isolation in tests*. With the tests as they are, every test is somewhat akin to an end-to-end test. This means that the test setup is lengthy and when something goes wrong, it will be time-consuming to figure out where the problem is.

Chapter 5, Dependency Injection with Monkey Patching

1. How does monkey patching work?

At its most basic level, monkey patching in Go involves swapping out one variable for another at runtime. This variable can be an instance of the dependency (in the form of a struct) or a function that wraps access to the dependency.

At a higher level, monkey patching is about replacing or intercepting access to a dependency to replace it with another implementation, typically a stub or a mock, to make testing simpler.

2. What are the ideal use cases for monkey patching?

Monkey patching can be used in a variety of situations, but the most notable are the following:

- With code that relies on a singleton
- With code that currently has no tests, no dependency injection, and where you want to add tests with a minimum of changes
- To decouple two packages without having to change the dependent package

3. How can you use monkey patching to decouple two packages without changing the dependent package?

We can introduce a variable of type function that calls the dependency package. We can then monkey patch our local variable instead of having to change the dependency. In this chapter, we saw that is especially useful for decoupling from code that we cannot change (such as the standard library).

Chapter 6, Dependency Injection with Constructor Injection

1. What are the steps we used to adopt constructor injection?

1. We identified the dependency we wanted to extract and eventually inject.
2. We removed the creation of that dependency and promoted it to a member variable.
3. We then defined the abstraction of the dependency as a local interface and changed the member variable to use that instead of the real dependency.
4. We then added a constructor with the abstraction of the dependency as a parameter so that we could ensure the dependency was always available.

2. What is a guard clause and when would you use it?

We defined guard clauses as a piece of code the ensured the dependency was supplied (in other words, not nil). In some cases, we used them in our constructors so that we could be 100% sure the dependency was provided.

3. How does constructor injection affect the life cycle of the dependency?

When dependencies are passed into via the constructor, we are sure that they are always available to other methods. As such, there is no risk of nil-pointer crashes related to the use of the dependency.

Additionally, we do not need to litter our methods with guard clauses or other sanity checks as any such validation only needs to exist in the constructor.

4. What are the ideal use cases for constructor injection?

Constructor injection is useful for many situations, including the following:

- Where the dependencies that are required
- Where the dependencies that are used by most or all of the methods of an object
- Where there are multiple implementations of a dependency
- Where the dependencies do not change between requests

Chapter 7, Dependency Injection with Method Injection

1. What are the ideal use cases for method injection?

Method injection is great for the following:

- Functions, frameworks, and shared libraries
- Requesting scoped dependencies, such as context or user credentials
- Stateless objects
- Dependencies that provide context or data in the request and as such are expected to vary between calls.

2. Why is it important not to save dependencies injected with method injection?

Because the dependency is a parameter of the function or method, every call will supply a new dependency. While saving the dependency before calling other internal methods might seem more straightforward than passing the parameter around as a dependency, such practice will cause data races between multiple concurrent usages.

3. What happens if we use method injection too much?

This question is somewhat subjective and depends on your opinion of both test-induced damage and code UX. Personally, I care about UX quite a lot. As such, making a function easier to use by reducing parameters is always on my mind (except for constructors).

From a testing perspective, it's far more flexible to have some form of dependency injection than to have none. Be pragmatic; you will find a balance that works for you.

4. Why is *stopping short* useful to the system as a whole?

Being able to stop processing a request when no-one is listening for the response is extremely useful. Not only does it bring the system closer to the user's expectations, but it reduces the load on the system as a whole. Many resources of the resources we are working with are finite, especially databases, and anything we can do to complete the processing of a request quicker, even when it ends in failure, is advantageous.

5. How can latency budgets improve UX?

Admittedly, latency budgets are a topic I have not heard discussed that often. Given the prevalence of APIs in our industry today, perhaps we should discuss them more. Their importance is twofold—for triggering *stop short* and for setting some bounds or expectations for our users.

When we publish our *maximum execution time* along with our API documentation, users will have clear expectations of our *worst-case* performance. Additionally, we can use the errors generated by the latency budget to return more informative error messages, further enabling the user to make more informed decisions.

Chapter 8, Dependency Injection by Config

1. How does config injection differ from method or constructor injection?

Config injection is an extended form of method and constructor injection. It intends to improve the UX of the code by hiding common and environmental concerns. This reduction in parameters makes the methods easier to understand, extend, and maintain.

2. How do we decide what parameters to move to config injection?

The key point to consider is how the parameter relates to the method or constructor. If the dependency is insignificant but necessary, such as loggers and instrumentation, then hiding it in the config improves the clarity of the function signature rather than detracting from it. Similarly, configuration coming from a config file is often necessary but not informative.

3. Why don't we inject all dependencies via config injection?

There are two significant issues with merging all the dependencies into one. The first is readability. Users of the method/function would have to open the definition of the config every time they wished to understand what parameters were available. Secondly, as an interface, users would be forced to create and maintain an implementation of the interface that could provide all of the parameters. While all config may come from the same place, other dependencies likely do not. The inclusion of the environmental dependencies is a little cheeky but their existence is almost ubiquitous, and their duplication across every constructor would be really annoying.

4. Why do we want to inject environmental dependencies (such as loggers) instead of using a global public variable?

As programmers, we like the **Don't Repeat Yourself** (**DRY**) principle. Injecting environmental dependencies everywhere is a lot of repeating.

5. Why are boundary tests important?

I hope we can all agree that it's important to test. Part of the value of testing is through running the tests repeatedly and detecting regression as soon as possible. To minimize the cost of running the tests often, we need the tests to be reasonably fast and absolutely reliable. When tests depend on an external system, particularly one that we are not responsible for, then we are putting the value of our tests at risk.

Anything can happen to an external system. The owner could break it; the internet/network could go down. Internal-facing boundary tests are similar to our unit tests. They protect our code from regression. External-facing boundary tests are our automated way of documenting and ensuring that the external system does what we need it to do.

6. What are the ideal use cases for config injection?

Config injection can be used in the same situations as constructor or method injection. The key deciding factor is whether the dependencies themselves should be combined and somewhat hidden by config injection and how that improves or detracts from the UX of the code.

Chapter 9, Just-in-Time Dependency Injection

1. How does Just-in-Time (JIT) dependency injection differ from constructor injection?

This depends a lot on how the constructor injection is being used; in particular, how many different implementations of the dependency exist. If there is only one production implementation of a dependency, then they are functionally equivalent. The only difference is UX (that is, whether there is one less dependency to inject into the constructor).

If, however, there is more than one production implementation, then JIT dependency injection cannot be used.

2. When working with optional dependencies, why is using a NO-OP implementation important?

When a member variable is not set by the constructor, then it is effectively optional. We cannot, therefore, be sure that the value has been set and not nil. By adding a NO-OP implementation of the optional dependency and automatically setting it to the member variable, we are able to assume that the dependency is always non-nil and we can forgo the need for guard clauses.

3. What are the ideal use cases for JIT injection?

JIT injection is ideal for the following:

- Replacing a dependency that would otherwise have been injected into the constructor and of which there is only one production implementation
- Providing a layer of indirection or abstraction between an object and a global singleton, particularly when we want to swap out the global singleton during testing
- Allowing dependencies to be optionally provided by the user

Chapter 10, Off-the-Shelf Injection

1. When adopting a dependency injection framework, what can you expect to gain?

This, of course, differs significantly between frameworks, but typically, you can expect to see the following:

- A reduction in boilerplate code
- Less complexity in setting up and maintaining the dependency creation order

2. When evaluating a dependency injection framework, what kind of issues should you being looking out for?

Beyond the gains mentioned previously, my primary criterion is the effect it has on the code; putting it a different way, whether I like how the code looks after adopting the framework.

I would also consider the configurability of the framework itself. Some configuration is expected, but too much can lead to a complicated UX.

The last aspect to consider is the health of the framework project. Is it being actively maintained? Are reported bugs being responded to? Switching between frameworks may not be cheap; it is a good idea to spend a little bit of time ensuring the one you choose is right for you in the long term.

3. What the ideal use cases for adopting off-the-shelf injection?

Typically, frameworks only support constructor injection. Off-the-shelf injection can, therefore, be used in projects that already use constructor injection.

4. Why is it important to protect your service from accidental API changes?

The API of a service is sometimes described as a contract. The word *contract* has been carefully chosen as it intends to convey how significant and binding the relationship is between the API and its users.

When we publish an API, we do not have control over how our users use our API and, perhaps more importantly, we have no control over how their software reacts to changes in our API. For us to deliver on our contract, it is imperative that we do everything we can to ensure we do not break their software by making unplanned changes to our API.

Chapter 11, Curbing Your Enthusiasm

1. What form of dependency injection-induced damage do you see most often?

For me, this is absolutely *excessive parameters*. After learning dependency injection and getting excited about it, it's easy to want to abstract and inject everything. It tends to make testing a lot easier as the *responsibility* of each object decreases. The downside is a lot of objects and too much injection.

If I find myself with too many dependencies, I will try to step back and check my object design, looking for single responsibility principle issues in particular.

2. Why is it important not to blindly apply dependency injection all the time?

Just because something is *cool* or new, doesn't mean it's the best tool for the job. We should always strive to fix the solution to the problem and avoid *cargo cult* programming when we can.

3. Does adopting a framework, such as Google Wire, eliminate all forms of dependency injection-induced damage?

Sadly, no. Given that it only supports constructor injection, it cannot even be applied in all situations. Beyond that, it can make the management of *excessive parameters* significantly less painful.

While that is a good thing, the fact that it alleviates the pain makes it less likely that we will feel the need to address the underlying issue.

Chapter 12, Reviewing Our Progress

1. What was the most important improvement made to our sample service?

This is subjective, and as such, there is no right answer. For me, it's either the decoupling or the removal of the globals. When the code becomes decoupled, it becomes easier for me test and each piece becomes a bite-sized chunk, which means it's easy to work on. Basically, I don't have to think too hard or remember too much context.

As to the globals, I've been bitten by this in the past, particularly the data races that happen during testing. I can't stand it when my tests are not reliable.

2. In our dependency graph, why isn't the data package under main?

We could refactor to make it this way, but at the moment we are using JIT injection between the model and data layers. This means the UX of the code is improved, but the dependency graph is not as flat as it could be. The data layer is also outputting DTOs instead of base data types, so any users will also be using the data package.

If we were determined to remove this as well, we could make a special package for the DTO and then exclude that package from the dependency graph, but that's extra work that does not gain us much as this point.

3. What would you do differently if you were starting a new service?

This is subjective, and as such, there is no right answer. After doing the UX survey, I would first write enough code to get a web server started, even if this was not yet using dependency. I would then design all of the endpoints and implement them with hard-coded responses. This would give me the ability to discuss, with examples, my deliverables with the users. I would also be able to put in some end-to-end tests to prevent any API regression.

My users would then be able to go ahead, with confidence and clarity about my API, and I would be able to *fill in the details*.

Other Books You May Enjoy

If you enjoyed this book, you may be interested in these other books by Packt:

Mastering Go
Mihalis Tsoukalos

ISBN: 9781788626545

- Understand the design choices of Golang syntax
- Know enough Go internals to be able to optimize Golang code
- Appreciate concurrency models available in Golang
- Understand the interplay of systems and networking code
- Write server-level code that plays well in all environments
- Understand the context and appropriate use of Go data types and data structures

Go Standard Library Cookbook

Radomir Sohlich

ISBN: 9781788475273

- Access environmental variables
- Execute and work with child processes
- Manipulate strings by performing operations such as search, concatenate, and so on
- Parse and format the output of date/time information
- Operate on complex numbers and effective conversions between different number formats and bases
- Work with standard input and output
- Handle filesystem operations and file permissions
- Create TCP and HTTP servers, and access those servers with a client
- Utilize synchronization primitives
- Test your code

Leave a review - let other readers know what you think

Please share your thoughts on this book with others by leaving a review on the site that you bought it from. If you purchased the book from Amazon, please leave us an honest review on this book's Amazon page. This is vital so that other potential readers can see and use your unbiased opinion to make purchasing decisions, we can understand what our customers think about our products, and our authors can see your feedback on the title that they have worked with Packt to create. It will only take a few minutes of your time, but is valuable to other potential customers, our authors, and Packt. Thank you!

Index

relationship, with Go 47

M

math/rand standard library package
  reference 110
method injection of context
  applying, to REST package 174, 175
method injection
  about 158, 159, 160
  advantages 161, 162, 163, 164, 165
  applying 165, 166, 167
  applying, to data package 168, 170
  applying, to exchange package 170
  applying, to model layer 173
  disadvantages 179, 180, 181
mockery
  reference 78
mocks 76
model layer
  method injection, applying to 173
monkey patching
  about 106
  advantages 106, 107, 108, 109, 110, 111
  applying 113
  applying, to ACME registration service 112
  between packages 124, 125, 126, 127
  error handling, testing 118, 119
  potential costs, considering 127, 128, 129
  with SQLMock 115, 116, 117

N

Network File Share (NFS) 10

O

off-the-shelf injection
  advantages 237, 238, 239, 240
  applying 241
  disadvantages 255, 256
  with Wire 234
open/closed principle (OCP)
  about 34
  advantages 35, 38
  relationship, with DI 39
  relationship, with Go 39, 41

P

package dependencies
  visualizing, with godepgraph 81
package-coverage
  reference 219
PMD
  reference 15
private dependencies, JIT
  coverage + dependency graph 220
  monkeys, chasing 221, 222
  unit test coverage 219, 220
provider sets
  adopting 236
providers 234, 235

S

simplified dependency creation 286, 287
single responsibility principle (SRP), using with Go
  functions 31
  interfaces 31
  packages 32, 34
  structs 31
single responsibility principle (SRP)
  about 26, 63, 91
  advantages 26, 27, 30
  relationship, with DI 30
  relationship, with Go 30
SQLMock package
  reference 113
SQLMock
  about 113
  using 114
  using, in monkey patching 115, 116, 117
stopping short 167, 286
structural typing 136
stubs 74, 75

T

table-driven tests
  about 73
  reference 119
  test bloat, reducing 120, 122, 124
test bloat
  reducing, with table-driven tests 120, 122, 124

www.ingramcontent.com/pod-product-compliance
Lightning Source LLC
Chambersburg PA
CBHW080619060326
40690CB00021B/4750